Let not a day pass without giving some inspiring nourishment to the soul. All hunger for higher knowledge but know not that it can flow from within, in the silence of your heart & mind. Be still & Know!

Blessings, mary

THE ELEVENTH HOUR

BY

COLONEL FREDERICK TIMMERMAN

THROUGH
LILIAS TIMMERMAN
AND DR. MARY MYERS

Copyright January 1991
ALL RIGHTS RESERVED

PRINTED IN USA

9/95

Gift
M.M.
J.D.

ACKNOWLEDGEMENTS

Never before in the history of spiritual development has a follower of Jesus made the rapid progress of becoming **One** with the Christlight. Through the special dispensation made by the Host of the Angelic Beings, the cross has been eliminated in the Piscean Age. A disciple willing to serve as the **Christ Light** leads the way as indicated within this book, The Eleventh Hour. In completing the eradication of the six states of consciousness through Etheric operations, one is transformed and enters into his own **Celestial Soul.**

Colonel Frederick Timmerman has dictated the book after completing his 360 Etheric Operations and has revealed how his ascension was accomplished through his own illumination received from Jesus the Christ, Raphael, Uriel, the Cosmic Holy Spirit and Sanat Kumara with Lady Master Venus Kumara, His divine complement. She is the Universal Mother with every ascended mother. All have contributed to this book in the various chapters.

With deep humility and appreciation, the great transformation took place in my spirit and soul as the revelations and truths that I received were dictated to me from Jesus the Christ. I progressed with the assistance of Raphael and Mary who also received from the Cosmic Holy Spirit, with His divine complement and the Great One. He is currently known as the **Ancient of Days,** who is Sanat Kumara, whose name bears the qualities of the **One Light.**

All these shining Ones or Angelic Beings, authored this book. The **One Voice** spoke through the Angelic Beings, and then the truth was transmitted by me, Colonel Timmerman.

Chapter after chapter discloses the inner Path of Light through the assistance of the Angelic Being, Raphael as he spoke to Mary. She received the dictation as Raphael gave it to me, and I now repeated the messages to his vessel, Mary. It was in observing Mary operate the Laws of Light by demonstrating them in the world that I rapidly understood these miraculous teachings which disclosed the inner Path of Light.

So willing and obedient to these teachings was I, Colonel Timmerman, that **I was willing to do anything directed by the Christ Light** to achieve my ascension. As a result of my dictation to Mary, she became illumined by my example, for it was I, known as Timothy in the past, who had searched throughout the ages for the Truth, and followed Jesus all the way to His Ascension into the spirit world. My Path of Light was so rapid and accelerated that never before in the history of mankind was a spiritual traveler able to enter into the inner dimensional levels to reach the pinnacle of becoming One with the Pure Light of God, just as Jesus had done when He made the Ascension.

Enormous assistance was given to Tim by his own wife, Lilias, and her best friend, Mary, who are both in communication with Sanat Kumara and Lady Master Venus Kumara. Mary assists them within the Etheric operations which transformed the states of consciousness I have gone through on my inner Path of Light journey revealed within this book.

TABLE OF CONTENTS

I. The Eleventh Hour   4

Tim's Version of Arlington Cemetery   7
Tim Speaks   11
Lilias Speaks   13
Tim Speaks Again, to Lilias   14

II. Jesus Shows Tim Who He was in the Past: 32

Tim, The Centurion (Jesus Teaches Tim)   32
The Angel Raphael Speaks   32
The Way to Peace   40

III. Tim's Book of Life 54

Tim's Book of Life   54
The State of Consciousness   62
The Great Adjustment   81
Early Stages of Development   94
The Birth of the Soul   98
The Christ Light is the Problem Solver   108

IV. States of Consciousness 116

The First State of Consciousness   116
Mary Magdalene   118
The Second State of Consciousness   119
The Third State of Consciousness   123
The Fourth State of Consciousness   128
The Consciousness of the Unsurrendered Soul   129
Herod   129
Herodias   131
John the Baptist   134
A Visit to a Prison   135
Tim's Continuation - Fourth State of Consciousness   146

V. The Fifth State of Consciousness . . 149

The Fifth State of Consciousness   149
The Spirit Body   157
One Year after My Transition   161
The Mysterious Wasp   165
Tim Speaks   178
Transition after Physical Life   185
The Transition of the Physical Body   194
God Proves Himself to his Seeking Children   197
The Fifth State of Consciousness Worldwide   205

VI. The Sixth State of Consciousness . 214

The Sixth State of Consciousness   214
The Higher Meaning of the Ten Commandments   223
 How the Third Body of Light is Formed   224
Thou Shalt Not Kill the Body of Light   227
Erroneous Concepts Shall Now Crumble   234
The Time of Illumination Has Arrived!   234
The Christ of the Earth   237
Test All Voices Heard Inwardly   240
What is the Truth?   243
He Who Loves God Will Obey God   252
The Description of the Heaven World   262
The Etheric Operations   268
Pure Love Begets Pure Love   275
What Do Spirits Eat?   276
The Great Second Coming   283
A Former Prince of the Church   286
Jesus Operates the Great Universal Law   290
Key to Illumination   291

VII. The All-Pervasive God Speaks . . 298

The Images of Man   305
Catastrophic Occurrences   309
The Keys to Answered Prayers   322
The Source of All Life   323
The Holy Cosmic Being   326
By-Laws   330
The Four Marys   336
Poem: "The Universal Mother is Glorified
        by Her Mortal Daughter, Mary"   340
The Ascended Mothers   341
Universal Poetry   359
Protected by the Blue Ray   367
Sanat Kumara Speaks   375
Sanat Kumara Speaks to Lilias   377
Love without Wisdom   379
Spiritual Darkness Covered the Earth   383
How to Come into My Presence   385
My Perfect Timing   396
The Supreme Deity   408

"ARISE, MY SON."

INTRODUCTION

THE ASCENSION AT THE ELEVENTH HOUR INTO THE SEVENTH DIMENSION

"**Arise, My son, and come to Me.** You are now on My spiraling stairway leading to the opened door to the starry heaven world. I have great need of you to pave the way to a New Octave of Consciousness. You have now been lifted to your own Celestial Soul, and you will now claim your Divine Birthright.

"The Angel incarnate who has been with you throughout your marriage made your ascension possible. In her soul she remembered that you had already played the role of a heavenly being, and she had surrendered you to your own Divine Heritage. You will no longer be bound by the illusory world of limited matter.

"It will be through you and the Celestial Angel with you, that your ascension will quicken the time for the mass awakening of thousands, even the 144,000 to find their way to the invisible door.

"The stairway to the door will be the passing through of your six states of consciousness to a higher plateau which was fraught with arduous labors in the past.

"But through the Grace of God, you have learned how the Laws of Light operate within the awakened multi-dimensional Light beings whom you mention in your book entitled <u>The Eleventh Hour</u>.

"You were taught these laws, and learned to operate them as they were practiced within the University of the Christ Light.

"Within one year's time of your continuous perseverance into the Unknown, and through the great knowledge revealed within your book, this book will serve our Purpose of bringing the planet and humanity into an increased awareness of the **Oneness of God throughout the earth.**

"The unification with this **Oneness** will occur all over the planet as news spreads swiftly, electronically, over the face of the earth that the higher Octave of the higher degrees are accessible to the people of the earth. The higher knowledge will be evidenced in the experiences you have so courageously manifested in all that has now been recorded between the human and divine world to full manifestation. These two worlds will be integrated, and separation from God will be seen as a limiting and confining self-creation.

"The Key shall be how one man made the **quantum leap so that others will know how to do likewise.**

"The large spiral of the Earth will give way to the unlimited spiral of the Universe. Myriads of starry Light Beings will be acknowledged in their harmonious, peaceful and loving ways, serving together to bring the entire Earth into the pulsations of higher Light frequencies.

"The invisible door has already been

opened into the heaven world. The Key will be given to the peaceful ones in the world. These peaceful ones will serve to assist in the task of unifying all the nations in peaceful spiritual pursuit by sharing the knowledge all over the world. This sharing of knowledge will usher in the higher state of consciousness, bringing in a higher state of happiness and prosperity all over the world. It is God who has been waiting to give his greater bounty to mankind as all recognize the **One as being the higher light encompassing the entire globe.**

"Each one will be a wheel within a greater wheel empowered to supply the Pure Light which removes all obstructions. This Pure Light will make the incredible dream become credible.

"Each one will be given the opportunity to choose whom he will follow among the Stars within the Invisible Dove now expanded to the four corners of the Earth. True seekers searching to find their way will be guided by the Starry Ones to each seeker's highest Celestial Soul within the **One.**"

I AM THE RESURRECTION

I AM THAT I AM is the Father Mother God of the Great Central Sun. Did I not say, it is the Father who doeth the works within the Pure Love of the Celestial Mother.

At the Eleventh Hour both of My daughters, Mary and Lilias released to the Christ in Jesus in prayer, the spirit of Colonel Frederick Timmerman. The Pure Love of the Mother lifted him into his own soul within the Sixth State of Consciousness.

In the past, Jesus demonstrated the Will of the Father to all as he showed the Way to ascension for the spirit to enter the soul. Once more, Jesus illustrated the Way and revealed in <u>The Eleventh Hour</u> all that Colonel Frederick Timmerman was to do within a year's time, to enable him to enter the Heaven World into the 7th day or the Seventh State of Consciousness where he too becomes One with the Christ Light.

CHAPTER I

THE ELEVENTH HOUR
June 16, 1990
10:00 A.M.
ARLINGTON CEMETERY

At precisely ten o'clock on the morning of June 16th, the door opened to the receiving room of the Arlington National Cemetery in Washington D.C. The relatives and friends of the deceased Colonel Frederick Timmerman were quietly entering the waiting room of the Administrative building provided for them until all was in readiness for the ceremony. There were eleven adults and seven small children wide eyed in observing those who were present. It was as though the children were all disciplined to be "good" by being silent and even the toddlers were subdued. The relatives and friends had flown to Washington, D.C. from California, Panama, New York, and North Carolina. Several army colonels were also present to pay their respects and to console Lilias, the deceased Colonel's wife, and offered to assist her in whatever help she would need.

The solemnity of the ceremony was evident to all. The warmth of a family reunion permeated the room as all embraced one another and engaged in quiet conversations until the time arrived for the ceremony to begin. The people filed out of the building into their respective cars,

4

and their attention was focused on the profusion of white crosses everywhere, even amidst the slightly rolling hills. Having arrived at the selected grave site, a hushed silence fell upon all.

Although the day was clear and sunny, momentarily the sun was shrouded by a few clouds passing over the area. Lilias was seated in the front row with her close friend holding her hand on one side, and Richard, Lilias' nephew, stood close to her, holding her hand to support her in her sorrow and grief.

The Eleventh Hour had struck! A troop of six ceremonial soldiers marched slowly and rhythmically, immaculately groomed in their uniforms, lifting their legs high in unison, showing their highly polished shoes. Their heads were held firmly while they looked straight ahead, marching toward the grave site. They stood parallel to the army chaplain, now prepared to give the eulogy based on the 23rd Psalm. When the chaplain recited, ". . .Yea though I walk through the Valley of the Shadow. . ." suddenly the sun pierced the clouds, and the brilliant light rays now focused on the chaplain's head. The sunlight now began to envelop the three, Lilias, her nephew and Mary. Powerful magnetic currents were now flowing which others could not define but all felt. The hand of Lilias was squeezed by her close friend as she whispered something in her ear. In a soft voice the chaplain continued the benediction and now honored Colonel Timmerman in his many accomplishments of extraordinary service in over thirty years with the United States Army. A fitting poem was recited, and he ended his sermon with a prayer.

The flag-folding ceremony began with the removal of the American flag from the urn. The soldiers then held it up before all and in turn folded the corners to the center forming a triangle symbolizing the trinity.

A soldier handed the flag to the chaplain, who turned towards Mrs. Timmerman and spoke of the significance of the American Flag and the democratic way of life.

"The United States flag is a memorable symbol of the continuous service for over thirty years of excellent performance within the United States Army by Colonel Frederick Timmerman. I know that his wife will treasure this memento lovingly as she has held the flag to her heart as I presented it to her. May we bow our heads as I give the closing prayer."

Tears trickled down Lilias' cheeks as she indeed held the flag to her heart. It was as though her husband's spirit was wrapped up in the American Flag.

Heads were now bowed as silent prayers were uttered. It was at this moment that Mary entered the dimension of her own soul and saw all that was happening within the higher dimension of the spirit atmosphere. She was astounded to see the spirit of Colonel Timmerman, dressed in his officer's uniform ascending slowly while "Taps" was being played. She nudged Lilias and described to her what was happening. The long, clear notes of the bugle resounded throughout the entire area.

Tim arose into a brilliant, pure Light. Suddenly the Light enveloped him and a clear Pink Ray hovered over him, sending forth a fragrance of the perfume of a Rose. The Pink Ray now enveloped all who were present and love and joy filled the air.

The three-gun salute then took place. The six soldiers obeyed the command to about-face, and they marched solemnly down the path.

After the chaplain completed the benediction, many of the guests gathered around Lilias to comfort her and express their willingness to assist her in any way she deemed necessary.

It became apparent to all that the sadness and grieving had vanished, and all began to embrace Lilias.

Tim's Version of Arlington Cemetery

The day was clear and sunny at the Arlington Cemetery, where so many of my closest friends and family members had gathered for the military funeral ceremony which had been prepared for me.

Now, although others know not what happens after one passes out of his body, few realize that the body holds the spirit. At the moment of passing, with the last breath of exhalation, the spirit leaves the body and enters the dimension of the spirit world. But the spirit world is not separated from the physical solid form world; it is as though the spirits are with the individuals, and yet separated by another atmosphere where the people in the world do not see us, but we see them.

Think of a glass window so constructed that the people in the spirit world can see through this glass and see all that is going on, but the people in the world do not have the glass to see through which is apparent to us. Thus, the people in the world know not the spirit world, because it is within a higher dimensional level.

Many sensitive individuals can feel our spirit and be vaguely aware of it, but the physical eyes do not see into this dimension of the spirit. Thus people believe only in what they see as being real.

Some imagine seeing our presence as they think about us. But they know not that as they are thinking about us, their thoughts flow into our spirit body and into the eyes and spirit ears. Our spirit body looks very much like our solid body.

It may be strange to many to think of us as being so light that we can float within the atmosphere of the spirit world. It is uncanny to realize that by just desiring to be some place, we suddenly are there. **This is the spirit world**.

Before the funeral services began, my friends were gathered within a waiting room provided for them in a building on the grounds of the cemetery for just the right moment that the ceremony was to occur, where all would be in readiness for the last rites to begin.

I, Tim, stood on the ground beside the casket, ready to watch the entire process. I heard every word and felt everyone's reactions. I observed all those true friends weeping silently and saw tears roll down their cheeks. But I saw their thoughts were not about **me**, but they were weeping for **my wife,** as they were thinking about her loss. The men too were wondering what would happen to their wives, as the husbands would pass on and the wives were left alone. Filled with compassion and understanding, the husbands suddenly took hold of the hands of their wives and held them lovingly.

The attention of the men were upon Lilias, my wife, who would feel the loss the most. All knew the care I had given to Lilias. All knew the extent of her reliance on me. I felt their prayers and saw how they were directed toward Lilias. All wanted to help her.

You, Mary, recognized how solicitous all were, and I saw the desires of all our friends wanting to help Lilias. The children who were there also wanted to help take care of her. I saw the thoughts of all wanting to do for us as both of us had done for them. I saw your prayers also, Mary. But I knew that you prayed daily as you understood and knew what to do for me. I recognized the hours you had spent in my behalf. I was aware that you had started etheric operations from the day that Lilias telephoned you and told you of my demise.

Lilias described what I had done at the time she was so ill and felt so distraught that I saw her thoughts of wanting to follow me. What would she do without me? In her condition, how could she cope with all that suddenly confronted her? It was all this that had enveloped her.

You, Mary stood by her all the way, and were now sitting next to her holding her hand while you were in prayer every moment during the services. Oh, dear one, I was in the light of all who were praying.

People do not realize how real prayers are helpful, and how we in the spirit world are benefited.

So melodious and inspiring was the rendition of "Taps" being played that the echoes resounded all through the Arlington Cemetery. After "Taps" came the three gun salute which ended the service.

It was then that I was enveloped into the Light as Mary described this to you, whispering into your ear all that she saw taking place within the inner spirit dimension.

Within a few moments I felt a strange sensation as though I were on an escalator moving slowly upward as Mary observed my silence and wonder in what was happening.

Then I ascended, and recognized that you and Mary were in a state of prayer. And Mary was looking directly at my spirit body as she witnessed my ascension. All the family were with you, Lilias, thinking of you while Richard held your hand all through the ceremony. This gave you strength to overcome your sorrow.

I AM THE RESURRECTION

Tim speaks to Mary: *"All that happened at the ceremony at Arlington Cemetery during the Eleventh Hour was according to the Divine Will of our Father Mother God. You and Lilias were already included in the prayer of dedication and were praying for the Will of God to take place. Furthermore, you, Mary, arrived several days early to spend time in prayer and prepare for the Ascension. I instructed you to keep silent and observe our works about the Ascension. Then at the Eleventh Hour, not only you and Lilias, but also the chaplain and all of the people who were present turned to God in silence and prayer in each one's own state of consciousness."*

At the ceremony, Tim was observing and recognized that all were in prayer and, at this moment, he too turned his mind on the Christ in Jesus. His own soul entered his spirit body, as you and Lilias were loving the Universal Mother Kumara, the Pure Love Principle of the Divine Mother. Her Pure Love became the Escalator that lifted him up. This same invisible Light enfolded Tim. This was the high frequency of Love in its pure state that enfolded Tim and lifted him to Jesus, who was within this Light.

Suddenly you, Mary, were aware of the vibrations that were lifting all who were present, according to each one's own soul light. Then you saw Tim arise into his own soul which turned his spirit to Jesus the Christ who enfolded him.

TIM SPEAKS:

The Eleventh Hour began after my transition when I realized the extent of my ignorance in these teachings you had followed for many years.

I disapproved of the teachings with all of my heart, but you, Lilias, stood firm and never changed your beliefs which I resisted by my unbelief. Only after my release from life did I understand these advanced teachings. I became enlightened and my understanding unfolded in my soul which was now awakened when I met My Father in Jesus. It is He who began to teach me. Great was my astonishment to learn that my wife and her friend had always followed Him.

From then onward began my purification, which was so unusual because I believed it to be arduous, and should be accompanied by long suffering, until I gave up this erroneous belief in suffering to overcome all the darkness, throughout my many lives. As you remembered, I suffered with my heart, and this was the reason for the pain in the heart of my conscious mind. My deep-seated beliefs which had accumulated throughout my many lives could now be dissolved by the Pure Light of the Christ in Jesus.

I was guided in all my darkness and ignorance to find the light slowly, for there was great suffering at first until I was enlightened. Each time I overcame one block, other blocks followed.

After the ascension, I had to stop for awhile to recover my spirit. Lord Jesus who was also known as the Christ, came for me, and began to teach me the new revelations, but first I had to undergo the dissolving of the great darkness that was still within my spirit; then slowly through admitting and recognizing what was stored within, I was determined to release all the darkness of my mind and spirit and soul.

We begin with the thought of **separation. Separation from our loved ones** occupies the minds of many who are close to transition. How will they be able to part with life itself, and all that belongs to that life? How will they separate from their families and loved ones?

The answer will be given for many to understand that there is no separation except in the physical body. At the time of transition there is a period of rest as though it were night time and one is sleeping.

The separation is only in the outer form. The inner form is the spirit form that takes over the life force, and life becomes different in its evolution. For life goes on eternally, ever higher in its growth and learning.

We will begin to write about yourself, Lilias, and how you felt when I left you, and this will give encouragement to all those women who lost their husbands and were left so distressed and distraught and fearful of being left alone in the world without the protection of their husbands. They had to learn to manage all of his affairs that became her affairs and how she was to cope with all the money matters. There was no one seemingly to protect or guide these women. But they did not know that their husbands never left them alone and guided them through all their difficulties. This was the case with Lilias.

Often they would feel their husband's presence and feel comforted and encouraged to go on with their lives. Many friends came to their aid in many ways.

They did not realize and did not recognize how often seemingly their problems were solved by others; however, the problems were really solved by their own husbands. Often they did feel lonely and forgotten by others, but changes did occur, and the women felt happy.

The husbands who loved their wives were always near to them and knew all their thoughts and desires which often were fulfilled, and slowly, the wives became independent and were able to live in the knowledge that they were never alone.

We will begin to speak about your experiences in the world without me.

Lilias speaks:

Everyone was very kind and helpful, but still there was that emptiness that I felt in the world when everyone else seemed so happily married and had their families and social lives, which gave them much to do. But soon I felt part of their lives, especially the children, now grown up and with their own families. I felt I was not alone. Barbara and Fannette took care of me with all the medical conditions, and the bills I had to pay were all explained and balanced.

When being with my friend Marge who had lost her husband Ray, she said he was always with her, guiding her and giving her encouragement to go on with her new life. She moved to a newly constructed retirement Air Force complex called "March Air Force Village West." She met many retired army wives and was happy, but very lonely at times. But she was comforted by the assurance that he was always there with her.

TIM SPEAKS AGAIN, TO LILIAS:

It is difficult to overcome fear, for it knows no bounds and is not influenced by logic. Now you are in a higher dimension. You must overcome fear, for it controls the whole mind, but I will take this fear from you, and you will be able to overcome any fear.

If you know the Light is stronger than fear and realize the fear is darkness, you will be willing to call upon the Light, and fear will be dissipated by the Light.

I know you are trying to write with Uriel, but you are still very much in the world and cannot hold to his Light. As you are cleared every night by the Etheric operations, you will be able to write what we say to you. For there is much to tell you.

You will never be at a loss to know what to do. Just turn inwardly and attune and write. You will soon feel my vibration, although you feel my presence, but you do not realize **why** you know

14

what it is. You will begin to feel the different vibrations of the ascended ones, and write always with the Divine Mother. This will open the way for you to hear clearly.

We will begin the lesson by your giving me your attention. Your attention is where your mind is and your spirit is whatever your thoughts dwell upon. There is your attention. And so, hold your attention upon your teacher. Your attention is especially intent upon the subjects that are unknown and completely new. That is how you begin, by holding your attention upon me. As you do more and more thinking of us, so your attention will grow, and you will be able to hold your mind upon your teacher. At this time, you are unable to hold your mind very long on any teaching, but you will be able to hold your mind longer as you listen centered on me when you do lose contact with my communication.

You are always to bring your mind back to me, and we will continue. You will keep this book for your lessons. Your lessons will be easy ones until you are able to hold to me for longer periods of time. Do not think about what happened fifty years ago, so much has happened within that time, and we are not to look backward in time.

Only the present time is important for you. Live only in this moment. You will see how your mind flits from place to place. Now you are with the violets, or the birds who have need of water, and so your mind becomes diverted, but in time, you will be able to be still, and overcome the outer, and only stay in the inner. So all your past life is now light and can be resurrected at any time within your memory which holds all your life.

Tim believes that family members are waiting for him to pass over into the spirit world. There have been so many books written about what is seen or felt about the spirit world.

Some have been out of their bodies in a comatose state. As they return to their bodies, after having been away from their bodies for a while, they will often not want to return to their world of darkness, or that which they believe to be darkness. Having seen the spirit world while they were temporarily separated from their physical bodies, the world in which these individuals had lived was believed to be the world of sickness and sorrow, tears and grief. This was the world of darkness in which the masses of people lived, described as the "other world."

"Ye are from beneath; I am from above. Ye are of this world; I am not of this world."

From the time these words were spoken by Jesus, the people began to believe that there were two worlds. But at the time, it was not understood by the people that Jesus was referring to the higher body of Light, the soul within a higher dimensional level. The physical body was within the world of each one's own state of consciousness. This physical world is the environment within which each one gravitates and has his being.

A doctor gravitates within the medical

world. A lawyer will often be within the political world; a teacher would be within the educational world. Each one creates the world within his own state of being and development.

The spirit body is within a higher dimensional level than the physical body. The spirit's environment would be the spirit world. The body of light or the soul is on a still higher dimensional level.This would be the world above the spirit world.

"Whither I go, ye cannot come."

None could come into the body of Light until the spirit body was purified and raised into the consciousness of the soul level. Jesus had become One with the Pure Light of the Father after he made his transition and was purified in his physical body, in his spirit and within the soul; yet he was unsurrendered to the Will of God.

But then he uttered the immortal words: "Unto thee, I commit my spirit; and, henceforth not my will but Thine be done." These words were the clue to his dedicating himself to God, his Father within the Pure Light.

All who learn how to follow the Wayshower, and dedicate themselves to God, as Jesus had done, are the ones who learn how to arise in spirit and come to the Father and learn how to hear His voice and obey His Laws.

Nevertheless, to this day, it has been believed that there are two separate worlds, and the interpretations of the human, limited mind have held man to believe that he is separated from God, and knows not where God is. Man knows he is somewhere, but where? And those who believe in two worlds, think the spirit world is somewhere in outer space.

The beliefs in two worlds have been engendered by descriptions given by the authorities of the churches. Throughout the ages the description was repeated as being one world where the saints abide. Included within this same world were all those servants who spent their entire lifetime serving the churches. The world of light was described as being a world free from all sin, turmoil, diseases and tears. This was a world of joy, where each one receives his reward for having given his life to the church and for obeying the doctrines of the church.

The church was of God; the ecclesiastical governing body of the church merited the world of light. But among the authorities of the church, only those whose hearts were pure and who would abstain from all evil and all that is impure were worthy of their reward. These are the virginal celibate ones who had sacrificed their lives in the world in order to be with their Lord.

Having been associated with this church within my lifetime, I believed all that I had been taught. **Because I was not serving in the church, besides not having consecrated my life to God, I did not expect to make the ascension.** I simply believed that I had served my fellow man in the world to the best of my ability. Therefore I believed and expected to be with those of my kind and would just be satisfied to have a peaceful rest and then return to Earth once more.

In my spirit body, I guided the chaplain in what he was to do for my wife in the church for he had come to visit her and pay his respects. It was after my demise that the chaplains in the church where my wife had served for so many years all now assisted her in whatever could be done to alleviate her difficulties in adjusting to all that confronts so many widows whose husbands would pass away. It was within this period of time that my adventures into the spirit world began.

I was relieved when my wife's best spiritual friend had flown from the United States to be with her in this foreign country. I did all that I could to guide both women in what was to be done in the move that would be made to the United States.

I was overwhelmed to observe from the spirit world the daily prayers offered by these two women; **it was uncanny that in their sensitivity they entered into my own dimension of spirit, within my own atmosphere or aura within the spirit world.**

Both of them heard me speak even as I called their names, and they would take notes on all that I would say. Both of them were so aware of my presence that they even discerned my own thoughts and felt my vibrations. While I was within my own home, in spirit, the vast amount of purification continued. I would describe this process as being comparable to viewing a movie screen while the scenes of my past rolled through my consciousness. I recognized everything taking place in exactly the way I had formerly experienced it within my own home environment.

Then the scenes of my past life continued every night. It was as though I were watching all that I had done within my entire lifetime being played back in a movie. But I was the actor and all revolved around me in a way that I was now watching my own drama being played.

But there was this difference: after I had watched the scenes pass through my spirit body, I could glimpse into my being and recognize the darkness slowly being obliterated. It simply vanished! I would compare this event to what I would see in the early morning hours as the night clouds were being swept away while the daylight began to appear.

After each purification, the negatives were removed, and I received more light. In my spirit body, I guided the chaplain in what he was to do for my wife in the church.

Little did I realize at the time that recorded on my wife's soul was the Biblical teaching that women were to turn to their husbands for all knowledge. At the time this was written, only the men were trained and educated in the world. Women were to have been taught by their mothers in the care, management and beautification of the home and all else that pertained to the operation of the home. But my wife believed that even in this, she was to come to me for supervision of everything.

She would come to me as a little child and look to me to do whatever she could not do and knew that I could do so well. She was a helpless and unknowing little girl. This was my wife.

Little did I realize the depth of her belief in God. At times, she believed that I was even as a God who took care of her.

On earth, I had experienced many trials in dealing with her ways, and great frustrations in not being able to change my wife. My expectations had failed. She believed the same truth I too accepted, that man had held the Spirit of God. For two thousand years the accepted belief was that man believed that man himself had held the soul, the Light of God, and that his wife would inhabit his own soul. Man would have the intelligence which he was to give to his wife.

At the time, this was mystifying to me. In my own realization, I was seeing my own beliefs reflected within my home, but I did not know how to rectify this. It was as though she would echo my ways and try to emulate what I would do. **But I did not recognize my own spirit within her own being.** Such an observation as this would not be clarified nor understood until after I had made the transition. It was after I came into the presence of Jesus the Christ, that I learned how he would peer into my spirit.

He would understand my every thought, all recorded deeds of the past, and all of my reactions which I had given to all manner of situations in the world, even within my own home.

For the first time, I perceived in myself

that I did not know, nor understand the **origin** of my own ways and beliefs, or why everything happened as it did.

Being an ambitious man, I would continue to learn all that I could of world affairs, and then I would consolidate all the knowledge I would gather together and pass along everything to my superiors. It was known that dedicated officers in the army would help one another in their promotions to higher positions. After each officer received his rewards, he would now assist those who were loyal and dedicated to him and reciprocate in many ways. Thus, others would be promoted to receive higher positions.

Although I had merited the position of colonel, I strove to gain the promotion of becoming a general. But no matter how I labored and how I excelled in all my performances, there seemed to be blocks placed on my path all the way. There were other officers whom I believed were not superior to me; neither had they served as long as I had, nor worked as many hours as I had; yet they received the higher positions and surpassed me.

Deep in my soul, I reasoned that inasmuch as my wife could not play the role of a general's wife, she could not measure up to the other women who had college degrees and supported their husbands socially and educationally. In her sweet humility, she could not compete with any of the wives. She was not ambitious enough to climb the "ladder of success" and had been totally absorbed in the study of spiritual knowledge. My wife had a silence in this that none could understand. While she supported me in her prayers throughout our entire marriage, her interests were not of this world. Nevertheless, she enjoyed the comforts and pleasures within the world that were within our means, in vacations and traveling in many countries. To further her own intellectual education in the world did not interest her. At the time, I did not realize that the only education she pursued and was interested in, and which she would strive to further her own progress, was the Knowledge of God. She was always seeking and buying numerous books that attracted her. All her spare time was spent in reading. She studied her religious books while I studied the foremost political books in the world.

It seemed we were studying on two different levels. It was as though each one of us lived within two different worlds, in two different states of consciousness.

In the earlier stages of our marriage she had been president of the Altar Guild; she had served as a Red Cross volunteer, and worked within the orphanages, distributing clothing and food and other necessities. In other assignments in Greece, Lilias had been decorated with the Order of the Phoenix, signifying service in the Greek military hospitals in Athens. Among other services, she was a volunteer nurse working with severely injured soldiers.

Still, she was not able to fulfill my

expectations of exemplifying the position of a colonel's wife within the social and community requirements often fulfilled by the wives of the higher positioned officials.

While Lilias would try to please me in my world, no matter what she would try to do, she simply could not give her full time to my world. She gave more and more of her time to her religious pursuits and less time to my interests. I became frustrated and aggravated in trying to change her religious pursuits. At times, I would believe she lived in a "dream world" filled with unreality. I could not understand her religious world and she could not comprehend my military, political world.

I was so filled with emotional exasperation that we began to drift apart. My negative feelings toward her seemed to increase in my own rebellion and animosity toward what she was studying.

Her studies had been so time-consuming that I now wanted to drown out all of my own turmoil in some way. Her evanescent and ethereal knowledge was useless to me. Talking to her about this was futile; her ideas simply made no sense to me. I rejected her teachings. I didn't understand the light. This was my state of mind that I began to hold throughout the many years of our married life. I tried to hold her to my world.

I observed how she despaired in trying to do what I would have her do. I imaged her again as a "little girl" who simply could not change, no matter how she appeared to try.

At times, I witnessed her suffering and this began to reflect itself in my own attitudes. I became aware of my own harsh judgments against her ways. In moments of compassion, I would try to ameliorate conditions by being good to her and would shower her with gifts that I knew she would love.

Then there were times when she would amaze me in her intuitive knowledge of me. I observed in certain moments, she would feel that one of my schemes or activities was about to take place which I discovered to be erroneous. At such times, she would show signs of being restless, anxious and worried. This gave me a clue that I was to change my course of action before I was about to embark upon what I had devised in my own mind. It was in changing my own approach and action, that I discovered repeatedly that **she was right.** From where did she receive this wisdom? Was this her intuition?

But this was an enigma I could not comprehend where she obtained this intuitive quality. It was simply there. My curiosity was piqued about her enough to begin to study her once more.

Over a period of years, I was astounded that she appeared illumined. Throughout our entire marriage, there wasn't a day that passed that she did not pray for me. Through her, I was enabled to follow the Will of God. Not only did I recognize His Will, but my Wisdom also came to me from God through her prayers.

Once more, I was overwhelmed in my

realization of all that I was witnessing: Lilias in all her sweet humility and childlike ways really believed in me and supported me. It was overpowering for her to have such a faith in me that she believed God was with me. With this evaluation of her, my own job performance increased in excellence and "right action."

Following this realization, I desired with all of my heart to show her my gratitude. So I planned trips for us all over the world. She showed me the desires of her heart in our travels. We went wherever her interests would lead us. In this way, we would see the "wonders of the world."

Lilias was greatly curious, and she sought places of religious significance so that we could observe first hand the religious centers of the Far East. Often she would precede our travels by studying in advance the knowledge of Tibet, Jerusalem, and Egypt--all rich in historic background.

I noted how knowledgeable she was, especially as she would tell me of the great prophets who wrote the books she had read. For the first time, this encouraged me to study the religions of the world. I, too, found such spiritual centers to be of great interest. But I did not associate any of the past religious leaders or prophets with saints or Ascended Beings. I knew some of the prophets who were the individuals known upon the earth such as St. Francis of Assisi, St. Mark, St. Luke and John the Beloved. All of these individuals had merited the ascension and became angelic beings within the Heaven World. All these were the brothers and sisters of Jesus. They were the men and women who learned how to follow the Will of God.

However, Jesus, the Christ Light who came into the world to play the role of the "One that ever was and ever shall be" was the True Light. Jesus was to show and demonstrate to mankind, the nature of God. Jesus was to portray the Light of God, and demonstrate what God was like. The son would blend with the Light of God and become the Lord in the world.

We were taught that Jesus was the "only begotten son of God" and that he was above all other prophets, who became One with His Father, the Pure Light that flowed to all men.

Each one's light was his own intelligence and was to be used in the world to serve God.

I believed that talents and intelligence were to be in service to the democratic way of life of the United States, in bringing forth the truth of God as I would interpret and perceive it. This was my way of serving the Christ Light. To me this Light was the supreme Light in all of mankind, because "this was the Light that ever was and ever shall be," and this is the Light of God.

To my way of thinking, in the Army, to serve the officers who were generals was like serving a higher intelligence. A general who had a higher intelligence from the other officers and whose performance was observed to be superior to the others, merited his superior position. As I too, would serve and perform to the best of my knowledge and intelligence, I believed that in time, I, too, would become a general.

I knew that I was indeed being considered for such a promotion at various times, but for some unknown reasons, others less qualified, were promoted. In my persistence, I still believed that if I continued to strive and do my best within my own talents, my time would come to merit the promotion.

Thus, I studied diligently through the years to reach my own goal within the U. S. Army. I believed the block was due to the deficiencies in my own wife.

The wives were so devoted and did indeed assist their husbands within their own community service. My wife served in the churches. Often she attended religious conferences. The women had gained social acumen while handling many parties and social activities. They were so adept in their social graces and had already been trained in the roles each one was to play as a general's wife. All along the way, such women were expected to assist their husbands with the social amenities within the military circles.

The economic level of such women set them free of the menial tasks performed by servants within the foreign countries. The generals' wives were supposed to train the servants to adapt to the ways of the military life. They were expected to perform in an efficient way to reflect the training each one had been given. It was within the homes of the generals in higher positions that a greater efficiency in performance was noted in all that was done. The highest officers were to be an example for all those officers serving the general.

This is not too unlike the role a queen would depict. She would have the housekeeper train the servants, but she would teach the housekeeper in what was expected of the servants. There were chefs in the kitchen who would be supervised by the general's wife. She would be adept in planning the meals.

The wife was in a managerial position with the staff of servants. The general too was in a supervisory position within his home to all of the servants, just as he was also in a higher position to all of the lesser officers. It was the general who would advise the wife in what was expected of her. Thus she would be able to play her role as a perfect hostess despite all the tasks that were done by others. She was still to oversee all that was done to be sure it was done right. All this was part of the way of life within the higher levels.

You, Mary, seemed to have the training to be a general's wife, and the parties in your home were observed by so many. The comments which were made were that you personally prepared the meals without any servants to assist you. All thought this was amazing. When Skippy Lynn flew from Washington, D.C. and visited your home at one of the parties, she saw the attractive home in which you lived. The efficiency in all that happened was noted in the delicious, well-balanced meals that were served to so many. You had the necessary training within the Home

Economics Department of the college and university you had attended. But your own husband did not fully realize your capabilities and had continued to hold you in a menial position as others had seen.

I am at this time now seeing how you will no longer tolerate his ways anymore. He, too, has changed even as you have through the teachings you are sending forth into the world from the Ascended Beings. He too would now assist you in everything. In your home you are operating the Law of Balanced Interchange and all in your home are taking part in this same law and now understand how it operates within the organization.

I am now seeing how this law works. But I also observed how you are aware of the flaws of so many. I see your own determination to do whatever is necessary yourself. You believed this reduced the stress and duplication of the work within the organization and in your home. You realized that others could not do as you do. Others too were aware of this and so they would step aside and let you do the work. I saw how you too, Mary, carried the belief: "If you want something done well, do it yourself." You recognized this in your own world as being a reflection of what you believed.

The time came, when you could no longer keep pace with the growing organization. You now relied on Raphael to do the works. I saw your joy in turning over everything to his right action in his Wisdom. You were willing to just have him show you what you were to do. You are now realizing what the balance is between the male and the female.

I too have learned exceedingly in just observing the way you work and have learned so much as I have listened to what you would say daily. By observing you, I know just what is to be released from my own spirit, especially as you work with Raphael and Sanat Kumara. This is the way I have been able to have a massive clearance rapidly.

At this time, Lilias prayed to Jesus and asked Him, "Who is Tim who was my husband for so many years?" Jesus now guides Lilias to read the chapter in the Bible about the Centurion. The many pages Lilias has received not only from Tim and Jesus, but also from Raphael, are printed here in the following chapter.

JESUS TEACHES TIM.

31-A

CHAPTER II

JESUS SHOWS TIM
WHO HE WAS IN THE PAST

THE CENTURION
Luke 7, Chapter 8

5 There came unto [Jesus] a Centurion, beseeching him,
6   And saying, Lord, my servant lieth at home sick of the palsy, grievously tormented.
7   And Jesus saith unto him, I will come and heal him.
8 The Centurion answered and said, Lord, I am not worthy that thou shouldest come under my roof: but speak the word only, and my servant shall be healed.
9   For I am a man under authority, having soldiers under me: and I say to this man, Go, and he goeth; and to another, Come, and he cometh; and to my servant, Do this, and he doeth it.
10 When Jesus heard it, he marveled, and said to them that followed, Verily I say unto you, I have not found so great faith, no, not in Israel.
13 And Jesus said unto the Centurion, Go thy way; and as thou hast believed, so be it done unto thee. And his servant was healed in the same hour.

THE ANGEL RAPHAEL SPEAKS:

The Centurion was a Roman, living in Rome and was sent on duty to Jerusalem   to protect the Roman conquests there of a portion of the Roman Empire.

He who was **Timothy**, the Centurion, is one and the same who has now made the ascension into the Heaven World. As my spirit is within my soul body of light, I have the memory of what happened during the time that Jesus was upon the earth.

. . .And so I was there with my soldiers, one hundred men who were all Romans. But our servants were of the Jewish nation. These servants cared for our home, and cooked our meals. The Romans enjoyed their duty in Jerusalem.

It was I who lived with the Jewish people and learned to love them even as I learned about their One God who is an invisible Holy Light. Therefore I built them a new synagogue, which endeared me to the Jews.

It was I who had won their confidence and trust and my devoted servant would keep me informed of what was happening among the Jewish people. For this servant was the one who kept me abreast of all that was happening among the Jewish nations whenever any prophet came to the areas where the Romans were residing. Therefore I was an informant to the Romans and, unknowingly, to the people of the Jewish nation. For at times I would attend the Jewish Temple and would ask my servant to explain his beliefs to me of the One God. In my own mind I would study this Jesus and also the God of the Jews and determine for myself whom I would follow.

When the healing took place with my servant, now this was evidence to me that it was the Father who had sent Jesus, and henceforth I would learn all that I could about this Prophet. Therefore, I gathered all the information not only from the Romans about Jesus but also from the Jewish people so that I could be knowledgeable in my own way of thinking.

During those times, all those who were the soldiers and officers within the Roman government were to give their allegiance to the Roman government and not to anyone else. For it was Caesar who claimed to be the representative of his own God Ammon.

Caesar's blood was royal and the oldest son was to have received the inheritance in divinity of his royal blood, to be next in line to rule as the father passed away.

Therefore, outwardly I could not show any loyalty either to the Jewish nation, nor to Jesus the Prophet. The subjects of Caesar were to follow only one God in his land, and Caesar represented this One God as being the ruler of the world.

Caesar represented the authoritative self, or the "Ego" who was prepared by his own father to replace him as the ruler in the land.

Caesar had the power of life or death over anyone, as all within his own empire were subject to him.

It was when I was told of the great silence of this Prophet that I personally could see his great wisdom and understanding of the Romans and of the Jewish nation. To me, he was a master of psychology and knew how to sway the people. For there was a great peace about this man, Jesus, and all felt the peace and kept silent to listen to every word he would say. Furthermore, I noted his supreme knowledge of His Father in Heaven of whom he taught. And he knew that none would understand him in the beginning since so few of the people had any knowledge outside of their own territory.

For it was only travelers who would bring to the people the news of other cities, kingdoms and other rulers. Communication was exceedingly slow, and travel was mostly done on foot, for the majority of the horses trained under the jurisdiction of the military were used to serve the purposes of the ruler. And all were in subjection, not only to serve their divine ruler, but all within the land, all the food, all the natural resources, all the talents, all the men, women, and children-- all belonged to God, the ruler in the land. And the best in all of the land was to be owned by the ruler. Even the most beautiful women were brought to the royal courts to serve the purpose of the ruler. He would choose who were to be a part of his harem and the women who would serve the royal ladies, who were as servants to the royal family. This was the way of life in the time that Jesus was upon the Earth.

During the crucifixion of Jesus, I was deeply pained that the Romans, under the rule of Caesar, had turned this extraordinary, able Prophet over to the Jewish nation. It was in my independent thinking that I could see his infinite ways of not being partial neither to the Romans, nor to the Jewish nation. He spoke of a Father over all, a Celestial Parent who loved all of mankind. And this now infuriated the Jewish nation inasmuch as they believed they were the chosen ones in the world to bring their God into the world to rule supreme over all of mankind. There was no other God to this nation but the invisible God, who was not form, but who was a Holy Flame, as Moses had showed them. And this Flame was the Creator of Heaven and Earth. For they would repeat in all of their Temples, "Hear Oh Israel, the Lord our **God is one.**"

And this statement had angered the rulers, who still followed the God of the Pharaohs whose name was Ammon. Thus there was great turmoil in the beliefs between the Romans and the Jews.

It was I who, as a Roman, observed the crucifixion and heard the words spoken upon the cross. It was I who would now follow this Jesus. I was convinced such a One was true. In my soul I bore witness to the Truth. And henceforth there would be no other God to me but Jesus.

Yes, I was there for his crucifixion, and sad and sorrowful it was. My heart was torn between my duty to Rome and what the Jewish rulers, through fear of the Romans, were about to do. The Jews convicted Jesus in the night with such cruelty. The masses were unable to understand what was happening because of the traitors spreading falsehoods about Jesus. And I was there and saw the terrible sight of such injustice to an innocent man, but was helpless to help Jesus. My life changed from that day onward, and I fought for justice.

You, Lilias, were not with me. I know now of your incarnation as the daughter of a very rich man who wanted you to marry a much older man. You rebelled and left with Miriam, your younger sister. You were lost in a desolate world, and within a short time, after great hardships (you and Miriam often were hungry) Miriam passed away; soon after, you did, too. After great suffering you passed on in the open air, the birds singing you to your onward journey.

Although it would be centuries before the teachings of Jesus the Christ, the Ascended One would be understood, it was as I came face to face with my Lord that I realized that I received the reward of my soul.

Now with the assistance of My wife, Lilias, and her dearest friend, the story of my ascension will begin.

Now I listened attentively, as you did, Mary, to every word that was spoken by the chaplain. You now recognized the Holy Spirit within the Resurrection Flame being with me. Others thought I was within the casket, but I was standing right there beside the casket looking at everyone, observing everyone's reactions to all that was now taking place.

In the midst of the great stillness of the people, "Taps" was played, as all were thinking of the departing spirit, when I suddenly felt as though I were enveloped by an atmosphere of

Love and my spirit was lifted up. Can you imagine standing on an escalator, moving up slowly? I was now on an invisible, Light-filled stairway that moved up in frequency.

I heard you, Mary, call upon the Resurrecting Angel, and you began to love the Divine Mother. It was Her Light which was the Escalator. You were, within that moment, within our dimension, seeing what was happening. For I saw your eyes upon me, focused on my body. You were seeing within the invisible atmosphere, as I slowly arose.

Then, Mary, I came into the Light of my Lord, Jesus the Christ. During this time, Lilias was dwelling on the Christ Light, Lord Jesus, who came for me. Suddenly, I experienced a joy that was overwhelming. You felt this Love--all felt this Love--but none could define what was being felt.

I knew that you knew because I heard how you described all of this to Lilias. She confirmed that she too felt the Presence of Christ. God is Love.

I know how long people have believed that the body is within the casket, but the masses cannot see the spirit once it leaves the body because their eyes are focused on what they believe. They do not realize the atmosphere in the world reflects the spirit of each one. The spirit eyes are seeing what each one believes; this holds one to the appearance world. Therefore, as the atmosphere is a reflective atmosphere, each one is given according to his own way of thinking

38

and believing.

One would believe there is such a thing as being resurrected into the Heaven World; while this is within one's consciousness, each one evaluates what he remembers about the one who has passed on. Most people believe that loved ones in the family who are already in the spirit world make their appearance at this time to welcome the one who has just arrived into the spirit world. It would be like a reunion of the family members who are already within the spirit world.

I know that records are kept in hospitals of when a person is expected to die, at times, the sick one will speak out loud as though he is seeing deceased members of his family and recognizing them by name.

THE WAY TO PEACE

By Our Lord

Jesus Speaks of Mary
(Lilias' Best Friend)

My own child, I have loved you as I have loved My own little lamb. You have followed Me, and loved Me in many lives, and searched for Me throughout the world.

My daughter, long have I waited until ye were so purified that you could feel My entry into thy soul. You are now aware of My Spirit, and you are seeing how My Spirit is like the great bodies of water which hold all the children in every country, in every land, in every religion--those who believe in Me, and those who believe in Me not.

You are to see how I say to you, "Believe in Me." For you believe that My Father is in My Body. And you, My child, have recognized the Father in My Body since you were a young woman. You understood how I had united with the Light of the Universal Body, which you at one time believed was located within the center of the sun. For many years, you worshiped the Light in the sun, as being The Father.

For many years you would come to Me in prayer and recognize this Light in My Body; you worshiped this Light. You believed that I directed this Light and performed all the miracles through this Light. Although you loved this Light, you were not aware of the Light in My Body being Pure Love. You were not aware that the substance which you worshiped as you felt the Magnetic substance in the air itself was My Body. You were not aware how many times I had come into your soul. Although you vaguely were aware of Light, as though it were a faint light in a dark room--still, you were aware to some degree of My Presence in the form of Light shining within your soul. You will now understand that I tried to come into your soul years ago as you were loving Me within thine own heart as I answered your prayers so many times.

You would feel My Light of great compassion and begin to weep. Many times you knew not why the tears would fall without your being able to hold them back. You at times felt such great sadness in My churches, and again did not know why you felt the deep sadness which so many feel within their own spirits. You did not know that as I held your spirit and you felt My Love and great compassion for you--it was as though you had come to your own child and longed with all of your heart to be recognized, but My child knew Me not within her own spirit.

Did I not show you, in My Parable, My own great sadness because My children, My own disciples who tried to follow Me, knew Me not within their own spirits. I said to them, "How long have I been with you, and you knew Me not!" Although I said these words and My

41

disciples heard them, they still understood not that **I am** within their own spirits.

How many times have you heard My sons say, "My Body is Spirit"? I AM that Spirit which is the Light of the Christ, the Universal Body which is in the world, and is known by many names. But it is still the One Body of the Universal Father Mother God, the threefold Pure Flame, which few realize is the Pure Light of Creation itself, which creates all things in the world. This Body of Light is constantly present within the center of one's own spirit, which holds the Flame of the Father Mother God.

I know that in the past, those who knew of this power held this secret to themselves, and considered it sacrilegious to give this knowledge to any other in the world. Man believed that this Pure Flame was guarded by the church itself and given only to those who had proven their own worthiness to receive this Sacred Holy Flame of Creation itself.

I know that it was believed only by the chosen of God Himself who looked into the hearts of all, and knew those of His children who were pure, and those who were not pure. I know that the ordinary man, or the ordinary woman were to receive the crusts of bread, which the chosen would give to them within the Temple.

This practice continued through the centuries in ritual form. In silence and sadness, I was present with My children among the laymen who knew Me not within their own spirits, who knew not that the sadness which they had felt within their own spirits, was **My Spirit** of sadness, as I was not recognized within. As I said, **Lo! I Am** with you always, many of My children still knew not that **I Am** always present with each one, with each man, woman and child in every nation throughout the world.

Others felt the sympathy in My Spirit as they heard the stories of the countless healings in the Parables of the Bible. All the healings which took place, took place first within the spirit. As the spirit was changed, the Body changed. The spirit receives the Light of the Father Mother God. The spirit receives the Light of the Universal Body which is The Christ. The spirit receives this soul Light which is the Light of My Body, which I filled with the substance of Love.

As it enters, the cells are so loved by this love that it is the same effect of reviving sick cells in the same way as a plant is revived, by putting it into the sunlight after a long period of being in the darkness.

I know that My children have waited throughout the world for My Second Coming--so that All would recognize Me. As I AM already here, and have never left the Earth, and have always been within the spirits of my children, My Second Coming is not of the solid, physical substance in the world. The first Body of Adam is the physical body, the solid body of substance, of a lower frequency, which looks outwardly into the world. My Second Coming is for the spirit body, the spiritual body, your body of spirit within your physical body.

At the right time, in my spiritual development, I gained an awareness of My Spirit. This would be considered the Second Coming into a higher state of consciousness within a little higher frequency.

The Second Coming is for the spirit body. As I descend from My Soul or Higher Body of Light, from a still higher frequency, I descend as an invisible light into the spirit body. The spirit body is the feeling body somewhat like a negative of a photograph. The spirit body likewise has nerves, and all the organs comparable to the physical body, as spirit organs. The spirit body is a replica of the physical body in spirit form.

The spirit feels My Light as a pulsating, throbbing Light in a Sea of Divine Love, which is the aura of Light in My Light Body or Soul. The soul lives and moves and breathes and has its being within a world of light, which is the frequency of the soul.

If ye, My children, come and sit in the sunlight and close your eyes, and feel the warmth of the sunlight in your spirit and body, My Light shining in your spirit will give you the same feeling of sitting in the sunlight with your eyes closed.

Now come into My sunlight, My daughter, as you used to do for many years. Close your eyes and feel My Spirit. Each of you who sit in the sunlight will feel My Spirit as you close your eyes. My sunlight flows into each one's spirit and warms their spirits just as I warm your spirit as you recognize Me in your second body. It is this recognition of Me within your spirit which will bring you joy. As you recognize Me not, your soul is sad.

Some of My disciples recognized Me within and spoke of the warmth in their hearts.

Some had to warm themselves by a fire. The spirit was cold; they had denied me. You remember how it was Peter who denied Me. You remember how he had to warm himself by the fire because he knew Me not within his own soul and spirit.

From now on, the moment you turn inwardly and close your eyes, and turn to your spirit as the place where you are thinking within your own body and mind, you will feel My Spirit in your spirit, as you sat in the sun and practice this. The sun may not be shining in the world. It is cold in the world. But you have turned inwardly, and you are feeling My Presence by admitting this light within your own self; you now feel as though you were sitting in the sunlight and you feel the warmth of the sun. You know the sun is not shining in the world, but you feel it shining within. You feel it as a peaceful feeling. You feel it as a gladness of spirit and joy; you cannot separate it from your own spirit. You are not aware that I have come into your world, your own spirit in your own body which reflects itself in the world.

Many of you will think of Me as being far away. As you think "far away," your own thought comes between you and Me, and shuts Me out of your own spirit.

Many of my teachers speak of the great privilege of My coming to them, as they are aware of Me in the different times of their lives. During the moments when My children prayed to Me, My Light surrounded them.

Millions have prayed to Me. While they were praying, My Light at that moment came into their souls. Each felt My Spirit of Peace. None knew that My Spirit was within their own spirit. The Peace they felt was My Spirit shining upon them as the Light of the sun is shining upon them and makes them sleepy. It is My Spirit that covers them. It is My Spirit that covers the mind and body and spirit--as when a child is in prayer.

Now prepare thyself for prayer, and be ready to speak to Me. Instead of speaking, just feel My Spirit with you as you turn within and think of Me within your spirit. You will find that this practice of feeling My Spirit will give to you the evidence which you have long been seeking from others because before you knew Me not in your own spirit.

The Son of God which is Spirit, comes from the one source of Universal Spirit. Since it comes from the Universal Spirit, it is only **One Spirit.** There is no other.

It is the **Spirit of God** which is Light and Spirit, the same substance of the Father, the same substance of the Universal One

My Body is not a body of flesh. It is a body of Light. But this body encircles the Earth and permeates all space. It is "the One Body that ever was and ever shall be." **One Body, Holy,** and **Begotten by the Father.** It is a Ray of the same Light being given from the Father which is from the Universal Light, the One Light which supplies all life, love, joy, wisdom, truth and all virtues from **the One Source of the Great Central Sun.**

All life comes from the One Source. Each child born into the world receives his life from the One Source. It is the **Only Begotten Source, the Father, the Christ, the Great Body** of **Light**--from which all things are made. There is no other source from which anything is made. It all comes from the One.

As you dwell on the Universal Body as being the Source of all life, all Light, you will see how "the only Begotten Son" is that Light that comes into the world, but comes not from the world. It is not of the substance of the world, but of the One Source of Light. All in the world, including the world itself, has been formed from the One Light.

This **Light is the Supreme Light** whom I have called **"Father which art in Heaven."**

Heaven is the place of the Pure Light of the Universal Christ, of which we are One, in which we have blended our own spirits to such a degree that there is no other spirit, but the Spirit of the Father. We dwell in His Spirit, with our minds centered on the Pure Light of the One Light. **As you look at My picture, notice My eyes. You will see how My eyes are thinking and dwelling with My Mind on the Pure Light within the Spirit--inward. Although I AM**

47

looking outward, I Am seeing My Father's Pure Light in My Spirit. Silently, I am now acknowledging Him, loving Him in My Spirit. Knowing that He is in My Spirit, I know also that He is Spirit; and as **He** is the **Father** of all--and is the source of Life of all--I see His Spirit everywhere.

In My great Love for His Spirit I recognize His Pure Spirit inside each one's own spirit. As I see this inward spirit in Me as being One and the same in thee--this spirit now shines upon the cells within your spirit, and you are healed by the very Pure Light, by the Purity of the Universal Body, in which there is no sin.

For it is Pure and it always was Pure, and always will be Pure. It is this Spirit which heals all the cells of everyone's body. The spirit is within the cell; there is no cell which is devoid of spirit substance around the cell, or within the cell. Spirit substance is itself Light. Each one feels the degree of light within himself as his spirit has been elevated, and he acknowledges the Spirit of God in his spirit.

To be spiritual is to be centered in spiritual things. You are centered in the Light which uplifts the Spirit, and which brings joy and peace and love to the mind, heart, and soul.

I Am the soul. **I Am** each one's soul. **I Am** the Universal One. The soul is "The only Begotten Son of the Father." It comes from the One. It is of the same Light. Although it is light, man knows not his own soul. If he knew his own soul, he would know Me. **I Am Soul.** All souls were created in the image of the Father. All souls will one day do what My Father will do. The soul is made of the substance of Light.

The soul is not to follow man. The soul is to follow the Father. The soul is the Son, "Begotten by the Father." There is only One. The Universal Body is Pure Light, that light which leads all souls to the Universal Body, its supreme Source.

I Am that Light from the beginning, and will be unto Everlasting. For the Universal Light is the Eternal Light of God--forever alive, forever present, forever upon the Earth, above, within and surrounding the Earth. The Earth is the body of man and woman in the flesh. The flesh is composed of the substance of Earth. The Earth in and of itself is only the outer substance of the spirit. The body is only the outer substance of the spirit within the body.

The Earth was without form until the breath of life was given to bring the earth's form into manifestation. Does not the Breath of Life bring a child to be a conscious living body into the world? For the Earth is made; then the breath of life is given to the baby; the spirit enters the body.Then, does not the body return to the dust as the breath of a living being has expired and is no more? With the breath, the spirit leaves the body and comes into the body. Spirit is life within the body. It is the spirit which has His Life and His Light. Light is Life.

Life is Light. All Light comes from the One. All spirits are "Begotten by My Father."

The seed of man contains the Spirit of Light. This seed is given to man by the Universal Body of My Father. All seeds contain light, and all light comes from the One.

I have been with many of My children and I gave My Truths to them. Those who hold power in their own spirits over the spirits of others knew that it was spirit which held the power. But those who knew not that the power of My Father is in spirit, feared the power as they understood it not.

The Truth has for many centuries been guarded from those who would be disobedient to the Law of Love within the Power of Light. These disobedient ones would use any means in the world to take that which they desired. They would use the power within their spirits to take what they wanted.

Some have discovered that the Power of Light is in their own spirits, but know not that the Power of Light is under the Law and operates according to the Law. No man can use this Light destructively. As one tries to use the Light in a destructive way, the same Light begins to destroy his own spirit.

No man can take hold of the Pure Light of the Universal One in order to take what he wants. Neither can any nation, nor church, nor organization use the Universal Light except this Light be given by the Father Himself. It is man's own human spirit which man sends out into the world as he would pray to use his Light to destroy. As his own spirit goes forth to destroy, it is his spirit which receives the destruction.

The spirit itself is under the Law. Whatever spirit is given out to any man, or woman, or group, or nation, that spirit will return to the nation. The man, woman, group or nation itself will receive the destructive energy originally sent forth.

Man has long justified wars and believed he had to defend his own nation. Those who believe in war, know not that the spirit of war sent out from any nation, will bring war to the nation, and all will suffer.

In the past, man has believed he would rescue his own brother from evil. As man sent out the spirit of evil, he was drawn into that evil.

It is the spirit of man which controls what a man will do and which may bring peace to a nation. The spirit of man is in the peace of the Father. The Father holds His nation in the peace of the Universal Light, the Everlasting Body around, above, and below man, centering and surrounding him.

As man gives his spirit to Universal Peace, no nation will have to go to war. The spirit of that nation will be in peace. This peace is the Universal Body of God. Peace or war is first within the spirit. It is in the spirit that wars are to cease.

Did I not teach mankind to resist not, but turn to the Universal Body of My Father--and love this Body in the enemy.

For the love to the Father will bring the Father into the spirit of the enemy. The power of evil will be removed, and Peace will come into his spirit.

The spirit of man is in his face. Man may choose Light, or he may choose darkness; he may turn to the right, or he may turn to the left. The right is light and the left is darkness. Darkness is of the world, as man turns away from the light and knows not the Light and he refuses it.

"The other cheek" is the right. This cheek knows that the Father stands on the right. It is this cheek which has the light, which has the knowledge and the truth.

The soul of light is on the right side. Man turns within to his soul as he turns his right cheek. But as he turns his left, he looks out into the world and sees only darkness, his enemy. His enemy is evil. He is seeing the darkness through his left eye, the eye which denies and refuses the soul, the light. The Universal Body of light surrounding every man, woman and child, and in all and through all, is the Father in the soul.

Did I not say, "Choose whom you will follow," the left or the right. Choose man or choose God. If you follow man in the world, you shall be in darkness. But as you follow God, you shall be in the Light and the Peace of the Universal Body of the One.

Now My Children, as I have long been known as "The Prince of Peace," My Peace will come upon all those who believe in the Universal Christ, the Everlasting Light of the Father Mother

God, which supplies the life of every man, woman and child upon the Earth. My Father is life. It is He who will bring Peace to the world as His children everywhere turn away from the control of man in the world, and turn to My Father.

He is in your spirit, your own Light, your own Life, and your own Love. You will feel the Light of His Spirit as you acknowledge Him within your own spirit and recognize your own soul--"His Only Begotten Son of the Father Mother God."

Blessed be **all** whose spirits are in His Peace! For you shall inherit His Peace, and receive His Peace. For your own soul will hold you to His Peace as you believe in Him in your own spirit--My Beloved children, whom ye All are.

Jesus

CHAPTER III

TIM'S BOOK OF LIFE

In the beginning of my spiritual evolvement, I believed in the light beings known upon the Earth as the saints, or the Angelic Beings, or the White Brotherhood, who had ascended into the Heaven World, just as Jesus had done.

The entire church which I had served followed the teachings of the saints which were for the dedicated few within the inner mystical society of the sanctified officers. These were the higher officers approved by the Pope; and then they received the highest teachings upon the Earth.

Among the dedicated women serving the church, many had been the female babies given to serve God within the church. These women were brought up and trained by the church teachers to serve the church in the highest, which was known to be following the angelic beings. What had been received from highly spiritual women in the church who were obedient to the church tenets, was now the property of the church, preserved and guarded by the Pope and reserved for the higher, inner mystical circle. Only those higher officials who obeyed the Pope and supported him in all the ways shown to them within the laws of the church, only these were eligible to receive these inner teachings preserved throughout the ages.

COLONEL FREDERICK TIMMERMAN

54-A

It was known that the preserved Word of God was indeed the property of the church since its inception so that the teachings would be propagated by the few until the masses evolved to the point where they could live in peace with their brothers and sisters within all countries of the world.

The secret teachings would be sacred teachings given to the authorities concerning the states of consciousness of all levels of society. Children are born to families in most cases, on their own level of consciousness.

But the stewards of the Church were the higher officers. Their Church was the one selected to accept all races, colors, and all who were ready to follow God. The stewards were to be the One Universal Church which would accept all races, colors, and all who were ready to follow God as they were to be taught on the level of each one's own progress.

Not too long ago, I was in the world within the services of the United States Army serving overseas as an officer in the capacity of colonel. Being fluent within the foreign language within the country where I served, it was my assignment to keep the government informed of what was heard on the television, radio and among the people. What was written within the periodicals of the land, newspapers and letters, would be briefly summarized to assist others in their understanding of the trend of the current thinking within the foreign country.

Furthermore, I was to circulate among the

political parties within the land and listen to all that was being said.

In continuing to absorb the news continuously, it was my portion of the work to interpret the trend of thinking within the land. Thus my attitude was to listen in a casual way to neighbors and friends who likewise spoke in their native tongues and passed along news as people would do concerning what was happening in the world.

During this period, under the existing conditions, my wife and her closest spiritual friend were studying knowledge on a spiritual level what I was gathering on a mental level. I was often aware within my intuitive nature of the prayers of my wife. She would pray for all of the people within the country and included all the people of the world.

It was in my study of the literature she was receiving that I became aware of her silent prayers. Even so, to admit praying for the problems which beset the people within the land where we resided was not the way of thinking of officers of the United States Army. Many considered praying a lack of one's own intelligence in dealing with problems. However, there were those generals whom I knew prayed for the safety for all of their men who were following the orders of the generals. These conscientious men felt the great responsibility of the lives of the men since the generals themselves would make the decisions of where to station soldiers, how much ammunition was needed, and how many men were needed, not only in war times, but to protect the people in the land lest any sudden surprise attack would happen. This so often would occur before a war was declared.

This was the environmental world in which I gravitated to serve the interests of avoiding wars. I was working within the interpretations given to the generals, who in turn, were to report to their superiors.

In the training of all military officers, all of them were to obey not only their military commanders' orders, but all of the lesser in command were to adhere to the principles of democracy in the operation of the U. S. Army.

The way of life for the officers was such that they enjoyed all the privileges the army could bestow upon the intelligent leaders who were in control and operated within their official positions in the army. This was the way of life for the officers in almost every country where soldiers were stationed inasmuch as it has long been known that the safety of a country depended upon the supply, training and amount of technology of war implements being used.

Throughout over fifty years that I had served, I had believed that at times, I contributed to the saving of many lives as I would seek out the truth which prevailed within many circles of command within the Headquarters areas. Although this work demanded most of my time, I likewise supported the churches, knowing that the presence of spiritual leaders was of great importance to the morale of the soldiers, their families, and all within the Army.

Where pastors, rabbis, and priests join hands, it was in this way they would assist in their ministry to the U.S. Army, Navy, Air Force, and all the dependents. It was believed that while God was with us, He was also with the generals and all who would officiate in all that pertained to the safety in life preservation in each one's country.

All were to believe it was the enemy who were the oppressors and the evil ones who fought for whatever it was that would enrich their own country. There were always so many purposes for which wars were purported to be fought. For all were instilled with the concept of the conquest of "good over evil." Therefore, in the eyes of the military, the evil was to be stamped out and this was done by killing the evil enemy. Thus, the propaganda would be aimed at showing the people the evils of the enemy through the news media and television.

It was known that the minds of the people could be swayed in whatever direction the media would take. Thus all that was reported was first to be approved by the General within the immediate area. However there were those highly intelligent reporters sent into the troubled areas by national news agencies. Again and again these reporters obtained that kind of truth which was embarrassing to the military. Not only were the officers scrutinized, but also the families of the military were also to be watched closely in what any one of them would say at every cocktail party or festive gathering. There were employed

58

foreign waiters acting as agents to report what was heard in casual conversations. But the wives of the officers and soldiers were taught to guard what each would say and confine their conversations to what was considered unimportant. Thus the women were controlled to keep silent, especially the intelligent women who were often the officers' wives.

Under this type of a system, the knowledgeable women learned to be cautious, silent as much as possible, and to limit their conversations to their own families. They were to direct what was being said by speaking of the community projects assigned to support the way of life which would be a credit to the government in the land.

Despite all the cautions which were used to control the women, there were always those independent women who would go their own ways. These intelligent women would give the appearances of obeying and being supportive; however, there were always such women who were innovative, perceptive and highly intelligent in operating in their own ways.

There were two such women in my immediate environment, who were close friends. In harmony with one another, they would spend their time in religious pursuit of the truth. In their own application of what they were learning, these two women in their sincere dedication, began to contact the angelic beings, and studied those great prophets who had made the ascension and were within a higher sphere which was known as the Heaven World. They had learned that the former prophets were now angelic beings. While my own wife continued to be very silent within our own home and studied the lessons concerning ascended beings, she began to learn how to follow these teachings within her own understanding, despite the military environment and way of thinking.

Along with my own way of thinking and believing in what I had harbored for so long, their studies mentioned names that I had never heard of before. I could not trust myself to follow that which was new or unknown within the spiritual circles. Therefore, I resisted following what she had accepted and believed. Quietly, I observed her ways and looked into her books, studying the materials she had been purchasing, in my own ways. It was now necessary for me to keep silent.

For in her determination to follow the teachings of her best friend, I too was determined to follow the Christ in Jesus. As My wife's friend was in our home, I would demonstrate my own trust in following the one who had proved himself to be true within the Christian world.

In my own interpretation, I believed that my wife was now following the One who was the Jewish God. For the Jewish followers were persecuted in every country until they would establish a country which would be their own land. Here they would be free to follow their own religion.

Nevertheless, I saw how the wars for

centuries were religious wars, often incited by the rigid disciplines and laws to which the selected few would adhere to within their own lives. And then, I saw the complete devotion and loyalty of this close friend of my wife, how she too followed this same God despite her leadership among the women devoted to the Christian religious circles within this foreign land.

To me, this woman was a mystery. How could she be a leader within the Christian world and likewise embrace and follow the Jewish God? Who was this Yahweh, known as "the Ancient of Days" in the Bible? I knew He identified himself as the **'I Am that I Am'** to Moses.

Yet, it was my wife who explained that this woman was brought up by those who followed the same God. This is an enigma. Was she a pacifist who would turn women to follow her God? Time would tell.

The answers would be forthcoming while I observed her in all that she would do and say. When she was visiting my wife in our home, I would personally listen to what she would say in a casual way. But to my great surprise and amazement, she believed in my God, while simultaneously she believed in her God. She revered both of them. I intuitively felt as though she honored and revered Jesus when I would pray and invite Him to be our invisible Guest at the table during mealtimes, since we would pray before we dined.

THE STATE OF
CONSCIOUSNESS

A state of consciousness consists of the total awareness of an individual, at a given place in time. It is one's own stage of development which an individual manifests in the world. Each state of consciousness is recorded upon a person's own light, within his own spirit.

Disciples have incarnated lifetime after lifetime within countries all over the world. Few realize that each country contains the national thinking consciousness of all of the people who reside within the area of the country. The customs, traditions, and laws of the land are part of the heritage of each one's state of consciousness, as he adapts to the national consciousness.

Consciousness can be compared to a child passing through all the grades in school. In each grade he has lessons to learn before he is promoted to a higher grade. The people themselves within the land, will pass through different stages and levels of development within their life spans. Each one has his own school of life, in which he will learn all that is to be required within that grade or level, before he passes into a higher level of spiritual consciousness. As the natives gained knowledge, experience and understanding, they would be able to overcome a previous state of consciousness to a certain degree. It is as one arises into a more elevated state within his own being, that he can now surmise what others must go through, to learn that which he has gained. Seniors in college will understand what freshmen will have to encounter to absorb the knowledge which they have attained. In their higher state, they will overcome their own previous lack of confidence, as they were freshmen. It is easy to see how, as one acquires more understanding, one can look back and see the immaturity and lack of comprehension of the past.

Many have noted that as a change occurs within a state of consciousness, frequently there will be a change in one's environment, which will often improve. Some will take up their residences in new lands, where growth and new knowledge will be gained. These now will enter a newer state of consciousness within the higher environment. As progress continues, one comes into the awareness of his own spirit. He will now be stimulated to learn all that he can find, which will give to him a greater understanding of himself. It is as so many have begun to learn the techniques of meditation that they have discovered their electromagnetic force fields within their spirits. The name "chakra" defines the light centers in one's being and brings the searcher into the study of his soul, which borders on his discovering his body of Light.

The seven chakras within the body which represent the different dimensional levels of one's spirit within, have their particular functions to perform. The mental chakra supplies the light from which thoughts, images and ideas are formed within the mental processes. The heart chakra governs the emotions in the body, and supplies the energy from which emotions are formed and felt. As a person feels love, the energy of love flowing from the Ray of Love into the spirit body, would emanate as flowing, pulsating light. Before chakras were discovered, individuals were not aware of these light centers within their beings. Nevertheless each one controlled his own forcefields of energy within the way the mind, heart, spirit, soul and body were utilized.

Moses depicted the role of that state of consciousness where the self would hold every chakra in his being to the "power of the self," within his beliefs, desires, and within the destiny he believed he was to fulfill. Moses would not understand his own state of consciousness which he portrayed, until he learned the higher state, as he would reincarnate into a later period of time. Nevertheless it was Jesus who surrendered the hold of his own power to the Will of God, as he had greater knowledge and understanding and had gained a higher state of consciousness than Moses. It was Jesus who received the interpretations from higher beings, known as the Angelic Host, who had access to the Universal Truths of God. They would now reveal them to Jesus as he obeyed them, in receiving their interpretations of the messages which came from God. These divine beings were known to have a higher state of consciousness than those who were mortal beings upon the earth.

Within the Book, <u>My Truth</u>, seven biblical characters were selected to portray the seven states of consciousness, which every seeker will eventually pass through. Meditate on each character. As you do this, then give that character to the Father Mother God in prayer. Spend some time in loving the Universal Love of the Mother, within the personality which holds the key to the state of consciousness each one has passed through. This will give each one an insight into his own former state of consciousness, known as the spirit of the past. There will be those who will recognize the country in which they had lived within a former period of time. As the Law of Love is operated within that state of consciousness which the character portrays, my Father will give the visions and enlightenment necessary for the disciple to comprehend his beliefs and himself in former times.

Many of my followers have wondered if Moses was the first one to bring forth the Laws of God, which were given within the Ten Commandments. We in the ascended state have shown our disciples in the past, that various prophets throughout many eras have brought forth Laws of God. These laws were recorded upon their own "rock," symbolized by the soul, the body of Light. This is the immortal body of Light, which is even as a rock, which may be thousands of years old. There are ancient stories of how prophets of antiquity were messengers of the Lord, who tried to show the people how to obey the Laws which came from the Lord, which they would teach. There are ancient, sacred writings which teach sincere disciples how to receive My Spirit into their own spirits.

There are those states of consciousness where men will portray the role of women, to serve some purpose. In later lifetimes, these same men or women would revert back to being males or females, as they were in previous lifetimes. Greater compassion and understanding would emerge as each experienced the opposite sex.

Thousands of my disciples have believed it was necessary to become priests, monks, or lead celibate lives. Those who experienced celibate lives, still within their souls would hold themselves to a state of purity. At the same time, these would judge the sins within one's own family, among friends, and even within their own nation. As these men or women marry, they are still carrying the beliefs of former incarnations, and would now judge their own husbands; or the husbands would be aware of the darkness of their own wives and silently judge them. Wives in former lifetimes, have left their husbands, or the husbands left their wives, to follow the Lord, not realizing that their responsibilities toward their children and wives were to be fulfilled. To abandon one's family to follow the Lord, was not in harmony with the Law of the Love of God for all of His children.

The Covenant of the Lord is purported to carry the Eternal Laws of God, which are repeated from generation to generation. The disciples of the Lord all over the world, would carry the Laws, even the Ten Commandments within their own souls, their body of Light, where these Laws would be preserved as they were accepted and believed. As Moses had heard My Voice and would try to be an example of obedience to the Lord, so too does this disciple hear My Voice, and shows the members how they too are to obey Me. Moses taught his followers how they too would be enabled to receive My Spirit into their spirits.

My daughter likewise carried the Laws of God in her soul from lifetime to lifetime. She too had held beliefs and former interpretations in the world as though they were everlasting truths.

Oh, my daughter, it was man himself who declared that "Thou shalt have no other gods before Me." At this period in time my children had all believed that the life of man was the God in man. No man, neither any woman, was to usurp the power of the Light of God, which all had believed was the sun. My children had held the concept that the sun gave fertility to man and to woman. Therefore, the Lord could not be a man. God was formless Light. All of my children need to meditate on this.

Jesus identified himself with his Father and became One with Him. It was this which was refused in man himself. All men were sinners. It was believed that none could be one with God. It was preposterous! Who could be one with a Flame? This power was too mysterious and unfathomable. This power was simply too great to be in mortal man. He could not bear this power; therefore it was apart from man. This power would guide man as a cloud, as a burning bush, or as an overpowering Light.

Within the indelible light, held and believed by thousands of my children, is written upon the souls of their earthlight, "Thou shalt not bow down before any graven image, or any likeness of anything that is in heaven above, or in the earth beneath, or that is in the water under the earth. Thou shalt not serve false images.

"For I, the Lord thy God, am a jealous God, visiting the iniquity of the fathers upon the children until the third and fourth generation of them that hate Me; and showing mercy to thousands of them that love Me and keep My Commandments."

Oh my own sons and daughters, man upon the earth would carve the faces of those upon the earth who were known to be kings, or angels, or leaders. They would give to them their love and adoration. This would be considered "hero-worship" and idolatry, which continues to this day.

God is not formless. God is form. Out of His own formless, primordial, creative Light, He created the form within the family of man. The form carries His Spirit which is His Light. But this Light was invisible and inconceivable. Man's own eyes were constructed within a lower, vibratory range. To see God with human eyes was impossible! The form was not God, and never will be. God is the Light of the Sun.

Consequently, there is no image or any face. It was futile to argue. None could prove God to the physical state of man's consciousness.

It was during this period of consciousness that Moses heard the Spirit speak to him which he believed was this Jehovah or Yahweh. He surmised that this was the great Holy Spirit of God that was a Flame, so powerful that only the "Good men and women" could approach this awesome, Holy Spirit.

The prophets directed man to worship this great God in reverence. This Holy One demonstrated countless miracles and intervened to solve perplexing problems in the world with such profound Wisdom that all accepted such a One to be divine.

Man deduced that since God abode in spirit, he should be worshiped in spirit. Thus chants and prayers were formed to be heard by this great Spirit. Petitions for all manner of needs were formulated to draw the attention of this omnipotent One. Thousands of believing children would supplicate and plead for the assistance so many needed in countless ways.

There were former prophets before Moses, who had taught that a time should be set aside for quiet meditation and prayer. Therefore it was decided that this should be done in the time of Moses. Moses recorded a law that a day should be named as a holy day, which would be spent in contemplation in the Lord. A name was given for this day, to be called a Sabbath day. It was agreed to have this Law recorded as having come from the Lord.

Man had not yet developed to the conscious awareness that he had Celestial Parents, who gave their own Light, Life and Love to their soul children upon the earth. Note, how long it has been written that, "the Lord giveth Light, Life and Love. "

Each one was blessed who would honor God as the Father, and God as the Mother. The Celestial Parents would one day be recognized, honored and loved by their own children. In time, the children would develop in sensitivity to feel the light of Love of their Presence, who watched over them as Guardian Angels. But alas, as neither men nor women had any knowledge of their heavenly Parents, they could not comprehend the "Eternal Life" of these Parents. Neither would they have the knowledge of what to do to receive it. It would be centuries before they would evolve to the place where they were ready to obey these highly evolved beings, who were their soul Parents.

It was the Light of divine Parents within the heaven world, which would shine into the darkness, which the children of the earth did not understand — "from whence it cometh." Note how it is written that, "The Lord giveth Light, Life and Love." He blesses each son and daughter as God the Father, and God the Mother would both be recognized, honored and loved.

The family of man did not realize that each one's own physical parents were often guided by the Celestial Parents. These were the divine parents of each one's higher body, the soul. The physical father carried the Love of his Celestial Mother. She was the Mother of his own soul, his own body of Light.

The physical mother had been unaware that she carried the Life of the Father embedded within the spirit of her husband, whose spirit was within her own body. What a mystery this is to realize so great a Truth. Imagine the Father's Spirit, His own Light, has been hidden all this time within the male spirit, inside of her own spirit in her own body. How can this be? Why didn't wives and mothers know this before? If this is a revelation from God, it must be true. It is worth investigating to ascertain the validity of so profound a Truth.

Man's spirit was closed to plausible or persuasive explanations that God is within. His ears were closed to any who purported to make any claims of God being within man. These were the ancient verities of Egypt. This was the state of consciousness when the Sun God "Ra" was worshiped in the world. He was the supreme God.

My children are now commencing to realize that it is not My Father who would have His children begin wars, or continue them, as though it is My Will. I have declared to My own children that, "I have no enemies."

My children are not to use My Name to retaliate against one's own enemies. My own children, in great numbers, have come into the startling awareness that one's own enemies are one's own spirit reflecting itself in the world, which has not yet been redeemed. The spirit of the enemy is a former spirit of a disciple, now being externalized and mirrored in the world. It is being exposed for each one to recognize, as being his own spirit, still embedded, waiting for the disciple to learn how it can be dissolved. To see this spirit in the world and recognize it, and then know what to do to banish it from his consciousness, without in any way being harmed, will be the discovery of the century.

The Lord does not hold any man or any woman to any form of darkness, guilt, punishment, retaliation, or evil of **any kind**. **God is pure light.** He is forever dissolving the darkness of man's own human creations, in what is negative. God is forever changing the darkness into Light.

Any man or any woman who uses his own energy in his own light against the Love of God for all of His children, understands not His Name. His Name is "Love to All." Those who pervert the Love of God into hate for anyone, are using His Name in vain; and turning His Light into darkness. This is the state of consciousness where man believes himself to be superior in power, to overcome the enemy.

There is the story of the two large and powerful goats who were tramping across a bridge from opposite directions. They met as each saw the reflection of the other in the water. Dashing their horns against one another, they both fell in the water and drowned. "Horns" have long been symbols of "the power and superiority of the mental faculties in the world." This is the state of consciousness, where there are those rulers who have gained wealth and position in the world to some capacity. There are those who would not tolerate a higher power, no matter who it is in the world.

To hold the power within one's own hand, no matter who's hand it may be--to be superior to all, is in vain. None can overcome the Light of God, which is pure Love for all of His children in the world. Man breaks himself in his own opposition to the Love of God.

One can see how man punishes himself with his own energy and his own power within his own light, as he would control this power and use it destructively. Those who believe in karma within their own guilt are condemned by their own spirits in the world. Using energy to destroy life is like hurling a flame into the world as a boomerang. It is belief in karma which returns the boomerang to the one who, in anger and hate, hurled it into the world. The darkness returns and settles upon his environment as his own light was used.

For centuries families labored in the world for their food, clothing, and the necessities of life. The parents would provide for their children. There were the animals to be cared for and the soil to be tilled. So much time was spent in providing a livelihood for all within the family, that it was only as man prospered and could afford servants, that he began to have time for the Lord. It was among the affluent that the time could be spent in the acquisition of knowledge, which was passed on through the generations from father to son.

Time elapsed. Man's consciousness evolved to the worship of "good spirits" in the world. These beneficent spirits manifested periodically as angelic beings. Miracles would abound as divine Spirits would descend from the skies. They were often compared to birds which would fly in the atmosphere. In the silence of man's spirit, he began to detect spirits speaking to him.

These spirits were defined as benevolent spirits who would teach man in such a profound way, that man associated them with divinity. They seemed to possess an indefinable, mysterious spirit.

Man was ready now to study the sun, the moon, the stars, and the light in the lightning. He felt the awesome power of the thunder. There were all manner of phenomena upon the earth which were inexplicable. Man began to believe that the spirits caused the phenomena.

Before the advent of Jesus upon the earth, the state of consciousness of the people had been that their God was a punishing God. The children upon the earth at the time, would stone one another for the same sins each one had himself committed. These were the same ones who believed that evil could be eradicated by stoning or mutilating the sinner. At times the "evil ones" were thrown into a deep crevice of the earth.

Meditate upon the parable about Moses, as he held the power in his hand, and commanded the earth to swallow up the children of evil. It was as the sinner was killed, that the killer had done a righteous deed in avenging himself. He rationalized that he would be favored in the eyes of God for removing the sin itself from the earth. Note how the parable depicted the beliefs of man in the world.

As man believed that God was a fire that consumed evil, human beings were tied to a tree, while branches were encircled around them to start the fire. Note how many centuries women had been burned. This dates back to the time sticks were rubbed together to create friction of heat which would start a fire.

Laws were interpreted in the past to mean that man himself should not kill another unjustly or for his own motives, or because he was jealous, or coveted the possessions of others. Neither was he to kill in anger. But the Law of retaliation continued to flourish in the land. It was the Law of an eye for an eye and a tooth for a tooth. As one killed another, that one should be justly punished by taking his life. The people still believed and followed their own Law of Retaliation. The authorities in the past themselves believed in a Law of Retaliation.

Even as there were marauders upon the land who would plunder and carry off the women and children, the rulers themselves formed armies to retaliate against those who would divest them of their possessions. To this day, there have been armies formed to pillage and kill those from whom others could enrich themselves. The Law of Retaliation has persisted throughout the world, as though it were a Law created by God. But throughout the centuries the layman could not discern which Law came from God, and which was made by the authorities in the land. To this day man's laws prevail upon the earth everywhere. Man understands not the Way of the Celestial Father Mother God, in knowing the perfect thing to do with each erring child. Our Creator knows how to remove the "evil spirit" within the body, without killing the man or woman. One day man will seek to understand God's Ways.

In the consciousness of man's unknowing, the pure Life of the Father and the pure Love of the Mother have been held in multitudinous perverse thoughts and beliefs, which have been formed by the human mind against My Life and against My Love. Great will be man's wonder as he discovers that the Father Himself purifies woman with His pure Life. Men and women will be amazed to learn that God's Love purifies each one.

When man finally understands the word "adulterate" to signify: As a husband is against the love in woman, or woman is against the life in man, it is *this* which turns the light into darkness and adulterates, by giving darkness to that which was given to man and woman from God. All the thought forms, negative judgments and images of evil are considered to be darkness, which mixes these as impurities, against My Life and against My Love.

Within the union of man and woman out of wedlock is felt the darkness of judgment against one another. Those who have taken marriage vows know when the vows are being broken. It is this which brings the darkness into the body, heart, mind and soul. My children are feeling the effects of this darkness as they become more enlightened.

In the gross ignorance of the spirit and soul, as countries throughout the world would be conquered, women were raped and the husbands were killed. So intense was the darkness, that there were those who so rejected men, hating them all, that these women would have such men killed and remove all of their possessions from them. The men abhorred these women and would retaliate against them and judged their love as being evil. It was this which brought serious suffering to the male and female.

The spirit of retaliation operated with men and women; and each gave the other that which had been given to them, in retaliation. Man saw the reactions of men and women and surmised that each one would receive as he sowed.

There were those in the state of consciousness who cared not for those from whom they would steal. It was the object which was desired which would be taken illegally. It was not realized that within one's own spirit, one would take from his own Father, the light of another, or the love of another. These would refuse to give God any recognition, that he was robbing the soul of another, the body of Light.

These unenlightened ones would take from their own souls and refuse to give any recognition that God is in man, or woman, or child. These would refuse to acknowledge God, in what God had given to His child. As any man or woman continues to take and gives not, now these are robbed in the world, no matter who that one may be. Long have my children controlled others to serve them often oppressing them, in holding them to continue to work and serve them. These are the individuals who would be robbed. Frequently they would be overcome, and their own possessions would be removed from them. Bandits and robbers would pillage and plunder, and hold the strong in the land under their own power of force.

For centuries the women and children were sold as slaves, until I gave to Moses those Laws which were to be obeyed. It was during this time that guards were trained to protect the people upon the land.

All have seen how stronger nations conquered weaker nations. As the stronger nation subdued the weaker nation through wars, monarchs, kings, presidents and pharaohs and all the authorities have broken the Laws of God in some way. When my children learn to give to Me as I would have them give to Me upon the land itself, and when my justice is obeyed, man shall not have crimes. This will continue until the spirits of the people have been redeemed and My laws are obeyed.

Now you know. Concerning false images in

the world, man realizes not that he is not to accept any darkness concerning any man, woman, or child, as though the darkness is a permanent truth. He is not to accept the darkness as being the person himself. He is not to accept or believe in the image of darkness created by observations, and by studying anyone, as though that which he sees is the truth.

No man, neither any woman, knows the soul of any other man or woman, or child. The knowledge of the soul is withheld until man learns to come to God for the Truth. The world itself, is so constituted that the images of darkness which are formed within the spirits of men, women and children, now reflect into the world and are confirmed. Man's own light is set to the Law of God: to give to man, or woman, or child in the world, according to the belief each holds within his own image.

It does not matter what the belief or image is. There is a lack of comprehension of man's own light. He is not aware that as he forms any image of darkness, he is within his spirit, perverting his light of life and light of love, which God gives to each one. All darkness passes away.

The false image, which is seeing the darkness against anyone, is perverting the light into darkness. My Father, who is the Alchemist, is forever changing the darkness into Light. Conversely, man is constantly changing the Light into darkness.

Within the spirit of the one who covets, that one is already breaking the law of Love and Light for all within his own soul, and the darkness now accumulates. As this spirit lurks in the darkness within the coveting of the object, the offender of another is already rejecting My Father, as though God is nonexistent in the one from whom the possession would be filched. The word "covet," means to desire that which others possess, no matter what it is. As anyone looks into the world and desires what others have, they are holding their attention within the world for their desires to be fulfilled.

Those who care not for laws, neither care for his neighbors, nor for my Father Mother God being with each one, these are the erring children who devise all manner of mischief in their spirits in the way the object can be secretly appropriated. Submitting to this desire and permitting this illegal act to grip one within the hidden areas of the spirit, will elicit a trembling of the soul.

When men and women deny My Father within themselves and others, as though no one will know what they have done, these realize not that all is recorded on the soul and the guilt is felt inwardly. It is my Father who would supply all the needs and desires of His children as they would learn how to come to Him for supply. He would show them the way the object can be obtained legally, and often in a delightful way, where one would now receive joy and satisfaction in the possession.

But as others use force and bring suffering to others, it is as though their own spirit becomes the jailer which imprisons the light of these short-sighted individuals, in their self-created, nefarious images which pervert the Light of God and flood their soul with darkness. Oh, my beloved ones, it is *this* which brings the cold and suffering to the soul, itself.

The soul is now cut off from the Light of God, as though that one had cut himself off from the sunshine. The spirit becomes as the night and the self has no food of Light in the world. His depleted soul is now like a wilted plant. For at the moment the object is attained by the self, the soul would be in a state of agony, proportionate to the suffering that one brought to others, and in the way the object was acquired. Instead of the joy and satisfaction one had envisioned, it would be like a heavy chain now was strapped around the body of light and the turmoil and nervousness mounts.

When my children, in their new state of consciousness, overcome the desire to covet that which legally belongs to others, and these have learned to recognize the Father Mother God as the true Source of Supply, great will be the Light which will open upon the earth as these children learn to obey this Law, first in the spirit, and then in the mind, heart, and soul. It is My Father who will teach these children how to obtain their heart's desire in the Love of the Father.

THE GREAT ADJUSTMENT

What I say will give encouragement to all

those women who have lost their husbands. They were left so distressed, insecure, and filled with fear in their being left alone without the protection of their husbands. There were so many adjustments to be made. The wife would now have to learn how to manage all of his affairs and all that took place within her own environment. Although the husband had the management of the money in the family, how would she now manage the money in the world? Who would protect her from the unscrupulous? Who would guide her? What was she to do?

The wives never realized that their husbands had left them only in the physical body. Many women have described how they felt the presence of their own husbands as though he were right there with them, and they felt his guidance through all in their difficulties in the very beginning. Although the fears were great, they often felt comforted and encouraged to go on seeking spiritual knowledge for their own understanding. Often others came to their aid in countless ways. It was not realized how often problems were solved by concerned individuals who understood their dilemma. But so many wives do not realize how their own husbands are aware of their problems, even in guiding them in what the wife should do.

At times they believed they were forgotten or even rejected by others. However, changes occurred to transform the situation.

The women in some uncanny way felt happy, but they knew not why they felt joy despite their belief that they were to continue to grieve. The light of the husbands, who gave love to their wives, are within the souls of the wives. They were always near and could recognize their thoughts and desires which were often fulfilled in some unknown way. As time passed the wives became independent and adjusted to their single state and were able to live in the knowledge that they were never alone, and the words would often flow, "Lo, I am with you always." But they didn't understand that this was the Light that was always with them.

In your particular case, Lilias, I will speak about your experiences in the world without your husband. I saw how everyone was so very kind and helpful to you, but despite all of this caring that was shown to you, you still felt that emptiness that I felt in the world.

I observed how so many seemed so happily married within their families and children, within their social life which kept them so busy in so many ways. But now the change in my being was felt since the children whom we cared for and brought up were now grown and had their own families. I began to feel that I too was not alone, and the two young women in our family were caring to such an extent that all the bills that had to be paid were balanced, and all the medical records were taken care of for you. Then my friend who had lost her husband said to you, that her husband was always with her, guiding her, encouraging her to go on with her life as she lived in a new retired Air Force Officers' Village.

This friend met many retired army wives and although she was happy, she too, understood the loneliness of these women. Nevertheless, there were others who felt the proximity of their husbands, and they too, were comforted by the same thoughts that in spirit he was always with her. It was his light again which was with the wife.

"Oh, my beloved wife, you have shown me your desire to hear me speak to you, and you have learned how to attune to my own soul. Thus in your silence, in your desire, and in your love, you were able to give to me your full attention, visualizing my being, thinking of my name, and now, waiting for me to speak in the still, small voice.

"In the beginning you had great fear of the spirit world, and did not want to have anything to do with spirits, not realizing that formerly the women were conditioned not to have anything to do with the spirit world, lest they become possessed. And so you wanted no part of the spirit world. But knowing that I had made the transition in your loneliness, you longed for my presence. And it is this that attracts the spirit to be near the wife.

"Oh, my dear one, it is difficult to overcome fear, for fear knows no bounds and at times is not even influenced by logic. But you have learned that the Love of God overcomes fear, and you learned as you loved the Light of God in a higher dimension, that you came into the peace of God; and now you could be still with the emotion that would grip you and then disappear as you began to think of God and loved his peaceful, loving Light.

"You knew that the Light of God is stronger than fear, and the Christ Light simply dissolved the fear. For fear is darkness, and you are to call upon the Light of the Christ to dissipate the enveloping current of fear that is generated from the beliefs of the past. Note how Jesus said, 'Fear not!' And as the disciple felt the love in his Christ Light, it was this love that now enveloped the spirit."

Today I will give you a message based on **"The Fear of Separation After Transition."** Your fear can be defined as a hopeless, helpless feeling of not knowing what to do. Your fear comes from thoughts created in your own mind that come upon you as you ask the question, "How is it possible to go on living after all is so changed?"

Many women have wondered, "How can it be that the one who has made the transition is with you, guiding you, in what is to be done?"

The thoughts hold you to continue in all the affairs that must now be in your own management. There are so many details to think about that you never realized before; neither did you understand, even as your own husband continued to do the works within your own marriage. There was so much that was not understood, but gradually you accepted that you were to confront everything, one step at a time, in order to live a normal life again, especially in the responsibilities of the estate which overwhelmed you.

All that had been written in my will and testament now had to be fulfilled. At times your mind whirled as life presented so many obstacles which you knew had to be overcome. But it was as the help came forth from so many directions that slowly life became orderly and peaceful. You were now able to face all that you had to do and confront the obstacles.

As your mind cleared, you entered a new joy, knowing that I was not only with you, but I was within all the activities around you. Your views had changed and you were now able to make the adjustments not only willingly, but they seemed now to become so much easier. There was a new confidence that came into your being. You recognized a sense of sufficiency in restoring your way of life. Now you joined into the activities of your dear family and all of your friends.

It was a daily occurrence for you to feel and acknowledge my presence as you heard me speak in the still, small voice.

After my ascension, as you know, I was to release all the darkness in my spirit, as I accepted the higher teachings given to me by my own Father, Lord Jesus. For it was He who was teaching me. I was able to learn about my soul, and about the light that was flowing into my soul. Slowly, as my comprehension grew, the darkness in my spirit was wiped out, but I still carried the great agony of my spirit and soul in what I had done as I was aware of my higher soul. In releasing the darkness and turmoil that I had given to each one in my own environment, my enlightenment dawned as I too was given the higher Light to see how people lived their lives without God, as compared to those higher beings whom I had now contacted, who blended with the higher Light within their own souls. What a contrast!

This greater Light, the Christ Light, sustained us all, without whom we would not be able to be aware of our own light. We were only conscious of the self. We imagined that the self was all there was in the world, and so the self began to live as if we were the lords of the earth, "the elite." Therefore, all nature was to give to us in all that was visible to our mortal limiting eyes. Now within the form world, within the mortal state of man, all that one sees with the outer senses has been created by the beliefs, the knowledge, and understanding on the physical level, gained in the world. Thus all that we recognized and understood were **our own creations**.

Here we see and feel the great turmoil of the spirit. It is in our present awareness that we have discovered so many false beliefs from our own analysis and reasoning and drawing our own conclusions, which now fall away as misconceptions and erroneous interpretations. I discovered that the belief is actually a darkness that has been formed, not only within the spirit and soul, but reflected also within the atmosphere of the environment.

In this age, mankind is receiving more understanding and within his comprehension is more light which is his own enlightenment. On a vast scale, man is beginning to realize that he is not alone in the universe but that there is a great power in control of the world.

"The earth is truly the Lord's and the fullness thereof."

It is in our own spirits that we are humbled as we now have the comprehension of the great wisdom of God. He is the answer to all the mysteries that seemed to be hidden within His invisible Light. Countless numbers are receiving the truth to understand "Man, know thyself."

The greatest realization in the beginning is to understand how the mortal mind, the spirit mind, and the soul mind of man have been controlled by the individual, to create his own environment, no matter what it is, in which he will live and breathe and move and have his being.

All that happens to the outer environment first is conceived within the spirit. It is incredible to realize that each one is responsible for his own thinking processes, his own actions, and his acceptance of whatever is believed.

It is incomprehensible to realize that everything within the spirit is reflected as a mirror within one's outer environment. This reflection returns as a boomerang returns when thrown out into the air.

Man will no longer be able to blame God for that which was conceived first within one's spirit, and then returned to plague the same one. The creator of what has happened will now recognize how his own spirit returns to him.

It is within this Age that thousands will be ready to learn the truth of God. The immensity of the revelation is great as man accepts that God's Light permeates the entire earth and all space, and is in all and through all. This one truth is overwhelming. Too long man had believed in two worlds: a world of light and a world of darkness, as though there were a separation; but God's Light is invisible and so pure, and of such a vibration, that it is hidden from the sight of man who has long believed only in that which he could see. But now, his own senses will have betrayed him. For in this Age there are sights and scenes man cannot see, but cameras are bringing forth the evidence; telescopes are playing a role in outer space to bring forth visions such as have never been seen before.

There are sounds that are higher than man can hear, and so the senses can no longer be believed as though it is the final truth.

Mankind is to learn that the Love of God governs all the laws inherent within his pure Light of Love. None can control the Higher Light of Love. And it is through the Love of God that man can receive more light and more truth, and the comprehension of his own life. Man is to learn how to control his own thoughts, his own will, and his own way, expressed in his mind in all that he would do. For it will be seen how thoughts will form images in the atmosphere itself. And thoughts are formed by the energy of one's own Light.

Therefore, the actions in the world will later be traced to their origins.

The cry in the world today is: How can one overcome the darkness which has been created? How does one change the thoughts from negative to positive, and how are creations dissolved?

As the mystery of life and death will be understood in passing through one's own states of consciousness, it will be understood that as one enters the spirit world, one now passes through that transition where he relives his life in the spirit world and recognizes the negativity he has given to all upon the earth. This is the hell that each one goes through in his own realization and suffering of what he has done, and what he has given to all others upon the earth. He will be knowledgeable in his own creations that through his positive works, good deeds, living a constructive life, and following a higher light, that he will indeed receive more light.

It is in the spirit world that the individual perceives the truth of his own creations in his thoughts and actions. It is his spirit which will gravitate to his own frequency, to that place of light which he has earned during his lifetime.

Those who desire to learn will merit the higher teachings, but it is imperative to persevere on his plateau until he receives the training and practices the disciplines. Much depends upon his desire of how long he will remain in his former level, based upon the degree of his learning.

With some, it may take years, depending upon the willingness of the individual to have dissolved all his debts, and accept the truth of God.

After making the decision to arise into a higher level of consciousness, in order to arise, one is to go through purification. Purification entails recognizing all the darkness that has been given to others when he was upon the earth in his body, admitting it within himself in the spirit world. It is this which is the suffering in one's spirit in the realization and knowing and recognizing what one has given, even to loved ones.

When the purification erases the past, one is now ready to begin upon a new path, where the mind is willing to learn the truth. Strange as it may seem, as there are classes in the world and instructions are given in a classroom, so too, in the spirit world are there classrooms and instructions. But the teacher is now an Ascended Being who has himself gone through and learned all that he is now teaching. The learning now is based on the inner life, the eternal life that flows from God, the Three in One, **Father Mother God.**

It is God the Creator to whom we all owe the Light of life, given to us within our beings.

As we learn about the self in the way we use our energy, not only for our own benefits, but as we use our energy for the benefits of all in the world, and each one accepts that every man is truly a brother, and every woman is truly a sister, now we can accept the **Father Mother God** as being the eternal parents of all mankind. The teachings are so vast in the study of the role each one plays in his own relationship to mankind, and to all the kingdoms of nature.

It is seen that each one born into the world has a mission to fulfill as he undertakes his responsibilities. When the lessons have been learned on your own level, you learn how to overcome the pull and desires within the physical self, and when the light grows stronger within the spirit, one is able to graduate to the next level. Within a higher level, you receive another teacher, and your lessons begin on the next new level. It is like graduating from plane to plane, or from class to class, as we would be promoted to higher grades in the school system of the world.

We are in a higher grade of the soul when our learning pertains to the laws of Light inherent in the Higher Light shining into our souls, just as it was written, "The Light is in the darkness, but man comprehended not this Light."

We are now being taught to comprehend this invisible Higher Light. One of the laws I have learned is the Law of Sacrifice. This is totally different from any laws I have ever learned upon the earth. It is operated through the Law of Love. As Jesus demonstrated, he could lay down his life for his friend; but he could also pick it up again. For the light you use to help another, you may pick up again, as you receive more light.

The Law of Sacrifice can be understood as

you give up some negative trait in your being for another; it may be your own child, or a husband or a wife. It is as though one recognizes the spirit of resistance to God in one's self, and offers up that resistance, now loving God in his friend. This is how one picks up his own light by recognizing the Law of God which is Love, and giving the Love to God within children, within relatives, with a husband or wife. For you lose nothing as you love God, but you gain more light, and this light is lifted up to bless all in your environment.

The Law of Love is the greatest Law within the Bible. But it is also exceedingly difficult to understand such a love. The Love of God is illustrated by the Universal Mother within the Trinity of God. In the beginning, one would start to love your family and relatives and friends and the whole world, but how can human love do the works? There is always a motive within the human love. It is limited, restricting, and confining.

To love the Universal Mother is to love the pure love in the Creator, in God, in the Christ Light. One is to hold one's mind steady in dwelling on the Love of God. It is accepted that there is a Universal Mother who portrays the Divine Mother in all mankind.

As it has been written, "God is Love," and as his love in its pure state is loved, now one will learn how to love the Lord Thy God with thy whole mind, body, spirit, soul, and strength, first within your own being, and then within your neighbor. Your neighbor is always all within your own environment. Each one will ultimately expand as one sees the great blessings accrue and as one loves God in the fullness of mankind.

For did the Creator not say, "The earth is the Lord's and the fullness thereof... " and the fullness is defined as being all the children on the earth--mankind.

We in the spirit world are learning another law called the Law of Precipitation. We are being taught that anything in the spirit world can be manifested and precipitated into our being.

The Law of Precipitation manifests in the higher realms of light, and we are gradually taught over a long period of time to understand how this law can be operated. It is as though man visualizes an apple, and the apple is created and reflected in the spirit world.

But it is only the Christ Light who is the Creator and now as we obey His Light in the images which we create, it is then that the Law of Precipitation operates.

Within the higher realms we are taught about the Ray of Peace inherent within the Light of the Christ in Jesus who was known as the Prince of Peace. It is in the loving of peace in ourselves. As one has heard in the world, "Peace begins with me," and one becomes peaceful within his own being, that one will ultimately learn how to work with the Prince of Peace in establishing peace in the world through the Love of God.

EARLY STAGES OF DEVELOPMENT

Although there have been numerous changes constantly taking place within these teachings, the greatest change yet to occur will now unfold as two women within the organization learn the way the divine Mothers operate within the ascended state. These two women have been together from the time the Holy Spirit came to this disciple and began to give to her beautiful poetry which thrilled her as words sounded like music, in a rhythm that danced within each line. Such poetry could only come from a divine being. Having loved poetry for many years, Walt Whitman's, "Leaves of Grass" fascinated her to such an extent that she believed the author was divinely inspired. Every nation claimed Walt Whitman as one of their own, so universal were his rhythmic lines. It was through poetry that this disciple was willing to follow the Holy Spirit.

In her mind, there was no doubt that the spirit's voice whom she heard, was a divine being. There was such a soothing, calming vibration which she felt in the beginning, that she would now listen to him daily, and write down the lines of poetry which she had heard.

The college which she had attended and studied journalism in class, here the students listened to her original poetry for the first time. Soon the college editor accepted her poems for the college newspaper to read her poetry before the student body. Following this honor, the newspaper editor of the local news office published her poetry. Not long after receiving local recognition, invitations were offered from ministers of varied churches to have her read her poems to the congregation. The poems were of a universal nature, which could be used by the ministers in their sermons to convey the same theme in her poetry. So beautifully presented were these poems that at times, the verses sounded like biblically inspired poetry.

Having already taught children within the Sunday school church classes for many years, this disciple was familiar with the Bible to such an extent that now there were some ministers who had invited her to give sermons in their respective churches. When such special days as Mothers' Day was celebrated she would compose special poems honoring the mothers and follow the theme with an inspired sermon which the people accepted to such an extent that now she was invited to speak in many churches. Among the prominent successful business women's clubs she entertained them by giving religious book reviews. At times, the women were spellbound as she entered the story as though she were acting the part and portrayed some of the characters in the book.

At one particular meeting as she was giving a review of the book, "Blessed Among Women," she seemed to understand the roles of the characters and acted out the part depicted in the story. But at one of the most luxurious hotels in the city, she was on a stage in a conference room about to begin another review of the same book.

Dressed in a lovely business suit, she faced the women and studied them. She noted how stylishly dressed the women in the audience appeared to be. They certainly were the intellectual, highly educated and sophisticated women. Unlike the women in church, their attitudes conveyed a superior boredom as though the collective thoughts she detected were evident on their faces: "What can she teach us that we haven't already heard?" The chatter among them continued to be noisy despite her patience to wait until the women were quiet.

During this time, she felt the imaginary butter flies flutter in the pit of her solar plexus. Suddenly she tried to gain their attention and started to speak, but her mouth became as dry as a sponge, and she trembled before them. At that agonizing moment she remembered just what to do from a passage in the book she had read recently, "Love Opens Prison Doors," by Starr Daily who overcame his own fear before an audience who were judging him. He disarmed his own enemies by loving the Spirit of God in all as he looked into their eyes and thought of the Light of God being with each one of them.

She now did likewise. She closed her eyes and began to pray silently. She practiced recognizing that God was with all and began to love His Presence with all the women. Immediately, her fear vanished. The "butterflies" disappeared, and a rush of saliva flowed into her mouth. She could now speak.

Opening her eyes, she saw the women

stamp out their burning cigarettes, turn away from facing one another, and look straight into the eyes of the speaker. There was a strange magnetic quality within the atmosphere and with this woman.

THE BIRTH OF THE SOUL

Since it was near the Christmas season, the story was about the birth of Jesus, being described as if the Mother Mary was present telling her own story. It began within the Jewish Temple where it had been foretold that Mary had been betrothed to Joseph, a highly respected elder of the Temple.

Although Joseph had been a married man, his wife had passed away. Joseph was left with five children of his own. He would portray the "father image" and protect and care for this young woman, Mary, whom he had learned was destined to bring forth a great prophet. And Joseph would be worthy and deserving to marry her inasmuch as he had proved himself within the temple to being a conscientious and "good man."

After he was betrothed to her, he learned she was already with child.

Mary described her encounter with the Angel Gabriel to her cousin, Elizabeth, when she visited her.

By this time, every ear was now attentive, listening to every word. Not a motion was made by the women as they sat so still, that only the voice of the speaker was heard. All became fascinated with the description that was given.

The Angel Gabriel now became real. But this was not yet understood to be the soul of Mary. The Angel portrayed was a being of Light. He entered the physical dimensional atmosphere of the world unseen by the mortal eyes of the physical body. It was his spirit that shone as the sunlight, and entered the room as a large beam of light. But the light extended from the sun and would be like a Ray of limitless magnitude that entered the room.

In the story that was told, the spirit of Mary was caught up into this magnificent glowing Light as it swirled and enfolded the spirit body within Mary. Her spirit body now entered into a higher dimensional level.

It was as though an eclipse had taken place, where the sun and the moon now polarized and became one light. She felt the magnetic currents sweep through her body. Her spirit arose as the essence of love had engulfed her within the higher plateau as she listened to the Angel speak to her.

The Holy Spirit that came upon her and entered into her spirit, was the Light that would be born into the world; "a son, carrying the Spirit of the Father, would come into the world and his name would be Jesus."

And Mary answered: "Be it done unto me, a handmaiden of the Lord according to the Will of My Father." Henceforth, Mary would have the conscious awareness of the Father speaking to her within her spirit. She would listen and obey what she was to do. She would be guided by the Will of her Heavenly Father as He spoke so lovingly to her in His still small voice.

Joseph, her husband, did not understand what had happened and he was ready to condemn her. But the Lord spoke to him in a dream and told him that he was to provide for her and protect her in the world. For the child to be born was sent from God; and Mary had been chosen even as she had been prepared since she was a two year old child, having been given to the Temple by Anna, her Mother. Therefore she was carefully trained and was brought up to keep her mind on that which was holy and pure. For she was destined to hold her son in the "Immaculate Concept" within the teachings of the Temple. She had long been overshadowed and prepared for the role she was to play. It was known by the elders in the Temple that Mary was destined to bring forth the Messiah.

Now although the women who were listening to this story were enthralled, there were poignant moments that brought tears to the eyes of these women as they saw what Mary had to go through when it was discovered that she was with child, but she declared that "she knew no man."

How can this be? It was a mystery to this very day. How can a light be a baby? How can an angel implant a light? The intelligent women were mystified. Who ever heard of this before?

But here was this young woman telling a story which had never before been presented in this way. Yet they had heard many times, that the Light was in the world, and Jesus was the

Light of the World.

Could this be another body of a higher dimensional level of light, called the soul? When one loses one's soul, is this the loss of the awareness of one's own light? What kind of a light is this? Is it visible or invisible?

The **Light Being**, an Angel, entered the room and spoke to Mary, "Fear not, Mary, for you have found favor with the Lord. For unto you, a Savior shall be born who will be called **"Christ the Lord."** But the Christ Light that ever was and ever shall be, would be depicted by Mary's son, Jesus.

For this purpose he was to come into the world and be the "Wayshower of the Path of Light" Jesus would walk, to point the way to the Father of mankind.

But this Path was not a trail in the world that he would travel upon. This would be a Path of Light which would show others how to be cleared of the density of the world which all accumulate. But the disciples were eventually to understand and also follow his example of purification. All who followed him were to give up their beliefs that God was only with one nation. As this was accepted, the spirit body on the cross would also be lifted up to the Universal Light. All of his disciples were to follow him all the way.

This was an inner Path of which he spoke and taught: "The Kingdom of Heaven is within." This was the light shining in the darkness but the disciples understood this not. For the darkness was symbolic of man's unknowing that this light was shining within the spirit body.

It was within the spirit body that woman gave birth to the light of her own soul. It was her own soul which was the Temple, which Jesus asserted would be built in three days. But those three days were in truth, three stages which each disciple was to go through within his own consciousness and comprehension. Each disciple would go through three states of purification within the self, within the spirit body, and also within the body of light, his own soul body which Jesus portrayed.

At the time, few were even aware of the inner body, the spirit body which was forever being made new as enlightenment dawned in man's continuous quest for knowledge. The learned knew that "Knowledge is Power". Thus those who knew this, would seek to know the truth about their own composition within their own lower and higher natures

It would take many lifetimes to learn about man's three bodies before man really understood himself and his own environment. For it was written: **"Man, know thyself."** But little did each one realize that he was indeed a miniature of his own small planet of light.

Centuries would pass before man realized that he himself created his own spirit body and reflected that spirit within his own environment or world. Years of probing, investigating and learning in the world would have to take place before man would be ready to turn inwardly to discover his own inner dimensional being.

Man would have to await for the New Age before he would find his own Universal Light. Furthermore, man would have to accept his duality of having the female aspect within and the male aspect in his physical body. For if the soul is made in the image of the Father, the **Christ Light** is the **Trinity: Father Mother God.**

Conditioned into believing that his own life and his own intelligence with his own strength was the supreme light, before he could begin to understand the supreme Universal Light, he would have to become humble as a little child to learn of a Wisdom that is of God. Man would have to accept that there is a Christ Light that is higher than his own light inasmuch as it is Everlasting.

A disciple would have to learn to trust his own higher soul to such an extent that he would be willing to give his own power to his own higher soul. And then when he learned how to love the Christ Light and accept this Light as being in all, now he would find this Universal Light, the Treasure of Treasures.

This will occur with thousands of men and women within this electronic age of operating with invisible atoms, molecules, protons, neutrons, and that Light which has already been found but seemingly cannot be controlled because the laws of the Universal Light are not understood. But nevertheless, the energy of light which prevails within the air itself, within water and within the atmosphere has excited researchers worldwide. Research centers now have central agencies where new inventions and discoveries can be disseminated. So rapid are new revelations flowing into the world.

The fascinating study of the mind and the way the brain operates, has led inventors to simulate this operation within a computer. While the computer now assists man in the vast amount of knowledge which is obtainable at his disposal, it duplicates the mind in the storage and availability of information and knowledge in practically every field of endeavor. All this study led to the eventual invention of the computer. At this very moment the computer is being operated by this disciple.

Just as a vast amount of knowledge could be stored within the memory of an individual, so too, was an enormous amount of data stored within the light of the computer. So rapid was communication and exchange of knowledge taking place within research centers in the world that man's knowledge of himself included entering into new dimensional levels unknown before.

My children worldwide are awakening to the awareness of the light pulsating within their own spirits. Recognizing the spirit body now as the inner body where one does most of his thinking, feeling and calculating, it is being perceived how each individual now sees according to the state of consciousness each one is within.

As a house shelters the physical body, the physical body shelters the spirit body. And then the spirit body shelters the soul. Note how solid a house is, in order to protect one from the elements. So too, does the physical body protect the spirit body. The physical body needs only to tighten up the muscles and the spirit body is likewise now tightened up. Likewise the soul becomes covered with a greater density as though a cloud covers the sunlight, when force is used upon one's own being over a lengthy period and fatigue sets in. The fatigue is an indication that stress has set in when one forces himself beyond the endurance of an individual and force is used to keep one going. The force now becomes defeating as the light of energy is blocked from flowing through the nervous system.

It is known that during sleep and rest, the soul replenishes the energy of the individual. But because the soul is within a higher dimensional level, man has believed that he generates his own energy through his food, through his exercising, through the invigorating fresh air breathed into his lungs, through the energy extracted from pure water, and in some other mysterious ways not yet understood. But so important is the soul, that the extension of one's life is dependent upon living according to the laws of light, hidden throughout the ages.

It is not too difficult to experiment with one's own body and spirit. Just as each one can close the spirit with the mind and refuse negativity within one's home so too can the mind close to new knowledge unconfirmed by authoritative ones who would pretend that there is no such body as a spirit body despite all the evidence collected in the world. Yet in the age-old beliefs in the world held by strong-willed leaders, the spirit body was long believed to be the divine, immortal body since the light was felt in the spirit body during prayer and meditation.

But this was the light shining in the darkness of one's own limitations. Although Jesus exemplified giving his spirit to the Will of God, he would henceforth be following the Universal Mind of the Father Mother God.

Although demonstrations were made to follow the ways of peace, which the Prince of Peace illustrated in order to acquire the higher soul, the strong desire to be the supreme ruler in the world has been the continuous struggle between the self and the higher body of light.

Was it not taught by the Master when he said, "What does it profit a man to become the supreme ruler in the world?" For as any ruler usurps the power of God as being the Father of all of mankind, that man will lose his own soul, his own light of life in God.

"The whole earth is the Lord's and the fullness thereof." All belongs to the Universal Light of the Christ, the Father of all of mankind. This is the Light Everlasting which created the Earth, in the first place. This is the Universal Soul, the Light of the Universe. But the light of the world was the son speaking before he made the ascension and became one with the Universal Christ Light.

But all this has been taught within the Bible. It is now being asserted that the trinity of God is three fold: not just the three covering the male aspect of God's being, but since God is Love, this is the feminine aspect that has been misconstrued. God is a Father and He is a Mother. All three of these aspects are within His One Body. And it is this aspect which was to be comprehended within the New Age.

It is this Universal Light of the Essence of His Love which will be the drama of the New Age. Since the Love of God is the Peace and the Healing Light within the body, spirit and soul. And man carries this love even as woman carries this higher love within the depths of her inter-dimensional being. But this love is to be given to God just as God placed this love as a lamp, deeply hidden within the depths of one's own feeling of love. It is in recognizing that the essence of love itself comes from the Love of God for his own child. This love would be like the love a mother has for her own child, or the father's love expressed for his own son or daughter. How much more does God love his son or daughter through the love which is His own Light, His Universal Light. It is Universal because His Love includes all of mankind. and as a disciple loved God with his own light of love, it would be God who would lift the spirit of man into the soul. But man is not to stop there. For the son, Jesus was made in the image of the ascended Angel who was Pure Light, whose Father was the Universal Light. It was this Light that ever was and ever shall be. It was this Light which was the **I Am that I Am**. It is this Light which was before Abraham lived upon the earth. It is the Universal Light of the Christ that created the Earth planet more than four billion years ago where countless civilizations have come and gone.

The light of the son, still bound to the physical mind, still unpurified in the spirit or soul, still going his own way in his own desires according to the way of the world, continues to receive his own turmoil within his own mental creations, according to his own state of consciousness. There are yet many members within this organization who still have a strong hold on their own beliefs and habits. There are still those who have not yet learned how to have their own immediate problems solved. For the Angelic beings remain silent and unobtrusive until a disciple is willing to follow. Thus each one is given a choice of "choosing whom ye will follow," his own will and habitual way or will he follow the Way of the **Christ Light** inherent within his own Celestial Teacher who is an ascended being already purified and blended with the **Christ Light**. It is this **Light which is the One Light** speaking within the **Light of the Saints,** who are the **Celestial Teachers** of the members of this organization.

THE CHRIST LIGHT
IS THE PROBLEM SOLVER

Too many individuals simply do not know how to have problems solved. They will reject, or avoid, or pay no attention to what is happening within their families or within their communities or in the world. It is as though a stance has been taken to be immune from the vibrations hurled into the atmosphere of the environment, and is felt even by the smallest children. But just trying to be immune and silent does not solve the immediate problem. My own light extensions will simply at times adapt the way of an ostrich as the head would be buried in the sand and they would not want to hear, see or have anything to do with threatening problems within their own neighborhoods. Some believe that by doing nothing, the problem will be solved, but this attitude does not produce any results.

Others will try mind control over offending parties with their own strong will and use their own light to oppress individuals. Some will scold, nag, condemn or punish others by using force to make others obey the wills of individuals and what should be done that is right. Prayers may be cited to tell God what he is to do to solve the problem. Sensitive individuals feeling the oppression and stress, will hurl invectives and resist the domination of others. But neither does this resolve the problem.

After feeling frustrated repeatedly, individuals at times, will counteract the mental domination with their own strong will, but this does not work either. Finally, after trying all the methods known, one will now be ready to try the Way of the Father Mother God.

As my children attempt these new methods for the first time, often it is just a mental fleeting attempt, done half-heartedly as though there is distrust in the new way. It has never been done before. Whatever prayers were given habitually, was done while being alone. But to practice these teachings in the presence of members of the family is like entering into another dimension while there are disturbances taking place. It was not too difficult to become calm where one is alone. The door is shut, as though the tensions of the world are sealed off from entering the bedroom. Here one can rest, be calm and attune. This is what is usually done by the members.

But how can one remain peaceful within the midst of turmoil? How can one center when one's attention is on the selves of everyone present? How can everyone in the room be silenced? A parent will often silence a child. Or the father will silence the mother. But what if a son's family has never heard of these teachings, how can one be peaceful while there is bickering, or crying or shouting. All experience the tensions in a home from time to time, even within places of employment, or out on the road while one is driving in the heat of the day when emotions can flare so easily. All confront opposition, discourtesy, criticism, resentment and judgment throughout one's day, or in whatever a situation that one may be surrounded.

How does one deal with strangers to remain peaceful and calm, centered and in control of one's own emotional upheaval?

In order to understand what to do, we have taken this disciple through all manner of situations within the home, on the road, amidst strangers, and even amidst members familiar with these teachings.

The same process of operation prevails in all cases. Once it is learned and practiced sufficiently to become an habitual knowing and doing, a great leap in understanding will be hurdled. Of course in this, patience is necessary. But also in the laboratory of life's experiences, one has need of daily practice. And this has been taking place for a longer period of time for this disciple because there is no precedent. It is first to be demonstrated.

The way is so new and different. It is necessary to have all the former ways removed. It is as though a new type of equipment has been brought into the home and one is now to follow the instructions carefully to know the way to use this marvelous appliance. It is so structured that it is operated by electric light and all feel the benefits.

Note how all feel without an air-conditioner when the windows are closed and the air is stale. Use the new appliance, the electric fan. Now open all the windows, turn on the electric fan and feel the vast difference in your body, mind and spirit. It is as though one would suddenly sigh in great relief to feel the calming effect.

Now instead of this being a fan blowing fresh air through the house from an open window, the fresh air flowing through the window would be the Light flowing from the Father Mother God. The blades of the fan are rotating so fast that the motion of the blades become invisible for the eyes to see. Likewise the light is of such a high frequency in the fresh air that one cannot see the Light. But since the soul is light, the soul passes on the light to the spirit and the spirit transmits it to the nerves which are like wires in the physical body.

The thought now should be on the Law of Recognition, and say silently inwardly, "**God** is in control." Attention should be on the **One Light which pervades all space**.

One becomes refreshed in using this great Law. To get this far brings confidence. Just holding the one thought, "**God**," brings the light into focus within the spirits of others.

G o d is all-pervasive but how can just knowing this, solve problems, no matter what they are? Where there is fighting, bickering, a clash of wills, judgment, blame, and condemnation, the atmosphere is filled with negativity and stress which returns to the nerves to bring all manner of discomfort, strain, and fatigue, followed by muddled thinking.

The greatest difficulty one encounters is judging others involved within the problem. While there is judgment, it is like a barrier covering the light with darkness which is a block to the flow of the Love of God, to operate with all who are involved with the problem. And judgment holds the spirit in a cloud while the light of God is above the cloud. It will be noted how difficult it is to love the Spirit of God in all while being held in the vortex of the whirling cloud of negativity.

But going through the magic of clearing away the stress and negativity and emotions within Etheric operations removes the negative frequency that holds others to the vortex of the swirling, dense cloudlike currents. Through releasing the layers of accumulated habitual behavior patterns in problems through purification, now the way becomes clear, to try to "let God" solve the problem in His Way of considering everyone and everything which is within the perplexing problem.

Peace and harmony will operate, besides "all things will work together in His Wonders to perform." While the members will feel a victory and learn to rely on the Christ Light with a feeling of greater trust and confidence in each one's own Celestial Father Mother God. Especially with all those who have learned to hear the still small voice through each one's own **Father Mother God**, the **Christ Light**.

It is like playing a new tune on a musical instrument. After the notes have all been learned and one has practiced sufficiently, now the concert can begin--playing the whole score without making a mistake in getting solutions to playing harmoniously.

The day of victory arrives. The scene is set. A beautiful dinner, succulent and delicious has been prepared. But a child spills his glass of milk all over the table as he extends his arm too far lunging for a hot corn muffin.

The anticipation of a successful dinnertime is ruined. The family and guests unthinkingly hold the child to the judgment of being undisciplined, grasping and careless. Before verbal displeasure is hurled, the mother quickly acts to wipe up the spilled milk with her apron. While she is doing this, her attention silently turned to **God**. He is with her son. This was a childish accident. And then, as she comforted the frightened child, all seated around the table became compassionate and forgiving. She saw the change instantly with her family and a few guests, and all resumed their dinner in a friendly manner, keeping silent to the child.

What others did not see or realize when this happened as each one's attention was centered on the accident at the table, was the mother used the Law of Recognition and called on the Universal Divine Mother at this moment and gave the entire incident to her. But this one person brought the invisible Light of the Love of the Mother to all. It was like lighting a candle in a temporarily darkened room. All were within the light of the candle. The glow of the flame was evidenced in the friendly guests and family members. Joy had returned and all relished the food as though nothing had happened.

Every reader may be able to write about his experiences and to describe how problems were quickly solved in the silence of the operation of attuning to the **One Universal Light**. Then he may be able to recognize the invisible Love of **God** with all involved in a problem, and tell how it was solved.

Oh My dear ones, it is necessary to start with little happenings that are not serious. But one grows stronger and more confident with victories as one continues to practice. For all have need of going through the experience of applying these teachings not just once, but a number of times before the act of remaining calm, centered, and holding to the **Love of God** for all, becomes a habit.

CHAPTER IV

THE FIRST STATE
OF CONSCIOUSNESS

MARY MAGDALENE

Mary Magdalene depicted the role of the physical awareness in the body of woman. It is that stage of consciousness where naught else existed except the body, the senses within the physical body, mind, and emotions of the heart.

Mary Magdalene simply imitated what she observed others do. She loved her body and accepted it as being natural. Having observed the effect she had on others, as she displayed her body as she had the opportunity, she had secretly been delighted in her own power to excite others as they found her appealing and desirable. Mary in her sweetness of the natural child had admired her own body and was attracted to handsome, virile, healthy men. She had beautified her body and believed that a healthy body tempted men. She sensed her own enjoyment of the power she exuded within her own love for men. As the men saw her beauty, she aroused their desire for her as she became flirtatious. Mary was tender-hearted and kind to little children. She loved the beauties of nature everywhere and especially the songs of the birds.

Although she learned the laws of the land, she would toss them to the winds and defy the laws. She catered to the freedom of expression in the body itself. It was made to be enjoyed. She cared not for the authority, nor for the law. As Mary Magdalene was introduced to Jesus and scrutinized his power, and appreciated his beauty, she discovered that he was exceedingly interesting and magnetic to be near. She listened to him with rapt attention. She wondered within her own mind if she could follow his teachings, to remain with only one man. She had experienced many enticing men as she was a young girl. Enjoying male company and loving their strength, she found men irresistible. It was she who was caught in the act of submissiveness to man and dragged before the priest. The disciples of Jesus, who stood before the priest, would act according to the laws in the land. Those who committed adultery were supposed to be stoned and killed.

Women who were known to be sinners, deserved to be punished because they broke the alleged law of God. Those self-righteous ones, who would punish the law-breakers, believed they would find favor with God.

Although there were those who had bruised and wounded Mary Magdalene with their stones, she silently pleaded to the Lord in prayer, to save her. It was Jesus who appeared. He understood the situation with one glance. He perceived what the disciples had done and knew the truth about each one.

All had broken the same law of God. But there was this difference: they were not caught. When Jesus saved Mary Magdalene, he set her free to go in peace and sin no more. Mary was filled with gratitude and fell in love with him. She would have willingly given herself to him, but he showed her that she was to remain true to God. Woman was not to give herself to any man outside of wedlock. As she listened to Jesus, in her gratitude to him for having protected her, she would now obey him.

Mary Magdalene

This story will be about Mary Magdalene, her path in life, and her trials and tests that she had to overcome. Slowly, as she struggled to overcome her many temptations, she came to that great change in her life, when she met Jesus at the temple. Here she was almost stoned to death by the judgment of the disciples who were with Jesus. Jesus said, "He who is without sin, let him cast the first stone," all put down their stones and walked away. Then Jesus turned to Mary Magdalene and said, "Go and sin no more."

This was a tremendous lesson for all involved; Mary was forgiven, and did indeed try, to the best of her ability, "to sin no more." This was a lesson for all, because the appearance of sin was before their very eyes, and for centuries the punishment for adultery was to be stoned to death. Many women were punished in this way.

For the disciples this was an entirely new concept, of not judging the women, when they themselves were as guilty as the women, and even more so, for they were the ones who often forced the women into submission.

Now we come to our own Age, where men

are still condemning women for the sins for which they themselves are responsible in raping women. It is in this Age that the men are being exposed for their own actions. Women are rebelling against the injustices of the men, who are set free from any responsibility at all, and leaving the women to take care of illegitimate babies while they face the judgment of the world alone.

How much suffering women have had to go through because of the lust of men. This will now be made **clear** in the new Laws that **both** are to be responsible and aware of the consequences of their actions.

THE SECOND STATE OF CONSCIOUSNESS

It was Mary Magdalene who became the wife of Zebedee, and later became the Mother of James and John. Mary had, through her marriage, entered the second state of consciousness. She would now depict the role of the "second" Mary, for she had been transformed by the Lord.

Her husband, who was deeply religious, likewise revered the Lord and would follow his teachings. Mary desired to emulate her husband and therefore became studious. However, even after reading the scrolls, she found it exceedingly difficult to obey the teachings. Throughout the years, her husband had understood the laws and had long practiced them. But obedience was contrary to Mary's nature, along with the beliefs she had cherished in the past. Nevertheless, she professed to follow her husband and turned away from her former ways in the world. She desired with all of her heart to be a respected wife and Mother in her own area.

She loved her husband, and for his sake she would now be a good wife and follow the ways of her husband. Mary could not comprehend the ways of the "invisible Teacher; " nevertheless she would now serve in the church. She became ambitious to attain the great goal set forth by the church. She would climb the pinnacle and accept the assignment given to her to do. She would strive to become obedient to man, for these were the teachings. The Spirit of God was in man, himself. As she had the two sons, James and John, she accepted the same belief that the Spirit of God was with her two sons.

Mary would now evolve within this second state of consciousness. She would dwell at length, on all that Jesus had taught her, and think about him lovingly as she remembered him. Desiring with all of her heart to have her two sons study diligently, she encouraged them to learn the scrolls well, which she would bring to them to study. They were to climb the heights with her and learn the Laws of God well. Even as her sons were very young, she would teach them patiently in all that she had learned.

Mary would eagerly listen to the interpretations of the disciples of Jesus, as they would now teach the people. But Mary could not discern at this stage of evolvement, what were the teachings of Jesus, and which were the interpretations now being given by the disciples. She became so trusting and believing, that she had believed what they had taught came from the soul in God. She was not aware that the disciples were continuing to teach their own beliefs, which they had not yet surrendered as Jesus had done. The disciples interpreted the scriptures according to their own interpretations, and taught as they desired to teach.

It is within this state of consciousness that women could not tell when God is speaking, or when the spirit of the self is speaking. At this point in her state of evolvement, Mary did not know that the Angelic Beings were bound by the Law of God to repeat to the disciples what had been created in their own minds, so that each one would know himself and know the thoughts which each one created. Therefore she was confused as she was led by the disciples to believe she was following the Spirit of God. But as she followed the disciples' teachings, she failed repeatedly to understand how to practice their teachings. She could not comprehend why her desires were not given to her, but she could not pray as I would have her pray. She had followed the male teachers in the world. She would repeat what others told her to say in prayers.

But she did not realize that the Spirit of the Father was within her own being. It was this Mary, who failed to achieve the awareness of the Love of God within her being. This is the second state of consciousness where Mary, who represented woman, could not overcome her physical body, even as she failed to remain true to her husband. She knew not what to do, as she was still bound in the flesh. She was overcome in her own temptations and could not remain true to her husband. It was this Mary who had failed in her pursuit to obtain the Spirit of God for her husband and two sons.

As my daughters dwell on the second state of consciousness, which all have passed through, where woman would follow man, it is this second state of consciousness in which woman would believe what she was taught. But even so, within the authority of man, as she would listen to him, there was something within her spirit which barred her from detecting the Spirit of God in the truth of God, as she followed the ways of man. This state of mind continued in lifetime after lifetime.

The progress of woman became exceedingly slow, as she continued the repetition of believing woman was to follow the teachings of man in the world. She repeated the same lessons, not knowing what to do. Centuries would pass before woman could gain the necessary education to be able to arise in her spirit. It was as she began to meditate and learned to turn inwardly, in quest of knowledge in her own soul, that she at last began to understand the Truth of God.

THE THIRD STATE
OF CONSCIOUSNESS

It was only as woman turned away from the world and the worldly teachings of man, that she had found the Lord as she turned to Him in prayer and recognized Him in Spirit and in Truth. Through her long hours of praying to God, her spiritual progress was kindled. She sensed the Light within her being. Gradually, she entered the third stage of consciousness and became the "third" Mary.

This was the Mary who sat at the feet of Jesus and listened to the invisibleTeacher speaking to her soul upon the Path of Prayer. He was the Spirit of God. It was at this point, that she had climbed "the hill of consciousness," and accepted her own soul as being her Master, her Teacher, and her Lord. This is the Mary who served in the churches for many lifetimes. It was this woman, Mary, the silent one, who would pray for her family. She prayed for her husband, her relatives and her friends. She prayed for her country, and finally expanded in consciousness to pray for all of mankind.

It was this "third" Mary, who recognized the male spirit in God. She discovered that as she discerned the Light within her own soul, she believed that this was her soul mate. She had reasoned that her own soul mate was her husband, in whose light she would abide and dwell.

As she persisted to serve God, she increased in progress, into the Light of the Presence of God within the male soul, and she began to detect the Love of God. As she would pray in deep reverence and in humility, she learned the great secret of loving the Love of God. As Mary continued to feel the Presence of God, her tears would fall automatically, in an uncontrolled manner which she could not understand. It was her soul which had travailed throughout the centuries.

It was as though woman had been in the desert and had thirsted for so long, and finally received a cool drink. This was the fountain which began to give to her from the depths of her own being.

It was the "third" Mary, who in the parable, met Jesus. Jesus portrayed the role of the soul of woman. It was he who appeared at the well and asked her for a drink.

When woman begins to love the Love of God, it is this which brought to her the soul in God. It was at this point of her spiritual progress that she learns how to receive her own Light. This was the Light which had waited until woman could love the Love of God in the Light itself. Such a discovery was colossal! Woman would ponder over this amazing revelation. As she recognized the Spirit of God in her own being, within the male soul, she was in the awareness of her Light.

As she loved this Love and breathed in this Light, the Light would begin to flow as a pulsating Light. Woman now learned that this flowing Light of Love is called the **Holy Mother** within her own being, and within her own soul which she carries. She had turned inwardly, meditating on her own male soul being present within her spirit.

Slowly this Mary learned how to love this Love in all of mankind. She has accepted the great Truth of her Lord that the Father is within all of mankind. She was amazed to discern how the Light flows within the Love of God as she loves God in prayer, in all and through all. She now feels the peace, the nourishment to her soul, the upliftment into a higher frequency. As she perseveres in following the great teachings from within her own soul, she comes into the Presence of the Father Mother God, within her own duality, within the Universal Light.

Woman now reviews her spiritual consciousness and realizes how she became disillusioned in the teachings, which mortal man in the world gave to her. She realized now, how it is that the self of man in the world and within her being is not true. She climbs the mountain through purification; and now sees how, she too, was not true in the past. Her compassion expands as she sees how all women, eventually would turn away from the world, and away from the self of man in the world, to find the Spirit of God at last.

All women pass through this state of consciousness where they lose faith in man, even as they lose faith in the power of their own physical love. She is aware now of her accumulated judgment of the ages. She has recognized this within herself, as the wife and mother in countless embodiments within the physical consciousness. She realizes how she did not understand the spirit body within her being. She confronts her own lack of knowledge in understanding her own duality, in which she carried her own soul.

Woman goes through a period of travail until she learns who her divine Mother is, and learns to love in purity. It is the divine Mother who now releases the darkness that her daughter had given to man in the previous states of consciousness.

In the parable of Martha and Lazarus, it was Martha who turned away from her husband and rejected him. With her own spirit she held him in the darkness of her own judgment. Martha was within the second state of consciousness, as her own husband's soul had passed away. For Martha had held his male spirit so long in the darkness, that the fumes of darkness enveloped him, and he lost the awareness of God in his life.

It is within the second state of consciousness where women learn to believe in the male principle. But these women still did not have sufficient knowledge, nor did they understand the duality of the soul. They did not yet learn how to operate the Law of Love to God. Woman will perceive how she has travailed through the ages, !earning a little here and a little there.

It was Jesus who appeared through the prayers of the "third" prayerful Mary when Lazarus died. When Jesus appeared, he commanded Martha to release Lazarus from the darkness of her judgment and forgive him. As she did this, now it was the Love of God which revived his soul as Jesus prayed to the Father.

There are many women who play the role of Martha within the married state. The soul is not yet understood by these women. In the past it was the daughter's father who would choose her husband while she was still very immature.

Woman had to travail in the world until she would learn how to come to God and follow Him, before she would receive her own soul in the world. As the "third" Mary serves the Lord from within her own soul, and fulfills the requirements of receiving her own soul, it is the Father who now shows her who her soul is in the world.

THE FOURTH STATE
OF CONSCIOUSNESS

Woman is still to travail until she becomes the "fourth" Mary, who learns to love the pure Love, and the pure Life within her own being. She goes through a period of training in operating the Law of Recognition within her being, and within the family of man, silently in all his own states of consciousness and on all planes.

She now becomes illuminated; and she is filled with knowledge and understanding of how man too passes through all of those stages which she has passed through. She learns how man has travailed as he too turned away from woman. Man also turns to God, and ultimately finds the Love of the divine Mother within his own soul. All are to understand how man and woman walk the Path of Light, to the consciousness of the Life of God and the Love of God; which is the purity of the Oversoul of each one's Father Mother God, their own Celestial Parents.

As these states of consciousness are studied, each woman who travels the Path of Light will understand what all other women have likewise gone through. Those women who are in travail in their own spirits, where the light has not yet come, will now be assisted by those of my daughters who have found the Way into the Light of their own souls.

As man is finally united to his own soul in woman within the world, and continues to serve the Father Mother God, their happiness now abounds in great joy as each one becomes enlightened and learns to obey the great Laws of God, which are within His own Wisdom and Love for all.

THE CONSCIOUSNESS OF THE UNSURRENDERED SOUL

HEROD

The character of Herod is that state of consciousness of the ruler within the world, which rules his own male principle. As the love within the male principle of Herod was not surrendered to love God, but perverted to the "love of the self," it is this character which has not been understood in the world. Herod believed there was another who was born in the land, who would become the king, chosen by God.

For centuries the concept was held that the king had the divine right to rule over the people, as the authority in the land. All were to be held in subjection to this absolute, divine rule in the land. This was the divine right because of a king's birth. Herod was the character chosen to symbolize the "life principle," which was believed to be in God.

The "royal blood" was the sanctified Life of God within the male. He was to represent the Christ Light upon the earth. This light was declared by the kings to be the supreme light which is to rule over all. Herod would be the absolute monarch within the spiritual kingdom. Man is not to usurp the power of the Christ Light.

Note how he professed to follow the Lord, and would desire to have the three kings find him so that he could go to worship the Lord. But in secret, he would not have any other being upon the earth to jeopardize his own light, which was supreme in the land.

It was this ruler Herod who would have all other lights cut off, as he gave the edict that all male babies under two years old were to be slain. As a child is under two years old spiritually, that one in his soul has not yet come into the love principle, which is the Love of God. It was the male principle which would slay the Love of God, which Jesus symbolized. Herod symbolized the "love of the self." All male disciples portray this spirit as they hold all to their own way, their own will, their own desires, beliefs, and creations in the world.

Note the struggles my children have had, in trying to obey Me and follow My Way. Note how each one loves his own supremacy in his own way, no matter what it is. Note how my daughters cannot give up their own love or their own light. Man too struggles to surrender his own light of Love, which is called the "Mother." He struggles and tries to give this Love to the Father which is the Universal Soul. All of my daughters and all of my sons have held to their own lights. All of my sons would be superior to Me until they surrender to Me, the Oversoul.

Meditate on the state of consciousness of Herod, who would stamp out the light of any other who would try to gain supremacy, no matter what that supremacy is in the world. This is the state of consciousness where the Christ Child has not yet been born into each one's own spirit. Each one will comprehend now, as they have never realized before.

HERODIAS

Herodias was a beautiful woman who loved luxury, and all the fine things in life. She loved being the queen, and believed that her role was to give to the king whatever he desired. She had been taught that women were to please the rulers in the land. The kings for many centuries had been accustomed to having many concubines, who were taught to give the pleasures of the flesh to the king, who was favored above all.

As Herodias desired to be the most favored among the women, she would try to hold her husband's love. She too had learned how to give the pleasures of the flesh to her husband. She was willing to submit to him in any of his desires so that he would love her above all of the concubines. She would not refuse her husband in any way, or in anything, no matter what he desired or asked of her.

As Herodias accepted the fact that the king was to rule in the land, she had been led to believe that women's place was to keep him happy. In this way he would be a good king. Therefore she catered to all of his desires in his appetites, in his comforts, and luxuries of the beautiful objects she would surround herself and her husband with. This devotion to him increased his love for his wife so much so, that he too would present her with whatever she desired. Each believed that life would be filled with happiness as all the pleasures in the world were satisfied. Queen Herodias recognized and loved the intelligence of her husband. She believed that the kings were God's favored sons and that He gave to them the intelligence to rule in the world.

The people themselves had long accepted that their kings were of divine birth, and to rule was the heritage of all kings. Therefore they were chosen to reign. The king was not to be opposed by anyone in the land, for he was the chosen authority who was the law of the land itself.

When the announcement was rumored within the royal court that there was one who had come to rule within the world, who was the true chosen one of God, even Jesus, this was a threat to the king. He would not that anyone usurp his power, no matter who it may be. As Jesus had been born into the land, and he was believed to be under two years old, this child must be found and destroyed before any attempts would be made to place him on the throne to be the future king.

John the Baptist knew that the previous king had lost his life, as his own brother fell in love with Herodias and desired her. The brother hired others to poison the king within the royal court. There were those powerful leaders who favored the brother; and so as the husband of Herodias passed away, the brother married her. He had long secretly loved this beautiful woman and would have her for himself.

There were those within the royal court who suspected that Herodias too had fallen in love with the brother. They believed Herodias plotted with the brother to do away with her husband. It was when these two married, that John the Baptist learned the truth and would now judge both of them.

King Herod depicted the role of "the rule of the world," which represented the mental chakra, the light in the mind. It is this chakra which would hold all of the other chakras in control, to give to the body all that the body desired, in the pleasures and appetites and wealth in the world. The self of the king would gain the knowledge of the world and use this power to give to the self in countless ways.

The daughter of Herodias, Salome, symbolized the "love of woman." She would dance to stimulate others to their passions in the physical body. The dancing daughter signified giving tantalizing, sensual pleasures to husbands or other observing men. The new king, who was the brother of Herod, was pleased with the grace of Salome, and was gratified with her dancing. After he received pleasure in watching her rhythmic and exciting motions of her body, he was ready to bestow any gift upon her in appreciation for the way she entertained him.

Herodias secretly despised John the Baptist

because he had judged her in the world. She knew that he suspected her of having plotted and schemed to have her husband poisoned. Herodias would have the head of John the Baptist placed upon a platter, to be sure he was dead. In this way she would silence all those who suspected the queen in the deed which was done.

THE FORGOTTEN FOURTH
STATE OF CONSCIOUSNESS

John the Baptist

The message is about John the Baptist, a cousin of Jesus. John was also an Essene and was brought up in the Essene teachings, so when he came to manhood, he began to preach to the people and exposed their sins against God. When Jesus came to him with his disciples, he baptized Jesus, with his disciples, in the River Jordan. At that moment, many were able to hear the words spoken from above: "This is My Beloved Son in whom I am well pleased."

John said, "I baptized Him with water, but **The Father** baptized Him with the fire from Heaven. I am not worthy to unlatch his shoes." John did not understand the Flame of the Love of God. At that moment, the **Christ Love** flowed and all felt the great peace within an indefinable love which enveloped them. Also at that moment, Jesus began his mission, to teach the people that God is Love. In time, John became more aggressive in his preaching against sin.

A Visit to a Prison

The story of John the Baptist's imprisonment will be revealed in the following story experienced in this lifetime by Mary as Jesus answered a prisoner's questions.

Mary was invited to speak to prisoners in a California State prison who were soon to be paroled and returned to their own homes. Would Mary assist these men to prepare them for the great changes which would take place as they would leave the prison.

Never having had any experience with prisoners, Mary's trepidations in feeling unqualified to know what to say to them, led her to pray and ask God if it was in His Will and Plan for her to speak before them.

"Go, Mary and just let come what may and you will see My works in My Way of handling this difficult task. Before you start, give the entire program to Me. Prepare no script, nor plan what you would say. Trust Me! "

Never had Mary seen such a beautiful prison as this one. Scrutinizing the newly constructed buildings, and the beautifully sculptured lawn edged with flowers, Mary assumed that this must be a showcase among prisons in California. She had compared this prison with so many of the dismal, ugly places which repelled visitors in the past. But this place was so attractive and clean that it would be fascinating to study the effect such a place had on the prisoners.

Before entering the lecture room, Mary remembered that she was to "Let come what may and she would be guided in all that she was to do." But having no script to follow, she suspected that she would now be tested and had need of operating the Law of Reliance. Thus she asked in a short silent prayer that the Holy Spirit hold her within His Light so that she could obey His own will in the role she was to play amidst prisoners.

Surrendering the entire program to His Wisdom, she cast off her lack of confidence and uncertainty in what was to be said. With an air of confidence and good will she entered the room where the men were already seated and waiting for her.

She knew they would look her over from every angle. She would have to be courageous in coming to California to speak to them. But she noted how surprised they were to observe such a humble, modestly dressed, attractive blonde. She sat quietly while the prison chaplain introduced her as a mother of four children, a teacher and writer.

The room was stuffy and although the men appeared to be restless and bored, before Mary could utter a word, a loud voice boomed out from the rear of the room as a prisoner asked, "Ma'am, do you mind if we smoke?"

Noting the closed windows and doors, she knew that fresh air was needed. In a calm smiling manner she answered, "Not at all. If there is good ventilation, the windows can be opened."

"Open the windows!" yelled the same

prisoner.

This was quickly done. A rush of fresh air pacified the men as many of them were now lighting cigarettes. The rest of the men studied Mary's reactions but she displayed no disturbance and waited patiently while recognizing the higher souls of all the men present. During this time, she thought of the Holy Spirit who would now show her what she was to say.

In a calm and sincere voice, she told them to regard her as a friend and a proxy mother. They were amused and some had smiles on their faces.

Before she could proceed any further, an American Indian prisoner interrupted her boldly, and in a challenging manner, asked her if she believed in the Great White Spirit.

She stood before all of the prisoners pensively, and began to love the Holy Spirit, in her sudden realization that this Indian was thinking of his own God and would challenge her to see what she would say.

Unhesitatingly, Mary answered, "Indeed I do believe in the Great White Spirit in His invisible Light which signifies the purity of light in the air everywhere, in the trees, lakes, rivers, and in all that lives and breathes. Is it not written that the Light of God is omnipresent?"

The American Indians were close to nature and often sensed this Spirit as it was invoked in their unique culture.

Often an Indian chief would feel the kinship of all men as he spoke of the Great White Spirit and thought of them as being his own sons within his own tribe. So ennobled would he be as the Presence of the Great White Spirit was invoked. With this answer, the cigarettes one by one were put out, and all began to listen attentively to this extraordinary woman.

The next question hurled at Mary before she could continue any further, came from a distraught black man. He asked in a disdainful way, "Why is it that when I am around women, they turn away from me, and don't want to speak to me?"

Mary answered, by asking another question, "Do you believe in good 'vibes' and bad 'vibes'?"

"Yes, " the black man replied. "I know all about vibes!"

"Would you care to stand up and define what 'vibes' are?" Mary asked.

"I cannot tell you what 'vibes' are, but I just feel and know when somebody hates me, and many women don't even want to have anything to do with me."

"How do **you** really feel about women? Do you have warm thoughts about them and think kindly of them?" Mary asked.

"Women are intuitive and also feel your own attitudes toward them. What they feel would be your 'vibes' flowing from your own body and spirit.

"Even children can feel the vibrations of others and will often cry as angry stinging 'vibes' are flowing. Sensitive ones feel this and react as though invisible darts loaded with destructive energy are jabbing their inner spirit bodies.

"'Vibes' are unseen vibrations produced and formed by your own life energy which you use to form thoughts and feelings. A camera today can take a picture of a clear image and a thought of an apple. There are some individuals who can visualize an apple so clearly that under given conditions, a picture of the image registers in the atmosphere and is reproduced by a camera.

"Feelings flow with thoughts and patients can observe their emotions on a screen observed on the television as they have been wired with electrodes. These are also considered to be invisible vibrations which all individuals constantly radiate. Whether the 'vibes' are negative or positive, they still flow out of your own being. When you visualize the selves of anyone, you direct your thoughts and feelings to the one to whom you are speaking or thinking about. You are using your own energy in a positive or negative way. "

At this point, Mary drew a spiral on the available blackboard in front of the room.

"All negative and destructive energies which have oppressed and depressed the spirits of all, will spiral in a downward motion. And then these depressing vibes will return to one's own spirit as each one will hear inwardly what he has said and done to others. If it has been negative, the individual is filled with turmoil.

"Each one will now understand why people in the world who have this knowledge are trying to form positive thoughts, sending forth good will which also returns to them and uplifts one's own spirit.

"A large box of books has been donated to the prison library to assist each one to understand himself, his spirit and his higher soul. Clayton, an officer of our organization, was the donator. His life has been saved several times. He was so filled with gratitude that he wanted to express it through these books given to all."

By this time, a short intermission was announced. Many of the men now came forward to shake Mary's hand. She learned that among the prisoners, there were so many nationalities represented. What surprised her was that some of them revealed to her that they were newspaper reporters, ministers, and there were even professionally educated businessmen.

Some were expressing their joy in being able to go home soon. Their period of discipline was now drawing to a close after having served their respective terms.

One of the deeply troubled prisoners saw Mary in the fenced in garden during family visiting hours after lunch and asked if he could speak to her. He did not have a chance to ask the question in the lecture room. Would she talk to him alone awhile? His spirit was so downcast as he looked sadly into her eyes, and spoke about his having been in solitary confinement for a long time. During this period he had suffered from untold darkness. It was as though everyone hated him.

He told Mary his name was John. "Wasn't

there a man by the name of John the Baptist? I never did understand why his head was cut off. Didn't Jesus visit him in prison? Why didn't Jesus save his life? This has bothered me so much, Mary. Is there an answer to my question?" he wondered.

Mary immediately became silent and gave this question in prayer to Jesus. He would know the perfect answer for this man.

In the parable in the Bible where Jesus visited John the Baptist in prison, Jesus spoke about how John the Baptist's strong judgment and hatred of the new ruler and his wife so inflamed both of them that John was put into prison. He had exposed the truth to the populace about how the younger brother of Herod had killed him.

But Herod's own wife who secretly loved the younger brother, plotted with him to dispose of Herod so that the younger brother would gain the throne and Herodias would become his wife. Jesus told John that his own hatred against the rulers and against society in his constant exposing of the evils of everyone in every area, had already bound his spirit in darkness and had cast his own light into prison.

Jesus knew that in God's Love and complete understanding of each one, that in His compassion and Wisdom He would be silent. God knew the beliefs which John had harbored in his soul. John had in the past been one who punished the people for their sins. Therefore, John had refused to accept the truth that Jesus had given to him in what John was to do to be set free.

John the Baptist was the disciple who could not untie or unravel his own shoes that had bound his feet. The feet have long been known as the symbols of one's own spirit in the way one walked in the world. And John walked everywhere telling everyone to give up his evils. But he himself could not give up his own former evils and believed it was his destiny to expose everybody. He would be superior in his own sight and so he refused to follow the Wayshower.

Furthermore, John refused to obey the law to "Love God at this time." This was impossible. Neither would he give up his condemnation and hatred toward the new ruler and Herodias, and toward all of society.

Jesus now explained in the biblical terminology: "Before ye can cast out the mote in thy brother's eye, ye must first cast out the beam ye are seeing from thine own eye. Otherwise ye cannot see clearly to know how to cast out the mote from thy brother's eye."

The beam which flows into the eye originates from the spirit, which is a reflection of what is believed within the physical or human eye. But now the human mind receives this beam and interprets what he is seeing from his own state of consciousness, from his own development.

Since the beliefs of man have been stored within the spirit, it is the spirit which clouds the eyes of the soul in what is being seen. But as the soul is recognized as the higher body within a higher dimensional level, it would be like having the sun light shining through the moon and reflecting what the shrouded clouds are to the spectator. In comparison, this would be the "mote" or the obstruction to the true light of the soul, just as the clouds obstruct the light of the sun.

But when the sun breaks through, it is like the early dawn of one's own enlightenment and understanding of himself, as being more than just a solid body composed of the elements of dust of the earth. But man has a spirit which is the blueprint or replica of his physical self.

One day, man will inevitably commune with his higher soul and then he will understand the "church not made by the hands of man, but by the Light of God who will transform and recreate the spirit body into God's image." And then, he too will become One with His Father.

Throughout the ages disciples have tried in all manner of ways to cast out the darkness within their own spirits and souls. But eventually the truth would be understood, that it is only God's Pure Light within each one's own soul that could change the darkness into light.

It is within His own Pure Love that the denser light could be cleansed. Jesus demonstrated this in the washing of the feet of his disciples, as he had already gained the knowledge of God's Ways.

Now Jesus knew that John had clouded the Love of God in his soul since this law was recorded in his spirit where all of his beliefs were stored, and had bound John to his own ways. Thus John refused to believe that God's Love would open the prison doors.

But the Divine Love which Jesus displayed was incomprehensible to John. It was this that he could not fathom, as in the parable about his not being able to untie the shoes on his own feet, because of his own lack of understanding. Neither could he comprehend his spirit body nor his own soul.

Jesus could not save John's Light of life as long as he used it to condemn others in rage and hatred vociferously. Jesus was under the law to keep silent. Jesus had to obey the Law of his Father: "To give to each disciple according to the disciple's own set ways."

It was the Love of God that saved the lives of millions of people through his legions of angels who represented God's Ways in His Love for all of mankind.

Often when a child is spanked by a parent, the child will harbor hatred against the parent who has injured him. This is a normal little child's reaction. Many thoughts of retaliation or revenge come into the minds of older children especially as they have been injured.

A mother may say to her son, "You are a bad boy!" These words enter into the child's spirit, and are repeated in the child's mind over and over. The same thing happens to mature adults. Whenever anyone is judged or held to be "bad," there are constant negative thoughts emanating from this person. And then if he believes this, he is held to the negative darkness of his own beliefs.

The honey that John the Baptist digested in the mind of his soul signified the sweet knowledge he had learned while he was in the company of the great Master and Teacher. Jesus depicted the Love of God in the miraculous healing John had seen him perform.

But John also ate locusts, and this depicted his own mental destructive nature of his judgmental thoughts and actions. Locusts destroy the wheat, and the wheat in the bread is the staff of life. But when life, even in the mind, is used to harm someone physically or mentally, his light or energy is perverted and becomes destructive.

Then his own turmoil returns to fill him with darkness in retaliatory actions and thoughts of those who have been offended. It is this which brings one so much suffering.

All who injure others mentally or physically, receive a multitude of thoughts that oppress the spirit and decrease the flow of life energy.

The prisoner who was in solitary confinement was shown that as he forgives all those who have hurled their negative, destructive thoughts and spirits against him, he would now know what to do to redeem his own negativity. He would understand how it is the Love of God which dissolves the evil thoughts and sets him free.

At last, the prisoner realized that it was not God who was punishing him, but it was his own beliefs. As he saw them now, his beliefs became his own worst enemies.

In God's way, as one forgives another, one can now love God in himself. And then God hears his prayer and can dissolve the evil he has given to God unknowingly in the past. But before the evil is removed, the one who has condemned others is to accept the truth that it is only God who can make the transformation in the dissolving of the evil which is the darkness.

In this way, God saves the life principle and does not destroy any one of his sons or daughters.

God is the Creator of all, and He has perfect understanding of all.

The prisoner's eyes were filled with tears as he heard what had been said. But now he understood, and asked if Mary would come again to talk to the prisoners. She did not answer this question. But Mary asked him to thank all of the men for being so attentive and ended with the words: "God bless them, each one."

"Tell them this, dear John," and she left the prison garden as he wept.

Tim's Continuation of the Fourth State of Consciousness:

As individuals pray as they are likewise walled-in with their own darkness, it is the Lord who will come to save that one who is heavy-laden, and give to him the truth of what he is to do within his own soul.

Myriads have unknowingly received the voice of the Lord within their spirits, showing them they were to turn away from the darkness and turn to God. They were to forgive those who had offended them. For all have in the past gone through every state of consciousness to reach their present state of evolvement. But few recognize their own darkness in the world being reflected in what happens within their own environment.

All go through the emotion of desiring to annihilate those who commit crimes against them in the world. As this spirit becomes evident under various circumstances which occur in the world, one will see the spirit of retaliation still festering within the spirit from the past.

It is often necessary to take disciples through many experiences where the Love of God for each one is proven. When errors are made, when impulsive actions take place, when others are suffering, these are problems which are to be brought to the Father to be solved in His Wisdom of knowing the right thing to do at the given moment. As individuals receive any evil in the world, as my children give the problem to Me, they will witness what I will do. Now they will realize that these are the human traits, yet unredeemed from former lifetimes.

The various characters of the Bible were selected to portray the spiritual stages which each one passes through. When the personality and the traits are analyzed and studied, one will recognize experiences each one has enacted and refused to forgive another for what happened in the world.

There are instances where each one will go through the state of life being a judge. It may be within a family, within a school, an institution, or under varied stage settings. Sooner or later, the disciple learns how to forgive as he gains the knowledge and the wisdom of the higher teachings which Jesus brought forth to the world.

There are those who have tried to forgive but found it was only a verbal forgiveness. But the resentment was still manifesting in their hearts against husbands or wives, or members of the family.

There are those who rely on the Spirit of God to help them forgive completely. It is in this Law of Reliance that they experience the complete removal of the spirit of resentment and rancor. They discover that their negative feelings and thoughts have been dissolved.

Love enters the spirit as the stone is rolled away, and the individual rises into the sixth state of consciousness. He has been elevated to a higher plateau. Feel thou my Love for All.

CHAPTER V
THE FIFTH STATE OF CONSCIOUSNESS

It is not generally understood that just as there are grades in elementary schools, high schools and colleges, so too, are there spiritual grades which individuals pass through. Oftentimes we are unaware of our own grade levels. It is within the Fourth State of Consciousness that the man or woman is totally unaware that he is more than a physical body.

There are those who will graduate from colleges and even have higher degrees while they are still within the consciousness of their own physical bodies. It is as the individual turns to the deity in some form that he first becomes aware of spirit. Myriads of people are within the Fourth State of Consciousness as they enter into the churches, temples or institutions of spiritual learning.

The Fifth State of Consciousness was symbolized by the character and personality of John the Baptist. It was he whose food was composed of locusts and honey. The knowledge which he had gained in the world while he was within his Fourth State of Consciousness, within the physical body and physical sense awareness, was the negative, destructive knowledge that locusts would destroy the grain or the wheat. The wheat often denoted the "staff of Life" which was the main ingredient in the making of bread. While bread was long known to signify the Light of Life within the physical body, it was this energy from life which had often been used destructively on all levels.

As one would break the Laws of the Love of God in judgment against his fellow man, he was using his energy destructively. All thoughts and emotions within the body can be used positively or negatively. To use one's energy negatively to harm another in any way, was doing as the locusts do when the wheat is destroyed and cannot be harvested.

John symbolized that spirit which was not yet aware of the laws governing his own Life force, his own energy. He had believed that by admonishing others of their evils and judging them vehemently, he would be following the prophets before him.

There were those prophets who likewise exposed the evils of the people and of the rulers upon the land. John did not have the understanding of the Love of God. Neither was he able to unravel the mysteries of how one should "love one's enemies." This was his own stumbling block which would hold him to the Fifth State of Consciousness until he learned the higher state of consciousness as presented and illustrated by Jesus.

It was Jesus who taught his disciples whom he knew were in the fourth and fifth States of Consciousness. Jesus was aware that his followers still believed in the law of his nation. He knew they followed the laws of the former prophets who had taught of the law of retaliation.

It was believed that for every evil that man would do, there was a law which meted out punishment according to the seriousness of the crime. The retaliatory law was exacting. Punishment would be meted out to the extent that one's crime was measured.

This was the law of an eye for an eye and a tooth for a tooth. The rulers in the land would mete out the punishment. This practice had been established in countries throughout the world. It was as Jesus was being taught by the angelic beings that he learned that there were higher laws than man's laws.

While he was being taught, he too had the laws of his nation recorded upon his own soul, his body of Light. It was as the angelic beings showed him which were God's Laws and which were man's laws that he was to relinquish the way of man and the laws of man. Once he would release his belief and acceptance of the laws made by the authorities in the land, now he could obey the Laws of God. It was the Angel of the Lord, or the Ascended Teacher of Jesus, who took him through his own beliefs while he travelled the Path of Light in his own learning process.

Jesus confronted his own spirit of the past as he was in the Temple. This took place when he lost his temper and whipped the money changers within the temple. Jesus believed that the temple was a holy and sanctified place where the Spirit of God would abide. He too had been taught in the temple not to mention the holy Name of Yahweh verbally but only to whisper this Name reverently. The Holy Name was to be spoken in spirit. The temple was not a place to carry on worldly business of merchants who would display their wares within the temple grounds. This was not a place where one should exchange money to buy and sell. This was sacrilegious. The house where the Lord was to be worshipped was to retain the sacred and holy atmosphere where spirits were elevated to be with the Spirit of the Lord.

It is this same belief which was propagated throughout the centuries. The origin of the belief that God was present only in the Temple or Church became established within the minds of religious people everywhere for many centuries. Once the people left the temple, they would be leaving God's Spirit there and now re-enter the world as they returned to their own homes.

The world of Light would now be divided by being associated only within the structures of places of worship. My children everywhere still have these beliefs indelibly printed on their own spirits. They will recognize this as they meditate on the origin of their own beliefs.

John the Baptist believed that he had entered the world of the Lord. It was within the temples that he would eat the honey. The honey was the food of the Lord which was sweet in the Peace of the Lord, the kindness, the simplicity and love which was demonstrated by Jesus. For the Knowledge of the Lord had long been associated as the food of the soul. This food was often referred to as honey, because it was filled with

Light and Life and Love. Considered soothing and pleasant to the taste, honey enhanced the tastes of other foods upon which it was used.

While John the Baptist taught the people the knowledge of God which he had acquired in his reading of the scrolls, he recognized that Jesus had the higher knowledge. Since Jesus was a messenger of the angelic beings and since he spoke the words of his Father, who was his Teacher within the ascended state, John revered Jesus. John the Baptist would herald the Presence of the Lord.

It was John who felt the Spirit of Jesus, and believed the Spirit of God had descended from the Heaven world, and was now with Jesus. Jesus was this son, "in whom Yahweh was well-pleased." It was Jesus whom John had baptized. When Jesus submitted to this practice, as he came out of the water where the baptismal service took place, it was John the Baptist who heard the voice of the Lord, who was Yahweh the Ancient One, say: "This is my Beloved Son in whom I am well-pleased."

It was within this ceremony that the sins were washed away according to the teachings within the Fifth State of Consciousness. At the moment Jesus came out of the water, the Holy Spirit descended from the Heaven world and now entered into the spirit of Jesus. This signified one's belief in God. Baptism was the act of pledging one's soul to the Spirit of God. John taught that those who would be baptized would be saved from the clutches of the evil one, known as

Satan. Henceforth the Angels would protect those who were baptized. These were the people who would now be known as the children of God. All others were to be condemned as being the children of darkness, of evil, of the Satanic forces. These were the beliefs incorporated with those who were within the Fifth State of Consciousness.

As Jesus studied in the temple of his nation even as he was a young boy, he had accepted the concepts that his nation was the "chosen nation" destined to bring forth the Messiah to reign upon the earth. This Holy One would one day banish all evil from the face of the earth. Dear readers, long had my children worldwide believed that a form would incarnate upon the Earth and fulfill this great prophecy. The disciples of Jesus believed that he had now come into the world through the son of Mary. As my children held this desire within their own minds, their hearts and their spirits, it was my Father who gave to them the image they had long held within their consciousness.

But even so, it was Jesus who portrayed the Sixth State of Consciousness which, at the time, was not understood. It was He who was to demonstrate to the world the way to the Seventh State of Consciousness. He was to ascend with his body of Light into that Universal realm of Light within the frequencies of the Angelic Beings. He was to clarify the image that the multitudes had adhered to for so many centuries. All had clung to the image of the male principle being God. This was yet the immature, limiting concept of the nature of God. How could a form hold the all-pervasive Light which flowed through all space, through the seas and the sky, sun and the moon, through all living things? He was not only Life but Love.

While Jesus portrayed the Life principle within the Love of God, it was woman who had first completed her cross. Did not Mary give her Light to the Father? Was he not her son, Jesus? It was she who had found her immortal soul, the body of Light as he arose. Mary met him and recognized him, at last. He was her Master, Teacher and Lord, the higher Self, the body of Light made in the image of the Light of the Father, the Universal Light.

When this great Truth can be accepted and perceived within the soul, each one will be quickened within his own Path of Light. It is woman who first goes through the cross. In surrendering her own Light to God, she has obeyed the Law of Balanced Interchange. She now loves her Father more than she loves her own son, the Light of Jesus. Mary obeyed the Laws of God and her Light ascended to become One with Him.

Her own husband, Joseph, who depicted the male spirit in the world, was now to receive his own soul as he followed the Laws of God and surrendered the spirit of Mary, his wife, whom he had carried.

Each man and each woman carry one another's spirit within the marriage state. Each one is male and female in spirit and within the soul. Each is given the partner in marriage to view one's own spirit, externalized by the male. All of the thought processes, attitudes, images, ways, beliefs within the personality, portrays the spirit of woman which the male carries. Eventually, his wife will awaken to the understanding of her own spirit. The male likewise will one day comprehend his own spirit, lodged within the physical body of his own wife.

Silently studying this spirit and meditating on all that he surveys in his wife, he will carefully examine all that is manifested before him. His knowledge of his own spirit will be profound as he scrutinizes the basic beliefs which he had clung to through the ages, being dramatized by his own spouse.

Although varied changes in his character and personality have occurred so that he does not recognize his spirit in his wife, still, she portrays the "spirit of his past." Her ways were his ways of the past lifetimes. Her reactions were his reactions of former times. His deep-seated concepts still unredeemed, are enacted before his eyes within his own household. What an enigma! What a revelation!

Great will be the spiritual progress as the husband and wife learn how to have all that each sees banished within the Etheric cleansing and erasing processes. What an immense privilege to have all that one has released completely erased as though it has been written upon a blackboard. Now the eraser would remove all that has been surrendered and was recognized. All this was impregnated upon the spirit. But now it will be eliminated with the Light of the Great Alchemist who changes the darkness into His own Light.

Those individuals who would embark upon a new path, willingly accepting the revelations being given to those who have enrolled within the University of the Twelve Rays of the Great Central Sun, will now forge ahead spiritually elevated higher than the masses. It has always been this way in the world.

There would be those courageous individuals who would leave the crowds and seek answers for themselves in their own pioneering spirit. Scientists have long been willing to experiment with laws which can be proven. Nevertheless, these laws are to be experimented within, not in the laboratory of others, but within the spirit and soul of one's own being. It is only this way that the scientist himself will be enabled to prove these teachings for himself.

THE SPIRIT BODY

The dawning in the world can be likened to my own dawning of my own learning. Within my present elevated state, the angelic beings began to speak to me. I not only heard with my spirit ears what was being said, but with the words spoken so silently into my spirit, I felt the flow of light waves like a soft breeze that permeated my being. It was an inner invisible light which accompanied their words as though a sunbeam touched my head and then entered interiorly into

157

my own mind.

The moment   an ascended light being entered my own frequency on my own light-dimensional level, it was like a beam of light extending from the sun above the cloud. This light pierced the dimmer light in the world. This is a mere comparison of what is seen in the sky at times. But the light was of so high a frequency that it could not be seen by physical eyes. My spirit eyes felt the contrast as though the outer aura light around me would be the cloud, and the diamond-like sparkling Ray now entered the spirit and filled me with new life which flowed into my spirit body.

Within my own spirit body within the spirit world, I have now observed this taking place with those who are hearing me speak to them. I can see how this light is transmitted to the physical body. Even while an angel is speaking to me, I am filled with a joy such as I had never known or felt before in my spirit.

While in the spirit world from my present higher dimensional level, since I have completed my own three stages of purification, now I have a brighter light that sees the denser light. Those in a higher frequency level can, with their higher light, see the manifestations of light of a lower frequency.   Since my own light was raised through purification, I now had the greater privilege of observing the prayers, thoughts, and visions of people from the physical dimensional level, a step lower in frequency.

I would describe this in the way one sees

printed lines cross a television screen horizontally, when a storm warning is given, for example, and the printing is seen while one is still watching the program. The lines now are super-imposed upon the screen and the message is flowing silently about an impending severe storm about to take place. I am seeing all this because it is registered on the light of the world. The light of the world is the aggregate light that everyone has gained within the entire world. When Jesus said, **"I Am the Light of the world,"** he was saying that the light of the soul is the Light of God. When one has become purified of the judgment of the world or refusing God in the world, one's own light is covered.

When one refuses to accept the Light and Life and Love of God as being in all space, in all living things, Omnipresent, and that there is no place, nor any space that He is not, one is seeing only through the limitations of the physical beliefs registered within the spirit body.

When God's Omnipresence is refused, one is bound to his own spirit of separation from God in the world. But as Jesus expanded his own light to encompass the entire globe, he knew that the Light of the world was in all space. Today this is called the electro-magnetic light within the entire atmosphere everywhere throughout the world. It is in this light that man lives and breathes and moves and has his being.

God gives to man according to his own beliefs in the world; just as Jesus reiterated: "Be it done according to your belief." Thus, each one creates his own environment within his own beliefs. And then this reflects in each one's own world. And it includes all that is believed and created within each one's own spirit which now reflects in each one's own environment or world. This light includes all of mankind. But there is this difference: the Light which is within My being has been purified by the Purest Light of the One God who created the entire earth in the first place.

While the spirit is within the light world, so visible are these thought manifestations, beliefs, images and feelings, emanating from the minds of people. It was easy for me actually to see the visions coming from the mind of my own wife and her spiritual friend, as both of them knew how to envision my being within the Christ Light. When they did this in light, His Light enveloped me. It is amazing to realize that in light, one need only envision an apple, and we would see this apple as though it were being shown on a television screen. But this was a reflecting atmosphere in which we were now surrounded and encompassed. Each one's spirit world consists of all that is created by one's own energies and all that has happened and manifested while in the physical body.

I heard my wife and her friend speak of the Divine Mother; but I did not know this Divine Mother of whom the women spoke. As I felt the love as a flowing light directed toward this beautiful angel, a glowing light appeared.

I was encompassed in a Light of Love. I felt

this Love as though, while in the world in a solid body, I was in the arms of the most beautiful woman in the world. This was the impression I had imagined in my own mind and feelings, but I could not see any woman in a spirit-form body. I just felt a brilliant, crystal pure Light lift me up, and I was held within an atmosphere of pure, joyous light. I remembered how I felt in the world when I was being loved by my wife, or by one who would give her love to me.

Another way of describing the reality of this love is like being in a room of fresh flowers in the springtime. The blossoms of flowers exude the fragrance of perfume. While breathing in this fragrance, thinking of the creations of God in the springtime, one feels an inexplicable joy, not realizing that this energy is the invisible magnetic light within the breeze. The essence of love is defined by what is felt in the heart. It is so soft and gentle. This was the same feeling I had when I was within the presence of the Lord Jesus or the Christ Light.

ONE YEAR AFTER MY TRANSITION

Exactly one year ago today, the 19th of May, 1990, I have been within the spirit world dimension, within a higher frequency of light since I have completed 360 light purifications assisted by my wife's friend with the great Angelic Being. This Celestial One changes darkness into light as I have released and surrendered all that I was shown by the Christ in

Jesus. It was this which enabled me to be lifted into the higher dimensional level within the atmosphere of the light of the "son of man", as an angel being takes you to the Light of the Christ. Is it not written: "No man comes to the Father (the Pure Light), except by Me?"

There are walls and curtains of perverted light created by one's own limited human mind that separate one dimensional level from another. Although it is a curtain created by the light inherent within one's being, it is still God who gives light to everyone, since He is the Source of all Light. But there are countless beliefs created in the spirit of man that are to be eliminated first by the Pure Light of God. None can do this, no matter what may be affirmed, or believed, or tried on a physical or spiritual level. It is only the Pure Light which can raise and purify a denser light.

It is not given to man in the world to change his own light. The transformation and renewing of the soul is the work of the divine beings, known as the Fathers and Mothers within the ascended state, who teach their own children what each is to do at the right time, to remove their own curtains or veils. This was illustrated by Mary Magdalene as she was purified after having passed through the seven veils or seven states of consciousness in the world of form. Mary went through the purification of the physical body, the spirit body and the body which held the light of the world, before she received her Universal soul.

Although the soul overshadows the physical and spirit body, the soul cannot enter and be one with the spirit until the spirit has been purified and reaches the same frequency of light as the universal soul.

The great revelation within this Age given by the angels is that while on the cross, Jesus portrayed the purification of the physical body, spirit body, and soul, His body of light. There were three crosses. Jesus spoke, telling the prisoner on his left on the cross, who illustrated the spirit body, that he too, would enter the Heaven World with him.

The three stages of purification, which I went through within a year of 360 Etheric clearings, removed the density of all three of my bodies. I have evidenced how within the spirit world, the eyes of the spirit body have become so purified that one can see the light within each mind beginning to form the thoughts, visions, plans, ideas and ways to accomplish what is to be done. All this becomes visible while being registered on the electromagnetic atmosphere in which all live and breathe and move and have their beings. Everything is being registered as though the atmosphere itself is a camera, taking pictures automatically, constantly. And then, the currents of the energy expended by the thoughts and feelings of people can be seen within the earth's atmosphere.

"Birds of a feather flock together," has long been repeated as an adage. Birds have been used in parables to show similes in the way thoughts fly, like the birds in the sky. Within the feathers created by the Light of God, would be the frequency of light which is given to like species of birds. Thoughts too, have varied frequencies depending upon the kind of an emotion which is carried by the thought. The energy within one's own being is used to create any type of a thought, whether the creations are positive or negative, uplifting or depressing, depending upon the state of mind within one's own knowledge and level of development.

Many are spiritually aware of these returned negative vibrations which often register as "stress" given out during the day to their own families within their environment. Stress accumulates with the turmoil, anger, dissention, or whatever has been done or said in a negative way. It emerges whenever peace does not prevail, and where criticism, judgment, and condemnation take place throughout the day or night.

The angelic beings have been teaching how to eliminate the negativity each day. All have felt this negativity and have received it on the rebound, oftentimes at night, to disturb one's peace. The "stress" can be eliminated and counteracted by laws that operate within the higher Beings of Light.

The physical eyes are so constructed within the solid form body to see all in the world that is solid and which has substance and form and can be seen by the "naked eyes." But often one will see in imagination what has been projected into the atmosphere. One believes he is seeing his own truth, but he has projected his image into the spirit atmosphere of his own imagination.

The Mysterious Wasp

Overseas in a foreign hospital where Lilias had just had an operation on her stomach, while still heavily sedated, her husband, Tim was sitting beside her bed, when Mary walked into the room to visit. Observing the sadness and solemnity of Tim, and knowing that Lilias was sleeping, she nodded a silent greeting to Tim and sat down at the foot of the bed preparing to pray. Lilias opened her eyes and gave a faint smile of recognition to Mary, and likewise said not a word.

Whenever Lilias had not been feeling well, she would visit Mary in her home and receive healings. But this time, Mary came to the hospital. Instinctively Lilias knew that she would now feel better, her dearest friend was now with her, and she could feel her prayers immediately. Although there was a sadness that Mary recognized within Lilias, she began to feel her morale lifted up as the loving vibrations coursed through her body. During this period, no words were exchanged between Lilias and Mary, and Tim understood and likewise began to feel the vibrations but did not understand them. He glimpsed at Mary and wondered just what she was doing in her prayers for he too, began to feel better.

As the peace enveloped both Tim and Lilias, now both of them fell into a deep sleep. It was obvious to Mary that Tim had been anxious and worried about his wife's condition, but in his own silence, he was grateful that it wasn't necessary to say anything. The smile and handshake from Mary was reassuring and brought an inner quietude and understanding, along with support to assist Lilias at this time of her need.

Mary silently called upon the Divine Physician, the Love of God within the Divine Mother which she knew was the Christ Light of Love in Jesus. Knowing that Tim likewise had been praying to the Divine Mother, she too had invoked the prayer to the Pure Love Principle of God, in the room as she had learned how to love the Pure Love of God in Christ's Being.

It was this which soothed and comforted Tim and Lilias. For two hours the healing Light continued to flow, restoring Tim to the peace which now lifted him out of his sadness and anxiety, while simultaneously Lilias was being healed.

Although Tim visited his wife daily while she was in the hospital, Mary would come to visit several times a week. Lilias' health improved steadily so that she could more rapidly complete her convalescense after she returned to her home.

Tim had evidenced the effect that Mary had on him and his wife; therefore, he welcomed her to his home whenever she would come for a visit. And, from that time on, whenever Lilias would become ill, she would travel at times, by train to visit and be healed by Mary.

Being very sensitive to insect bites, Lilias suffered exceedingly when bitten by a wasp, and at times, had to go to the hospital for treatment. The poison of the wasp entered her blood stream so rapidly that she would be overcome, and she developed an intense fear of wasps. After an encounter with a wasp, while she was still recovering from having been bitten, her husband agreed to let her stay a week within Mary's home, a few hours away by train. This delighted Lilias for she knew that in some way there would be a permanent healing and so she held this thought in her consciousness.

During her visit with Mary, while the two women were alone in the evenings, they were free to commune with the Cosmic Holy Spirit, as they had in the past. Mary's husband was supervising the USO shows throughout the week and thus would be very busy at night. Knowing that it was necessary to be alone to commune with the angels, both of the women were delighted to have the opportunity in Mary's home, and anticipated the evening meetings joyously. They would, at such times, receive messages and enlightenment, along with healings.

What happened the first evening was totally unexpected. While Lilias and Mary were in a state of meditation and prayer, a wasp flew into the room. Where did it come from? All the windows had been shut. There were screens outside the windows, and a wasp had never flown into the room before.

Lilias' face became white with fright and she became horrified as the wasp buzzed and hovered around her.

Mary quietly directed Lilias to lie down on the couch and be very still. "Don't move a muscle," she commanded.

Lilias obeyed while Mary prayed, knowing just what to do. But the look in Lilias' eyes was so fearful and she was so alarmed that she believed she would faint if the wasp bit her. Keeping her eyes now on Mary, Lilias became perfectly still in her body and in her mind. Although the fear was evident, slowly she relaxed and became confident that the wasp would not bite her. The moment this state of mind occurred, the wasp flew directly to the window pane and disappeared as though the glass was not there.

Where did the wasp go? This was an enigma to both of them. But the women reasoned within themselves and now believed this phenomenon was manifested by the Holy Spirit to serve the purpose of understanding the relationship of her intense fear of wasps, to her intense reaction in her mind and body to the venom of the wasp.

Lilias and Mary repeated what had happened. Both had heard the buzzing of the wasp and followed the path of the wasp while it was in the room. Neither one was hallucinating because each one saw the same thing.

In communion with the Holy Spirit, it was demonstrated that the wasp had been manifested to teach Lilias what she was to do. Lilias was told that it was necessary for her to overcome her fear in the confrontation with the wasp as it flew around her body. She was shown that as she released her fear and became very still, the wasp did not bite her. It simply flew rapidly toward the closed window and disappeared out of sight.

Having learned this, Lilias sighed in great relief, and then she became very tired from the emotional turmoil in her body and relaxed on the couch to such an extent that she fell into a deep sleep. It was during this time that Mary prayed, and all the tensions were alleviated. When Lilias awoke, her eyes were clear and bright. Her cheeks were rosy and a big smile showed Mary how joyous she was. It reminded Mary of the way a little baby awakens from a refreshing sleep and would smile when the mother appeared.

Once more Lilias was healed just as she had believed she would be in some permanent way.

The following night, Lilias and Mary dressed as though they were going to church. They expected invisible guests again and wanted to look lovely for the occasion.

Mary spoke audibly to Lilias and told her what she had seen in spirit. And then, Lilias sensed the presence of more than one being. Mary attuned to the one whom she often called," "the Holy Spirit." But in entering the inner dimensional level, Mary sensed a host of beings encircling the room and knew not who they were. No sooner had she invoked the prayers and operated the "Law of Love" now this Pure Love lifted her to the presence of the Father. He saw her thoughts within the white mist that emanated from the spirit head and began to answer her question before she had asked him about the beings in the room.

He told her that there were newly ascended beings who had become discouraged because they could not contact their loved ones within the world. Therefore, the Holy Spirit showed them that these two women would play a great role in the world in the near future.

The Holy Spirit said that he brought some of the newly ascended beings with him to meet Mary and Lilias. Because the light beings discovered within the spiritual realms that none seemed to hear them speak in mental telepathy to the friends or loved ones. They became discouraged because no apparent interest was detected by those within the world. It was seen how so many had feared making any contacts into the spirit dimension. These newly arrived beings learned that many deserted those who had passed on, believing that they were not to be disturbed, nor contacted.

It was soon discovered that very few individuals knew how to communicate with others and so now they were deserted for awhile. But the Holy Spirit brought them to these two women to show them a great change would take place as the organization in the United States would be established, and so the time would soon come when hundreds would be taught how to commune with the angels.

This prophecy has indeed come to pass as a teaching and training center was established and has been operating for twenty years in Charlotte, North Carolina. Scores would find their own divine souls through this organization. This too has already taken place.

In simplicity change has been defined. To understand changes of varied dimensional levels, note the change that ice goes through. The ice is the solid form, and then it changes to water as it is warmed. Heat the water to the boiling point and the water changes to steam. The transformation takes place by raising the frequency of light in the water to a higher level by heating it. The emotion of Pure love would be the catalyst that warms the light so that one can enter another dimensional level. One may learn and understand how to enter varied dimensional levels.

The spirit body could be compared to the change from the solid body to an ethereal body, which in the case of water would be raised to a higher state in the transformation and would now be steam. The spirit body would be like the mist of steam. Continue to boil water and the water disappears into the air, now unseen. So too, does the spirit body disappear and cannot be seen. Note how the body is composed of 92% water. Although the spirit body is a replica of the solid body, it also has all the organs, all the senses, all that is within the physical, solid state but now it is within the higher state within the atmosphere on its own dimensional level. The transformation through the change that has occurred as the body was left behind in the world will now be understood. **The spirit body has eyes with which to see according to the amount of light he has earned within his own spirit body as he was in the world**

While I, Tim am in the spirit world, my spirit body is also with my wife. This is a mystery. But it is solvable, because the spirit body carries the same frequency inherent in the wife. As a man marries, and the words are spoken in the marriage ceremony: "To have and to hold," the spirit body of the husband enters the wife's spirit; thus it is the same frequency; and the wife's spirit becomes one with her husband's spirit because she too would have and hold his spirit within her physical body. But as the body passes away, the spirit body now enters the spirit world.

The spirit world into which the spirit arises is a degree higher than the frequency of the physical body. But it is the frequency of the soul, the light in the body, which determines to which plateau each one gravitates within the spirit world.

Did not the Lord say, "My Father has many mansions?" This refers to the varied plateaus to which the spirit gravitates. It is known today that the spirit body is very light, as light as the wind. But this too varies, as weight varies in each one's physical body. But the spirit body would be measured in ounces since it is so light. And here again the law of "Like attracts like" prevails. The amount of light each one has within his own spirit body, determines the frequency within each one's own spirit. And the spirit itself will have its own degree of light. **For all gain light as God's laws of light are followed and obeyed, according to the interpretations the angels give to what these laws of light are, within the inner dimensional levels and plateaus of light frequency.** This could be called a school or educational center in the spirit world.

The husband who has made the transition into the spirit world can enter his wife's spirit within the atmosphere of the earth.

Often because of the desire to be with her husband in her love for him, the wife will often draw his spirit into her own spirit. Women are unaware how even in their longing for their husbands, this too will attract him to be with her. However, as women grieve and weep, and hold to the negative aspect of the feeling body, these women are unaware that their spirit is dimmed by sadness and grieving. These negative emotions can often be painful to the spirit of the husband.

The electromagnetic atmosphere is a multi-dimenstional layered atmosphere in which the people in the world live and breathe and move and have their beings. **Each one, unknowingly, creates his own spirit body.** This body stores the cumulative knowledge of all that the individual has learned while he is living within the physical body on earth.

In describing that which is unseen, often an

illustration will give the enlightenment to an individual. Therefore, parables have long been used to tell a story which brings understanding.

To have a vision of a three-storied house in which an individual lives, would clarify the images of higher frequencies of the physical body, spirit and soul. Envision the first floor of the house as the level where the physical body would reside. As one learns to climb the inner stairs and go to the second floor, higher than the first, this is where the spirit body would dwell. Now arise into the third story by seeking the light within, and you learn how to open the door into the third story.

"Seek to find your own light." Once you have learned the way into the spirit and into the soul, you will be aware of climbing higher to the third floor described by Jesus as the "Upper Room."

All the knowledge one learns from teachers, parents, friends, relatives or anyone in the world would have the vibrations of that which is learned in the world. But within the third body, one learns how to arise in spirit and go to the third floor; the Light of the world is referred to again as the third body within each one's body of light or soul body. This was depicted by Jesus. Jesus often said to his sons and daughters, "Arise and come to Me."

Was it not written, "In the beginning was the word and the word was with God and the word is God." His own Spirit is in His own immortal words. And he who incorporates the

Spirit of the Pure Light of God in His own words, into his mind and spirit, receives more Light. But God is a living Spirit and those who contact Him in prayer, in reverence and in love, will receive His Living words, not just in a book, no matter how sacred, but given in a way to be applicable today.

If the Light is always present, is He not present today? Is He not with the ONE who is ever present and "who ever was and ever shall be"?

The soul body is composed of all that the individual has learned about God. But as the knowledge is given within one's own human interpretation, within the limitation of the mortal, the receiver opens his own spirit to receive the frequency of light of his teacher. Note how the listeners gathered around Jesus, often just to feel the vibrations and the light, even though many did not understand what he was saying.

Within the second floor of each one's house would be the place of privacy, where one meditates, rests, prays and is often alone with his own thoughts. The moment one is thinking quietly, one is already on the second floor within one's own spirit. Here one makes his plans, reviews his own ideas, and thinks of what he should say to family members. The moment he speaks to others, he is back on the first floor, within his own environment. But his own world includes his place of employment, in fact, all the people around whom he gravitates and with whom he communicates. The vocal speaking is heard outwardly, but the spirit speaking is heard inwardly. One will hear in spirit, often, what has already been heard in the world reviewed in his mind.

The self or the physical individual would control his own speaking based on his own knowledge and way of thinking within the ego of the self. But there is still more; all of his own processes of acting within his habit patterns at each stage of his development, are reflections of what is already in his spirit body. Furthermore, all of his future plans and ways of responding or reacting in the world, based on all of his observations of others, his own reasoning acquired from his own individual training. All this becomes a part of the self which is expressed in his own world of what is created, whatever it is. And then, there are all the achievements which include his economic status, his educational achievements, his talents which have been recognized within all the honors and degrees he has earned. All this would be within the merits and recognition of the individual in the world, or take place on the first floor of his dwelling.

Little has been known about the second house in which man lives within his spirit. For centuries it was believed that the inner body of spirit was composed of the Light of God because God is Spirit. But within man's spirit flowed the Light, as silently as the dawn of the day enters the world, and none can hear a sound of the change from darkness to light.

For too long in the world of awareness of

one's spirit, the spirit was shrouded. Man believed this was the private domain which was hidden from the world. Inwardly, he and he alone, could think his own thoughts, plan his own destiny, and choose the way he would go in whatever interests he would have, or whatever field of endeavor he chose.

It is within his own mind and his own spirit that all that is done within his own hidden thinking processes, is first devised and imaged within, according to the motives and desires he would follow within himself. He believed that all his ideas, thoughts and beliefs formulated within his own secret hiding place. His spirit had no substance in the world. None would know what goes on within the head. But the spirit atmosphere of the world receives all thoughts, all that goes on within the mind of man, woman and child. All becomes registered upon the electro-magnetic atmosphere which can be seen within the spirit world by those who have the light with which to see within the higher spheres of light. It was this which was now being experienced within the spirit world by **this one** who came into the spirit world and arose into a higher light.

Since being within the spirit world, great changes have taken place within the thought processes of this former colonel. In examining his own thoughts about his wife since the time he was ready to share his life with a woman, little did he realize that the woman he married was a composite image of what he believed about women, what he had imaged about them. The traits which he loved had long been formed in his mind first of all. What was most important to him in a woman is that he would be loved, esteemed and cared for in the same way that he experienced in his own mother. He would seek the same type of a woman, devoted and loving. He had already imaged an attractive woman in good health, who possessed a pleasant disposition.

Having found the woman of his choice, in introspection he recalled the words uttered by the minister during the marriage ceremony. The husband is to have and to hold his wife until "death do us part." It was while these words were being given that the union of the male spirit with the female spirit occurred.

Tim Speaks:

Henceforth, we (my wife Lilias and I) became one in spirit. She belonged to me, and I belonged to her. In our marriage vows, we were to forsake all others, in loving only each other.

Thus, we were bound to each other on Earth. And whatever is bound on Earth, is likewise bound within the soul, the light inherent within my spirit, so I believed, according to the words which were spoken.

It would be years before I would realize that joining the spirit body to my wife, she would now receive my "hidden thoughts" and I would be able to discern her hidden thoughts within her own spirit which I now carried within my own body. No longer were my thinking processes secret, but after awhile, it seemed uncanny to recognize how many of my thoughts and images flowed into her mind through my own spirit into her body. In the beginning of our marriage this was suspected, but my own refusal to believe that thoughts have any substance, and remained within one's own mind, prevented my understanding of "the intuition of sensitive women," especially my own wife. While simultaneously, I believed in my own intuitive nature. But how was this done? This was a mystery at the time when we were living together in our home.

In my own interpretation of being joined together, I believed this meant the conjugal union with one another. Nevertheless, her thoughts would enter into my own mind as silently as my thoughts entered into her own mind from my spirit mind which she held within her own being. There have been many sensitive women who described to close friends their own recognition of the spirits of their husbands still being with them.

My wife was the greatest influence in my life from the moment of the Eleventh Hour. Prior to that time, she was an enigma to me. All the influences which have played a role in forming my attitudes of her in all that she would do, in her own ways of thinking were based on the beliefs I had held of woman. All of my beliefs were recorded within my spirit, **which**

body she now held. To my spirit body, she would now reflect and depict all that actually took place within our environment. It was as though whatever I had created first in truth in my own mind and spirit, she now reflected one by one, all of my beliefs and attitudes before my own eyes, in our own environment.

How astounding it became to me that my wife and I lived and breathed and had our own beings within the atmosphere of our own making. But in my spirit body at the present time, it would be as though I were now living in a spirit body on the second floor of the same house with my wife, within the spirit atmosphere of our own spirits. But while she was still with her physical body within her own environment, she would be residing on the first floor of the same house in the world. **But now I too experience, within her current environment, her own state of evolvement and development,** based on all of her background. All of her influences, and all that she experienced in her realms of achievement in her mental and spiritual acquisition, in her own learning processes, I now reacted to her spirit in my being. This is the spirit I am now recognizing, which I am carrying. But there is this difference: **My understanding was vague until I made the transition into the spirit world.**

It has been written in the Bible, "It is better that the wife does not remarry after her husband passes away." Many widows have suspected that the spirits of their husbands are still with them.

The husband's spirit within the wife, which she still carries, would try to guide and direct his wife in thought form. His thoughts would simply enter into her own spirit mind and he would try to show her what to do, especially when she had relied on him so much of the time, within his own intelligence in directing her in the right action he had previously performed. But now he sees her need and would still try to help her as he did in the past.

Observing the physical body from the spirit plane, it is seen how the physical body is a replica of the spirit body. It is amazing to view the solid physical body and now compare it to the finer body of spirit.

The spirit body has often been called "the ghost," because it is invisible, but it is seen as a body made of an ethereal substance. Oftentimes, as a spirit body would be shown on a movie screen in theaters, the spirit would suddenly appear and disappear, but none would know where it came from or where the spirit would go. The spirit body within a higher dimension usually could not be seen except under given conditions, where a sensitive individual already knew how to enter the same dimensional level and where the laws of light were known. The eyes and the dimensional level of the eyes of the physical body were confined to the solid form world of seeing. But the eyes of the spirit body, apart from the physical body, now see everything that is solid in the physical world. So another dimension is added to one's knowing in the spirit world.

All that is solid also has a spirit counterpart. It is the counterpart that is not seen with physical eyes. All that is composed of spirit substance is the world in which the spirit now dwells and has his being. It is the spirit essence which is the real world of the spirit. Since thoughts are composed of energy which in turn is light of a given frequency, **the light of the thought is perceived**.

This would not be too unlike the wisps of mist seen in the atmosphere which are of varying shades and colors, depending upon the thought, whether it be of a high vibration of light or a lower negative thought which would have the denser shades and lower vibrations which people throughout the world have sensed, but did not have the specific vocabulary to define.

It is very easy now to define the spirit world when observing what is happening in both worlds by comparing the two worlds as one would two houses. **While the spirit is within the spirit world, that portion of the spirit which is of the same frequency as the spirit within the wife is now accessible to the husband.** For while death separates the physical body from the spirit body and the soul body, the spirit is still held in the world by the wife and she does not know, in most cases, how to enter the spirit dimensional world at will. But my own wife learned how to do this and therefore was able to communicate with me.

Although the marriage vows are no longer

applicable, and the husband or the wife is set free as one or the other passes on, still, as the women have lived with their husbands for so many years, the women now believe they are all alone when the husband makes the transition. As millions of women have cherished their husbands and devoted their entire lives to caring for them, it is better for these wives who have been left ample means to live comfortably, to spend the rest of their lives in religious pursuit to develop their spiritual qualities.

As such women remain in a single state, they now feel at peace and believe they will be reunited with their husbands whom they have loved throughout their entire marriage. When the time comes for them to leave the solid physical body behind, their spirits will once more be joined to their husbands.

There are no rules or laws to govern any situation, for within each individual case, the spiritual development of the soul varies to a great extent. There are those women who have been true to their husbands on the Earth and lived a productive life; there are times such women will receive their own divine souls. Such women have learned how to be true to one man, thus they are ready to follow the Will of God as it is understood. These are the women who are greatly blessed. At other times, women who loved their husbands to such an extent that they wanted no other, will be true to the one and believe that it is better not to marry again.

Each woman is given according to that

which she believes, and creates, and holds in her consciousness as being the truth. For one day, as women learn the Great Magnitude of God's Love, these women will follow the Spirit of God and ultimately be guided to the place where each one will understand His own Truth within His own **All-Encompassing Light.** Little by little within the human love of the self will be whittled away. Her Light will eventually expand to include all within mankind within God's own **All Pervasive Light.**

Now her light will grow into the image of the duality of her own Soul within the Oneness of the **One God.** It is then that these women will be ready to follow the Wisdom of the male aspect of their own Soul. By this time, there will be a loving willingness to follow the Path of Love to God within the male aspect of her Celestial Soul, depicted by the Celestial Teacher, Master and Lord within the Father Mother God.

At this point each one will understand how it is that God knows the Perfect Thing to Do in His Way, in His Will and in His Timing, considering all involved in all of her difficulties and problems which will be solved in God's Love. Such women are called "blessed."

Transition after Physical Life

The Eleventh Hour began with my transition when I realized the extent of my ignorance in these teachings you, Lilias, had followed for many years. I disapproved of them with all my heart, but you stood firm and never changed your beliefs. I know you suffered by my unbelief; only after my release from life did I understand or acknowledge these teachings. My awakening began by meeting my Father, in the Christ Light, who began to teach me. Great was my astonishment that you had always followed Him. From then onward began my purification and great suffering in overcoming all the darkness throughout my many lives.

As you remember how much I suffered, this was the reason for the pain in my heart and conscious mind through my beliefs which had accumulated throughout my many lives. I was guided in my ignorance to find the Light slowly, for there was great suffering. Each time I overcame one obstacle, there were other obstacles.

My life appeared before my eyes as if it were wholly contained within a beam of light. This beam of light held all I had done and experienced on earth. Receiving the Etheric operations from Mary upon the earth had prepared me to overcome all the darkness I had given to anyone upon the earth. Then began my instructions and higher teachings from the Ascended Beings. After great suffering of my soul, shedding all the darkness, I began to feel the Universal Light of the Father Mother God of the Great Central Sun.

I met Raphael and began my mission of helping all souls in the spirit world and in the world of turning to the Light of God and becoming One with Him in the Great Central Sun.

You had the military service for me at Arlington Cemetery including the playing of "Taps" and the salute of the firing squad. Then Mary witnessed my ascension.

All the family were with you and Richard held your hand all through the ceremony which gave you strength to overcome your sorrow. After the ascension, I had to sleep for awhile and recover my spirit. Lord Jesus came for me, and he began to teach me the new revelations, but first I had to undergo the dissolving of the great darkness within my spirit. Slowly through understanding, I became able to release all the darkness of my mind and spirit and soul.

The Light overcame the darkness. I was shown the false beliefs I had followed for many lifetimes. Now I began to see the false ideas that were given through indoctrination within the church. My life in the church was revealed to me. The church had held to the rigid laws of good and evil. The stress that the priests gave to the people was negative in their interpretations of the Bible. For I was in one lifetime a prince in the Catholic Church in Rome and was aware of the erroneous interpretations given to the people, the seeds of which led us astray and were difficult to follow. Those that rebelled against these laws were excommunicated and supposedly lost their souls.

Then I released this darkness from my soul, and through great enlightenment I was able to have the darkness in the world dissolved. Slowly I ascended and with great anguish of my soul, I was given the understanding of how to help the many who are suffering in the spirit world, and through the ignorance of the Laws of Light could not overcome their plight by themselves.

Through my own great sacrifice and determination, I began to feel the power of the Light and to understand the minds of men and women.

My work now is to bring the light of understanding to those who are seeking release from the darkness of the world and to give them the understanding of the power of the Light and how the Light of the **Father Mother God** can obliterate all the darkness in the souls of men by their acceptance of the invisible laws of God. This is the glory of His Light and Love for all mankind, the Creation of all the world of the living, and all life in heaven and earth. It is time now that mankind be given the Light of Understanding of the Laws of God and to follow the Laws of Peace and Harmony and begin to receive the Truth and Revelations herein to all mankind.

After my ascension there were many obstacles to overcome to release all the darkness in my spirit. As the teachings were given to me by my Father, Lord Jesus, I was able to slowly learn about the Light. Slowly, I had to have dissolved all the darkness in my spirit, with great agony of my soul. I had to love God to release the darkness I had given to each one in the world. Now my eyes were open to see how we lived our lives without God, this great Light which sustains us without whom we could not live. We were only conscious of the self, and imagined the self was all there was in the world, and began to live as if we were the lords of the earth. All nature was to give to us in all that was visible to our eyes.

Now the world man has created is illusion, recognized only by the outer senses. All that can be seen and recognized and understood are each one's own creations.

When man is illumined, he becomes aware of the false beliefs and darkness within and without in the world. Man now receives more light and understands himself. He is beginning to realize that he is not alone in the universe, that a great power is in control of the world in which he lives. This prompts him to seek the wisdom of God. He searches for answers to all the mysteries that are hidden within himself.

Many are receiving the revelations with enlightenment. Truth is being given to those who are seeking, especially as they are searching to understand themselves. Many have been astounded to discover that they create their own environments with all manner of mental images and projections of their own mental states of development which become their own worlds in which they live and breathe and move and have their beings. Their mental states are based on the beliefs programmed into their own spirits.

All that happens to one in the world, is first formed within the subconscious mind from thought formations, even though the thoughts appear to be hidden but still flow into the atmosphere and enter the spirits of those whom each one visualizes. These thoughts may be charged with emotional anger and begin to reflect back to the individual in the way others respond and react in their retaliatory ways within the same environment. But because thoughts are unseen, others cannot understand why they are treated by such an angry outburst that returns to them and is being displayed by family members. But the recipient of such anger has received the thoughts of one's own negativity, in such resentment and hatred that the effect and reflection of the thoughts first created within but not vocalized, are now taking place for one to see the evidence.

In a democracy where individuals have the freedom to pursue happiness and freedom of religion and speech, these are the same people within their freedom loving country who are to become responsible for their own thoughts, ways and actions to learn how to receive the happiness and peace of mind within their own families, among their associates, friends and neighbors in each one's immediate area.

Although the freedom is given in speech

and in religion, there are laws of decency and respect for one another and discipline of the uncontrolled mind should be part of the training within religions and psychological studies that should go with democracy. But the discipline should be self-discipline which will be a primary factor in achieving the happiness within a democratic country.

As the **Christ in Jesus** is followed, the issues of the heart or emotions even hidden, may continue to accumulate over a period of time to bring on all manner of illnesses which is simply described as stress by doctors; but it is not understood how the stress is formed or how it is to be handled.

Everything people create first in spirit, returns to them from the mirrored world and God should not be blamed for all that happens to people. For it is the energy of light that is known today that is within the thought and spirit that each one uses in the formation of whatever vibrations flow outwardly into the world.

One cannot use the same laws upon all of mankind in every country because of the varied states of consciousness, indoctrination of various religious beliefs and the discrepancy in the ways people react to one another as traditional patterns of behavior are exemplified by the rulers of varied cultures and traditions.

It is within the democratic countries that the people have the freedom to follow one's own higher soul. It is this great freedom that will bring each one of his own volition, to the place where there are thousands who desire to have peace, harmony and happiness. Now these are the ones who are ready to learn the truth--that all is Light--that God is Light, and Light is in and through all of mankind. And light is used to form thoughts and travels with the speed of light within the electro-magnetic atmosphere in which all live and breathe and move and have their beings.

Mankind is to learn in the world that "the Earth is the **Lord's** and the fullness thereof" which is all that **God has created in the world to bless mankind.** All the resources in the world, including all the minerals, forests, lakes, and oceans, are for improved ways of living in His Planet Earth. And all the richness of His Bounty has been given to mankind in **His love to all.** Each freedom loving individual will one day learn the truth that through his own Love to God, he will desire to follow God's own Truth.

The young people will realize that they cannot do whatever they desire to do without having the consequences of misused thoughts and actions return to them from the electro-magnetic atmosphere. But eventually, it will be realized that one can receive the Light and Truth to reach one's own goal of Peace, Love, Happiness, Prosperity and all the blessings of **God** as one obeys His great Laws of justice for all.

He can learn how to control his own mind in all that he does and each one will accept the truth that one is responsible for his own thoughts and actions. As this happens, man is enabled to be guided by the Light in how to overcome the darkness he has created, and how to be within the Love of his own higher soul, and know how God balances and erases the negatives and dissolves his own creations within himself.

The mystery of life and death will be understood now, that as one passes through transition, he relives his life, and now he must learn how to dissolve the negatives he has given to all upon the earth. Only through his obedience to God's Love and His Laws does he receive the Light, and is enabled to perceive the Truth of his own creations in thoughts and actions. His spirit then is renewed and he receives the Light he has earned from all that he has done while upon the earth in his physical body.

After man's transition, he has much to learn in the spirit world. "As a man is ready for higher knowledge, the Master appears." He receives a teacher who will guide him in the path he is to follow. **He remains in the spirit world until he has become renewed and transformed, and prepared to return to the earth for his next stage of evolvement where he is now given the opportunity to redeem his debts to God.**

In his choice to "choose whom he will follow," he may now overcome and gain more light, or repeat the lessons he will have to go through before he can receive the Light within his own soul in God. If he wishes to walk the Path of Light and advance to the next plateau, he will go through the training and the experiences to progress in the Light.

The teaching will be given in such a way that the realization that one is receiving the truth, will now be acknowledged.

Within this book, one will begin to understand these teachings after purification since one's spirit becomes sensitized and these teachings will give each one his own evidence. He will receive the knowledge in his spirit of all that has been recorded from within his soul and he will recognize his own thinking and behavior patterns.

For ages angelic beings have lived in the Heaven World with God and followed the Laws that were given to them. But man in the world became superior to God and followed his own will and desires and that was the parting of the ways. Man followed the self, and created his own laws and chaos followed. To this day, countless numbers are still living in chaos and turmoil.

Now the time has come that so much destruction to the planet and to mankind is taking place that all life is endangered. It is being seen that there are those in high positions who are not recognizing that there are God's Laws to be reckoned with, and that through their own power, there are those who would try to use any means and use force if necessary, to gain their own desires in the world. A great question repeated for centuries by spiritual leaders still applies in the world today: "But what does it profit a man to gain the whole world if he loses his own soul?"

God knows that in time each one will be

ready to learn directly from the angelic beings, and through them, will be taught to understand the Laws of God and be ready to follow Him. The angelic beings are all working together to raise the Family of Man to a higher consciousness. The darkness surrounding man in his resistance to God, will slowly be lifted and dissolved.

The higher Light is already flowing to lift man into a higher realization that **God** is in control. When man has reached the lowest depths of darkness, he must turn to the Light of Truth and begin to follow the Path of Light inwardly, and learn how to follow and obey Celestial Parents. One by one finally gives in and then wonder why it has taken so long to follow **Him**.

There are many lightbearers on earth and many are now serving God to help mankind learn the magnificent ways of Peace. Although there is chaos in many areas of the world, the way is open for thousands to find the leaders who know the way to Peace and many seekers are already finding **God**. These leaders of the New Age, are bringing forth the great Truths from the Angelic Beings within this present Age of Light.

The transition of the physical body into the spirit body

All mankind must pass through the physical awareness into the Light of the spirit. Many souls in the spirit world have been very ill and must sleep and rest before going to the place each one has earned and has created for himself by his good deeds on earth. And there are those who have increased the light within their beings through their services in the world which have improved the conditions for others and blessed so many in their own kind deeds as they helped so many people in their hour of need. There are highly evolved teachers in the spirit world who will instruct him in what he has to do, in order to have his soul wishes fulfilled.

There will be others of like mind whom he will meet in the spirit world. He will be given his freedom to follow the higher Path of light as he meets the radiant beings. If he wishes to go onward into a higher Light, he must begin his purification before he can be raised into a higher frequency of Light. As he wishes to go onward, he may submit to the removal of all perversions and negatives accumulated within his past life, have dissolved the heaviness and density in his spirit in what he has given to those on earth, and those who are already in the spirit world. Many are filled with remorse in their souls as they see their actions and condemnations of the past, despite having forgotten about them.

But scores of disciples will receive the understanding of how negative thought processes and actions are dissolved in the Law of Love to God. Many then go onward to the next level as they are raised and renewed in spirit.

Each one sets his own pace as to how long he will remain in each degree of learning. This may take years of earth time depending on each one's willingness and diligence in learning how to have all former debts dissolved when he learns the truth that all have debts to pay.

By this time, one learns about the inner life, the real life, that all comes from **God**, the **trinity**, the **Father Mother God**. It is **God the Creator** to whom each one owes his life and all light in his being.

Each one is to learn about himself and all that is given to bless each one. The disciple learns how to use his energies constructively within his environment, not for himself alone, but he becomes illumined in the way to improve all of his relationships with people within his family and with all in his world.

Thousands of people seek the way to bring people together and discuss their problems and come to decisions about solving problems, to find a peaceful solution to perplexing situations. The Peace of the Christ Light brings harmony and understanding to all who call on the **One who is in peace.**

All who learn to follow the Wayshower, and dedicate themselves to God, as Jesus had done, will learn to arise in spirit and come to the Father and learn to hear His voice, and receive the training in the way to obey His Laws.

To this day, it has been believed that there are two separate worlds, and the interpretations of the human, limited mind has held man to believe that he is separated from God, and knows not where God is. And those who believe in two worlds, think God is somewhere in outer space. The truth is that "there is no place that He is not."

GOD PROVES HIMSELF
TO HIS SEEKING CHILDREN

The prophets of the past would go apart from the multitudes to commune in silence with the Spirit of God. So likewise, is one to learn how to commune in the silence with the Spirit of God within a peaceful area which he would choose. To meditate is to turn inwardly in the silence of one's own soul. The thinking processes are done as one is in a contemplative mood. All within this University of the Christ Light with the 12 Rays will be taught how to hear the voice of the Father, the Oversoul, **the One** who speaks through the ascended beings.

As the voice of the Lord is heard within, now the recipients of His Voice relay His messages to those upon the earth. The sound is not heard by the ears of the physical body. The sound is heard by the ears of the spirit body which hears in spirit. The physical body ears were so constructed that the sounds of the earth can be heard on the dimensional level of the physical body.

The spirit body is within the fifth dimension where the audible sounds are of a spirit nature. The sound would be as one memorizes poetry and hears the words repeated inwardly in spirit, and enters the mind within the physical body.

This will all be understood as psychologists

and psychiatrists study the voices of the spirits within their own beings. As one has retired, one will frequently hear in spirit what others have said during the day.

Conversations in dreams are given in the spirit while the physical body is in repose. The voice of God is heard as one gives his attention to the Spirit of God and is willing to recognize that His Spirit pervades all space. But as the sound waves flow, they first flow through each one's own dimension which is the body of Light. This body of Light is the Lamp of each one which lights up the spirit.

As God speaks, His Light lights up the spirit with every word that is spoken. The words flow softly, magnetically, lovingly as though your best friend is carrying on a conversation with you while you are at rest, listening peacefully. To hear what another would say, one is to give one's attention to the individual speaking. So too is one to give one's inner attention to the Spirit of God being within the All-Encompassing Light present everywhere.

As you are thinking on this Truth, your mind is centered on God, with but one thought: God. Hold steady on this thought lovingly and reverently.   You are now in a state of listening. But be relaxed and strive not to do any thinking on your part, just as you would keep silent as another is speaking. Your mind is likewise to keep silent and listen.

Be aware of what traverses the mind as though a wave of Light is flowing through the mind, and so it is. Take note of what is being said and write it down. Throughout the centuries, millions of my children received inner flowing thoughts but did not give these thoughts full attention. With some it would be vague, as though they were day dreaming. It is in a quiet state of mind that the light waves can enter into the spirit of the mind.

To continue to form one's own thoughts and images and think of other things, is like keeping your lines busy. The individual is to learn to listen in spirit and in Truth. The **Truth** is that **God is Spirit** and **He speaks in spirit** to the one to whom He is speaking. As **His Spirit flows,** it is like a soft flow of warm sunlight that touches the body. Study how weightless this touch is as you are in the sunlight. Note how silently this light wave operates inwardly. It would come and go as a breeze. But he who is aware and pays no attention to the world but inwardly listens, with one's mind on God, will hear the voice of God.

Do not others who speak to you, often cease speaking as your attention is given to something else? So too does the voice of God cease speaking as you turn away and turn your attention to someone in the world.

My Father knows that his children are still so overawed and mystified in the seeming supernatural experiences disciples are having.

In the past, as one heard the voice of the Lord, that particular one was investigated by the church. When found to be authentic, he was set apart from all others as a "chosen one of the

Lord." Oftentimes, the people considered these chosen ones to be candidates for sainthood. It was the natural and expected offer of the church to admit such individuals into the temple to continue their service to God. They no longer belonged to the world. These "favored ones" now belonged to God and to the church.

This was the procedure of the past which was accepted by the people as the authority of the church remained supreme in the land. God was the highest authority. God was in church. The world of the church was set apart from the world of the "common people." The royal courts of the past were deemed to be the world of wealth and opulence, power and rule. Rulers were placed in a different category. This separation was conditioned into the spirits of the masses.

Beliefs, opinions, and all manner of hidden thoughts accumulated among the people. Here was the origin to the separation of the world of the people and the world of the church and authority in the land. As the might of the rulers was used in the laws which were formed to discipline the people to an orderly and safe way of life, so too did the churches form their own laws to favor their own institutions among the people.

What happened to those who broke the church mandates within the laws propagated by the church were observed by all. Many lost their lives. Certain ones were chastised by the church. As laws were enforced, fears spread over the people. The populace were so gripped in their spirits by these fears of punishment that they suffered silently in varied ways. To counteract the ailments and reactions of the people which were studied by the royal court and church psychologists, leniency was adopted by the church as a "God given Grace."

Those who were filled with remorse and were ready to change their ways, their sins would be expiated in confessions to the priests. Forgiveness was possible. Known for ages that God had forgiven sins of His children, hope was kindled. Jesus forgave the sins committed by men and women. The great prayer, which was the Lord's Prayer, illustrated that people were to forgive others as God forgave them. This Truth was implanted within the souls of disciples everywhere.

Not only the sanctified of the church but also even rulers within the royal courts, all sinned. None were without sin in the world. But the church was granted the authorization by the Lord to forgive the sins of those who admitted them. With confession of one's sins, atonement was now possible. Human weaknesses inherent within the self, were to be admitted to the priests. The "chosen of the Lord" and the sanctified were to overcome the sins of the flesh of the physical body by subjugating the self to the spirit body.

The spirit body was believed to be the immortal body which was made in the image of God who was spirit. These were the alleged verities promulgated by the teachings within the structures of the religious institutions and organizations.

For centuries, the churches held the iron "rod of power," to the extent that none were to usurp the power of the leader of the church, no matter who it was. Neither was any man or woman to believe in the power of the divine rule, by right of their royal blood. These beliefs are so indelibly recorded upon the spirits of disciples throughout the world that there are still many who suffer from their deep-seated fears.Many understood not the origin or source of these fears. The fears were usually hidden and were not to be expressed openly. However, thoughts will continue to emanate from the subconscious mind to convey to the people that they are still recorded and they receive the "feedback" into their conscious mind. At times, scores of people will perceive these hidden fears. Note how the deep seated beliefs have not yet been eradicated.

This spirit of the past is awaiting each ones own recognition. One will learn to"know thyself" by the reactions which well up at varied intervals to reveal to each one what has still been embedded within the spirit. These are the beliefs which have lurked within the depths of one's being as though they were stored in the basement of the lower chakras. The Etheric operations are great blessings which eradicate all that is recognized and released willingly, gladly, gratefully. It is as though a genius has entered your home to remove all the cobwebs, dust and pollutions, to clear the air with fresh, invigorating radiations which uplift all who reside within the dwelling.

Being in a state of humility and

thanksgiving makes erasing the fears, the terrors, the worries and condemnations a much easier task. Be done with the past and "let it go" with a sense of relief that it has been dissolved.

Now be about your Father's business and repeat the words inwardly and love the words while thinking of God and loving his spirit in the words that have been given as His creations.

"We do not live by bread alone but by every word that proceedeth out of the mouth of God." Therefore, the words given to us are called **new creations.** It is the spirit of God now creating in His Words as we love His Spirit in each word. It is this which will bring to us new life and new light. This is the building of our temple within our spirit. His words would be the building blocks of our temple.

As we receive the new truths from our Father, we now have an insight in what we are to release of the erroneous concepts of the past. Some of My beloved disciples brood over the past, not realizing that they believed they were to be filled with remorse and sorrow over what has been done. **It is not My Father's will to have His children carry the burdens of remorse, tears, and persecuting one's self.** We are indeed "to let go of the past." Here one is to rely on God and ask Him in prayer for help so that the past can be overcome to release "looking back and continue in brooding."

It is not My Father's will that his children condemn one's own light which is the soul, which **I AM.** My sons and daughters realize not that as they turn against themselves, they inadvertently are turning against me. This has been done for many centuries where some of My children have tried to destroy themselves. They did not realize their own lack of understanding within former beliefs that became their own stumbling block of not knowing how to look up, as they dwell on the past.

Be aware that these are former, erroneous concepts of self-abnegation, self-abasement, and self-excoriation. To turn on the self is inadvertently to condemn one's own light which is the soul, which **I Am**. My children are not to turn against themselves. It is this which has been done for many centuries, where there were those who would destroy themselves. These would entertain suicidal attempts at times. They did not realize that they lacked understanding of their beliefs which were deeply affecting not only the mind but the spirit, body and soul.

All are to meditate on the Love of My Father and Mother for each child. Note how I have said, "child." All over the world, children do not have sufficient comprehension of their spirits. Neither are they aware of what transpired within their previous lifetimes.

It is as my children have believed that my Father is a retaliating God that these children would retaliate against themselves, so entrenched are some of these attitudes and concepts of the past states of consciousness. These children need the assistance of others to reassure them, to love them, to demonstrate the kindness many of these have never known. All have, at times, under varied circumstances, perceived their own thoughts along these same lines. Although that period in time has been forgotten, the devastating thought forms may still be lodged and arise under varied conditions.

THE FIFTH STATE OF CONSCIOUSNESS WORLDWIDE

It is not generally understood that just as there are grades in elementary schools, high schools and colleges, so too, are there spiritual grades which individuals pass through. Oftentimes we are unaware of our own grade levels. It is within the Fourth State of Consciousness that the man or woman is totally unaware that he is more than a physical body.

There are those who will graduate from colleges and even have higher degrees while they are still within the consciousness of their own physical bodies. It is as the individual turns to the deity in some form that he first becomes aware of spirit. Myriads of people are within the Fourth State of Consciousness as they enter into the churches, temples or institutions of spiritual learning.

The Fifth State of Consciousness was symbolized by the character and personality of John the Baptist. It was he whose food was composed of locusts and honey. The knowledge he had gained in the world, his Fourth State of Consciousness, were those negative, destructive thoughts and emotions. Accumulations of destructive thoughts can destroy one's own light in God just as the locusts can destroy the grain or the wheat. The wheat often denoted the "staff of Life" which was the main ingredient in the making of bread. While bread was long known to signify the Light of Life within the physical body, it was this energy of his own life which had often been used destructively on all levels.

As one would break the Laws of the Love of God in judgment against his fellow man, he was using his energy destructively. All thoughts and emotions within the body can be used positively or negatively. To use one's energy negatively to harm another in any way, was doing as the locusts do when the wheat is destroyed and cannot be harvested.

John symbolized that spirit where he was not yet aware of the laws governing his own Life force, his own energy. He had believed that by admonishing others in their varied evils and judging them vehemently, he would be following the prophets before him who had taught others to repent.

Certain prophets likewise exposed the evils of the people and of the rulers upon the land. John did not have the understanding of the Love of God. Neither was he able to unravel the mysteries of how one should "love one's enemies." This was his own stumbling block which would hold him to the Fifth State of Consciousness until he learned the higher state of consciousness as presented and illustrated by Jesus.

It was Jesus who taught his disciples whom he knew were in the Fourth and Fifth States of Consciousness. Jesus was aware that his followers still believed in the laws of his nation. He knew they followed the laws of the former prophets who had taught of the law of retaliation.

It was believed that for every evil that man would do, there was a law which meted out punishment according to the seriousness of the crime. The retaliatory law was exacting. Punishment would be meted out to the extent that one's crime was measured.

This was the law of an eye for an eye and a tooth for a tooth. The rulers in the land would mete out the punishment. This practice had been established in countries throughout the world. It was as Jesus was being taught by the angelic beings that he learned that there were higher laws than man's laws.

While he was being taught, he too had the laws of his nation recorded upon his own soul, his body of Light. It was as the angelic beings showed him which were God's Laws and which were man's laws that he was to relinquish the way of man and the laws of man. Once he would release his belief and acceptance of the laws made by the authorities in the land, now he could obey the Laws of God. It was the Angel of the Lord, or the Ascended Teacher of Jesus, who took him through his own beliefs while he travelled the Path of Light in his own learning process.

Jesus confronted his own spirit of the past as he was in the Temple. This took place when he lost his temper and whipped the money changers within the temple. Jesus believed that the temple was a holy and sanctified place where the Spirit of God would abide. He too had been taught in the temple not to mention the holy Name of "Yahweh" verbally, but only whisper this Name reverently. The Holy Name was to be spoken in reverence in spirit.

The temple was not a place to carry on worldly business of merchants who would display their wares within the temple grounds. This was not a place where one should exchange money to buy and sell. This was sacrilegious. "The House where the Lord was to be worshipped" was to retain the sacred and holy atmosphere where spirits were elevated to be with the Spirit of the Lord.

It is this same belief which was propagated throughout the centuries. The origin of the belief that God was present only in the Temple or Church, became established within the minds of religious people everywhere for many centuries. Once the people left the temple, they would be leaving God's Spirit there and now reenter the world as they returned to their own homes.

The world of Light would now be divided by associating God to be only within the structures of places of worship.

My children everywhere still have these beliefs indelibly printed on their own spirits. They will recognize this as they meditate on the origin of their own beliefs.

John the Baptist believed that he had

entered the world of the Lord. It was within the temples that he would eat the honey. The honey was the food of the Lord which was sweet in the Peace of the Lord, the kindness, the simplicity and love which was demonstrated by Jesus. For "the Knowledge of the Lord had long been associated as the food of the soul." This food was often referred to as honey, because it was filled with Light, Life and Love. Considered soothing and pleasant to the taste, honey enhanced the tastes of other foods upon which it was used.

While John the Baptist taught the people the knowledge of God which he had acquired in his reading of the scrolls, he recognized that Jesus had the higher knowledge. Since Jesus was a messenger of the angelic beings and since he spoke the words of his Father, his Teacher within the ascended state, John revered Jesus. John the Baptist would herald the Presence of the Lord.

It was John who felt the Spirit of Jesus, and believed the Spirit of God had descended from the Heaven world, and was now with Jesus. Jesus was this son, "in whom Yahweh was well-pleased." It was Jesus whom John had baptized. When Jesus submitted to this practice, as he came out of the water where the baptismal service took place, it was John the Baptist who heard the voice of the Lord, who was Yahweh the Ancient One, say: **"This is my son in whom I AM well pleased."**

It was within this ceremony that the sins were washed away according to the teachings within the Fifth State of Consciousness. At the moment Jesus came out of the water, the Holy Spirit descended from the Heaven world and now entered into the spirit of Jesus. This signified one's belief in God. Baptism was the act of pledging one's soul to the Spirit of God. John taught that those who would be baptized would be saved from the clutches of the evil one, known as Satan. Henceforth the Angels would protect those who were baptized. These were the people who would now be known as the children of God. All others were to be condemned as being the children of darkness, of evil, or the Satanic forces. These were the beliefs incorporated with those who were within the Fifth State of Consciousness.

As Jesus studied in the temple of his nation even as he was a young boy, he had accepted the concepts that his nation was the "chosen nation" destined to bring forth the Messiah to reign upon the earth. This Holy One would one day banish all evil from the face of the earth.

Dear readers, long had my children worldwide believed that a form would incarnate upon the Earth and fulfill this great prophecy. The disciples of Jesus believed that he had now come into the world through the son of Mary. As my children held this desire within their own minds, their hearts and their spirits, it was my Father who gave to them the image they had long held within their consciousness.

But even so, it was Jesus who portrayed the Sixth State of Consciousness which, at the time, was not understood. It was He who was to demonstrate to the world the way to the Seventh State of Consciousness. He was to ascend with his body of Light into that Universal realm of Light within the frequencies of the Angelic Beings. He was to clarify the image that the multitudes had adhered to for so many centuries. All had clung to the image of the male principle being God. This was yet the immature, limiting concept of the nature of God. How could a form hold the all-pervasive Light which flowed through all space, through the seas and the sky, sun and the moon, through all living things?

God was not only Life but Love. While Jesus portrayed the Life principle within the Love of God, it was woman who had first completed her cross. Did not Mary give her Light to the Father? Was he not her son, Jesus? It was she who had found her immortal soul, the body of Light as he arose. Mary met him and recognized him, at last. He was her Master, Teacher and Lord, the higher Self, the body of Light made in the image of the Light of the Father, the Universal Light.

When this great Truth can be accepted and perceived within the soul, each one will be quickened within his own Path of Light. It is woman who first goes through the cross. It is her male principle who is given to the Father. In surrendering her own Light to God, she has obeyed the Law of Balanced Interchange. She now loves her Father more than she loves her own son, the Light of Jesus. Mary obeyed the Laws of God and her Light, her son, ascended to become One with the Father.

Her own husband, Joseph, who depicted the male spirit in the world, was now to awaken to his own light in the awareness of his soul within. Joseph had not yet learned the higher Laws of God. He would one day understand the female spirit which he carried, and learn to surrender the female spirit to God, as woman surrendered the male principle to the Father.

Each man and each woman carry one another's spirit within the marriage state. Each one is male and female in spirit and within the soul. Each is given the partner in marriage to view one's own spirit, externalized by the male and female. All of the thought processes, attitudes, images, ways, and beliefs within the personality, portray the spirit of woman which the male carries.

Eventually his wife will awaken to the understanding of her own spirit. The male likewise will one day comprehend his own spirit, lodged within the physical body of his own wife.

Silently studying this spirit and meditating on all that he surveys in his wife, he will carefully examine all that is manifested before him. His knowledge of his own spirit will be profound as he scrutinizes the basic beliefs which he had clung to through the ages, being dramatized by his own spouse.

Although varied changes in his character and personality have occurred so that he does not recognize his spirit in his wife, still, she portrays the "spirit of his past." Her ways were his ways of the past lifetimes. Her reactions were his reactions of former times. His deep-seated concepts still unredeemed, are enacted before his eyes within his own household. What an enigma! What a revelation!

Great will be the spiritual progress as the husband and wife learn how to have all that each sees banished within the Etheric cleansing and erasing processes. What an immense privilege to have all that one has released completely erased as though it has been written upon a blackboard. Now the eraser would remove all that has been surrendered and recognized. All this was impregnated upon the spirit. But now it will be eliminated with the Light of the Great Alchemist who changes the darkness into His own Light.

Those individuals who would embark upon a new path and willingly accept the revelations being given to those who have enrolled within the **University Of The Christ Light with the Twelve Rays Of The Great Central Sun**, will now forge ahead spiritually and be elevated higher than the masses. It has always been this way in the world.

There would be those courageous individuals who would leave the crowds and seek answers for themselves in their own pioneering spirit. Scientists have long been willing to experiment with laws which can be proven. Nevertheless, these laws are to be experimented within, not in the laboratory of others, but within the spirit and soul of one's own being. It is only this way that the scientist himself will be enabled to prove these teachings for himself.

CHAPTER VI

THE SIXTH STATE OF CONSCIOUSNESS

Two thousand years ago, as the scribes recorded the words of Jesus upon the cross, they would not that the Truth be given to the Gentiles. If the Gentiles followed the words of Jesus, as he spoke them word for word, they would have discovered the great Truth of how to contact the Lord of Hosts.

This secret was jealously guarded by that nation who would not that the Pharaohs obtain the sacred Truths. These were to be unobtainable to those who misused the power of God. Therefore, how to contact the divine Spirit of God had been guarded by the inner circles of the authorities. These were the elders of the "chosen nation."

It was seen that so much of what had been recorded in the past, was added to the library of the rulers, so that the royal family would have access to the highest knowledge brought forth by the prophets, who knew how to contact the Spirit of God.

This knowledge was not to be written so that it could not be passed on to the royalty. For, as this would happen, the people would follow the pharaohs instead of the true messengers of God within their own nation. It was in this way, that their own people could be protected to preserve the truths from generation to generation. Only those who were dedicated and worthy to receive the Word of the Lord, were to have access to knowing how to contact Jehovah. Even the holy Name "Yahweh" was not to be spoken orally.

It was taught among the trusted few that His Name was to be silently uttered in spirit, in reverence. Only those who revered God were to speak His Name. It was known that addressing Him by name brought His Spirit to the people. Consequently, they were taught not to mention His true Name anywhere, except within the silence of the temple.

Since the temple was consecrated, all who entered therein were to recognize that the temple carried His Holy Spirit. It was this knowledge which eventually spread among the people everywhere. The ground upon which the temples were built was considered holy.

In the Far East, it had long been the custom to remove one's shoes before entering a home. It became obvious that the shoes carried the soil into the homes. It was this practice that had become the custom especially where beautiful carpets had adorned the rooms. Designed upon these carpets, mystical emblems were frequently interwoven, deemed holy. Sitting upon these carpets, the people did not desire to soil their carpets nor their clothing. Thus it became the custom to remove one's shoes before entering a home.

Before long, this custom was adopted in many of the temples in the Far East. This same custom prevails to this day. Those travellers who have visited the temples would often see shoes placed together before the entrances to the temples or homes. As the Jewish Nation had long been following the Angels, it was known to them that these great beings had formerly lived upon the earth and eventually received their own souls and made the ascension. Questions had been asked by the people: "Is Jesus the one and the same as Elijah who had ascended?"

There were those ascended beings who would speak to their own former children upon the earth. These spiritually advanced divine spirits often spoke to a son or a daughter whom they had known in previous lifetimes. These were now considered to be the "Holy Parents." Individuals whose parents had passed on and were within the spirit world, would often hover near their own children, trying to assist them, gain their attention and speak to them.

Thousands have carried on conversations with their departed parents in dreams which were so vivid and often remembered. So too, would divine Parents try to contact their own children and assist them in their spiritual growth. The divine Parents would overshadow their children and give to them of their own Pure Light.

Often these Celestial Parents would protect and guide their sons and daughters throughout the ages until their children would finally grow sensitive enough to recognize them. But even though my children would acknowledge them and accept them, they did not understand that their own souls were as little children. The soul was now to be given to the Celestial Parents so that the body of Light would receive the higher Light and be taught by this purer Light.

The self or physical body had been under the tutelage of the physical parents throughout the centuries and understood not the Parents of their own soul, the body of Light. This was utterly new. None had taught them of their own Parents within the Heaven world.

Although there were those scribes who were given the assignment to record the messages of the prophets, it was not known that the scribes themselves would not that the people obtain the advanced knowledge. Were the "common herd" to have access to such knowledge, these would no longer be the servants to the wealthier people. These would now desire to be treated as equals and this was impossible. For the masses were not educated. They were not refined. They were uncouth. These were the law breakers, the criminals, the thieves, the rapists, the evil-doers in society. These teachings would have to be guarded from the "herd."

The writers of the sacred word would eliminate those passages which gave the clues to opening the doors to the soul, to the Heaven world. Deleting and eliminating portions would not be detected by the layman. For these received what the authorities chose to give them. The superior ones gave very little knowledge to the world. These knew that Knowledge is Power and so it would be withheld from the masses.

Throughout the centuries, those of the upper classes would educate their own children and relatives. But educational opportunities were denied to the poor. Such privileges were withheld even to the middle classes. These would serve the knowledgeable, the superior, the educated and the refined. In every country where individuals showed signs of being highly intelligent, these were commanded to serve within the royal courts. However, their services were rewarded, at times, very handsomely.

The intelligent would often count it a privilege to be invited to the center of political activity in the courts. This was the way of life in so many countries in the world. Populations everywhere were increasing. It was evident that of necessity the land would have to be divided into provinces. The king would now select those who would be subservient to him, whom he could trust to assist him in ruling over the land. Those who merited honors of esteem were now given titles as his colleagues would govern the province of the area assigned to him under the king's jurisdiction.

The stage of the great drama of the entry of Jesus into the world was now prepared. The Messiah was the promised One who would enter the world and at the right time, assert his power and receive his throne in the world. These were the cherished beliefs of the multitudes who had long followed their Lord, the Great Yahweh, who was to come into the world through His own son. There was great hope and expectancy that their own beliefs would now come to pass. The countless miracles and healings which Jesus performed strengthened the credulity of the people in him. Here, at last, was the true prophet, the Messiah, now come into the world.

It was as Jesus did not retaliate against the soldiers and against the authority in the land that this act of non-resistance baffled his disciples and the people. His silence was mystifying. The people believed he would use the same kind of power which Moses had used when he lifted up his "Rod of Power" to destroy the soldiers and overcome the Pharaoh in the distant past. The actions of Jesus were contrary to what his nation expected of him. His behavior when the soldiers captured him, had been peaceful. He admonished Peter to lay down his sword.

"Those who live by the sword will themselves die by the sword." But others did not understand that as an implement is used to take a life, at that moment, man loses his own light. He is no longer aware of his light and it is now filled with darkness. The act of killing another brought the death of his own soul, his body of light.

It was this that Jesus was showing his disciples. But they understood not the soul. Neither did they know the Laws of God as Jesus knew them. He had been illumined by the Angelic Beings who interpreted the Universal Laws of God to give to him the understanding. The disciples, on the other hand, would interpret the laws from the human mind, according to the way they were taught by the spiritual authorities, even the prophets.

For centuries, the prophets themselves had relied on their own interpretations. But it was

Jesus who was taught by his own Celestial Parents from the time his soul was a small child. He had spent time daily in communion with the Angelic Host. It was known that Lord Maitreya had been his teacher. But this knowledge was hidden from the world. The names of the Angelic Beings were not to be uttered in the world.

God so loved the world that He gave His own Light of Love to those of His children who obeyed the Law of God. Mary obeyed that Law as she loved the Lord with her whole heart, her mind, spirit, body, soul, strength and with her own will. It was she who obeyed the Lord and gave her own Light to God as she gave her own son, who signified the Light of God. As she committed her Light to the Father, now she received her own soul, her body of Light, into her own spirit within her being.

As the soul descended from the Heaven world, it entered into her spirit and now became a "living spirit," as the spirit now lived within the Light of the soul within her body.

It was the Father who would now do the works within the soul. This was the seventh day for Mary. Jesus, her son, was this Light of her own soul. Did she not call him, her Lord, her Master and her Teacher? Did she not recognize the Father within the soul of Jesus? It was He who had been her Teacher. This was the Light now, which spoke to Mary in the still small voice. This was the Light which guided Mary, which filled her with the Peace and Love of God. It is this Light which is the "Pearl of Great Price."

As Mary completed her cross in the world, it was now Joseph, her husband, who placed the Light of God into his own rock which signified "his belief in the Truth of God." Was it not written, "Upon this 'rock,' I will build my church?" My church was the soul, not made by the hands of man, but fashioned by the Knowledge of God, by the Truths of God, which came from the still small voice from within one's own soul.

Did I not say, "Thou shalt have no other gods before Me?"

The pure Light of God which enters the soul, is like a lamp that receives the Light from the Power which flows into the lamp. As a lamp is connected to the socket and the flow of electricity comes from the outside of the house through the wires so too, does the Light of God flow from the outside of the individual, from the Celestial Parents who give their own Light to Light the lamp as the Laws of God are obeyed.

THE KEY IS WITHIN
THE GREAT LAW

The "Key" to lighting one's own lamp is in **obedience** to the great Law of Balanced Interchange.

Jesus dramatized the role which signified the "Lamp" which holds the Light. The soul likewise holds the Light. The soul is the Lamp. The Father Mother God, the Trinity, is the Light of the Lamp. As light flows through the nerves, so too, does electricity flow through the wires. The wires would be comparable to the nerves. One can see the analogy of the lamp to the soul. Meditate on this, dear readers.

Illumination will come into your spirit as you love the Creator within His revelations. His Truth is written within these pages in simplicity so that all may read and understand.

You have now been prepared to realize how the writers throughout the ages would write their own beliefs in what each would view in the world as being the truth. It is now evident that their knowledge and information from other sources were often quoted. This is the world of illusion, reflecting through the state of consciousness of the writers. Scribes view the appearance world and this now becomes the truth. But my Father, hidden in the depths of His children, observes all that takes place. He cannot be deceived by any man, woman or child in that which is written in the world.

My Father is showing my children the Truth which has been hidden for centuries.

THE AWAKENING TIME
HAS ARRIVED

My children have been asleep in their souls long enough. The time of awakening is at hand. All, who accept these teachings within their souls, will now receive the Light within the Words written upon these pages.

THE HIGHER MEANING OF
THE TEN COMMANDMENTS

My children are now ready in the world to receive the higher interpretations of the **Ten Commandments.**

It is My Father who is even now interpreting the **Ten Commandments** through this disciple who is preparing this book.

1. THOU SHALT NOT KILL

As man has long believed this Law applied to the physical body, he was given the interpretation which applied to the physical body. But as man is elevated into his third body, the soul, a body of light, it is this body which is not to be killed. This is the body which is made in the dual image of the Universal Light: male and female. This is the Light of the Trinity: **Father Mother God**, all three within the third body of the soul. Note how the Universal Light is also Father Mother God, the Trinity, with the duality of the male and female. This duality is within the Light itself.

HOW THE THIRD BODY OF
LIGHT IS FORMED

The Body of Light is formed by the Celestial Parents, just as physical parents form the physical body of the babe. But instead of receiving a solid, material body of the substance of the earth, which is made up of the elements of the earth, the body of Light is formed by the same Light as the Light of the Creator. This is the Light which is **immaculate**, since it is the pure Light which unites with its own pure Light. A being is now formed from this union and is made in the image of the Light in which it has been formed. This is the third body.

It is presented to a man or woman who gives his own spirit body to the Light of God, to be taught, trained, and nurtured just as physical parents teach and nurture their own children. So too, do the ascended hosts nurture their own children of Light.

For centuries as sincere disciples gave their spirits to the Creator, they received their own souls. These individuals would begin to hear the voice of the Lord. When this would happen among the laymen, the authorities within the institutions everywhere could not tolerate any layman, who would usurp the power which was to be awarded only to the sanctified of the present church.

These disciples were frequently excommunicated. They were given the option to leave the church, or continue to be among the sanctified. It was in this way that the church would be protected within the policies and beliefs adopted by the church authorities. This same practice prevailed during the period that the baby Jesus was whisked away from the rulers, to be hidden in Egypt until it was safe to return him to his native land.

Jesus portrayed the Light that was being protected. When the Light is exterminated, the body of Light would be killed. This has been taking place throughout the centuries. It is, as the individual loses his awareness of his own Light, that this Light is as though the body of Light is dead within the individual. He now loses his sensitivity, his life in God, and is returned to the world to live within his former spirit which is of his own spirit. It is **not** the death of the physical body.

It was Noah's own body of Light, his soul, which had spoken to him in the past. What was said was recorded in the Bible. The soul body repeats what has been recorded on one's own light, or his own stored beliefs. This is what took place with Noah as his soul spoke to him and exposed the beliefs written within, so that he could understand his own reactions and thoughts and behavior within his own environment or world.

Preachers throughout the world have sounded the alarm that the world was coming to an end, that it would be destroyed. At times the newspapers record these predictions. Thousands have heard these stories that the world is coming to an end. This belief now would be released to the self of the individual, since it had been recorded within his own soul by his own light.

The belief and image was held within the consciousness as though this holocaust would actually take place. The soul would show this image and belief to the individual. The thoughts would also be released for the spirit within to realize. Prophets all over the world would not comprehend their own spirits, their own consciousness. The consciousness contains all that they have accepted, stored within and held as though it were a truth. As it is held, it is recorded by their own lights. It is this which had been dissolved and eliminated from Noah as the soul released what he was to view inwardly.

The Father teaches his son who is the self. He shows the self what is recorded upon his soul which he believed and accumulated. These conjectures, suppositions, images and worldly creations would block the disciple from entering into the gates of the Heaven World. This Heaven is composed of the Universal Pure Light of the Father Mother God.

Noah had not yet evolved to the place where he would have received the great Law of Balanced Interchange. He like Moses still had those laws from his own nation impregnated upon his own spirit.

In the future, within a New Age, these laws will be released. Nevertheless, Noah would come to the Father and ask Him what he should do, repeatedly, under all manner of circumstances. He would also bring his problems which had beset him, to the Father, as he recognized His great wisdom. It was in relying on the supreme Knowledge and Wisdom of the Father that he progressed spiritually. It was because of his loyalty and reliance on the Father that he became an esteemed leader of his own people.

Note: Once more all the people in the world were not destroyed in the Flood, as it was presumed, because the story itself took place within Noah's spirit **first**. That which takes place within later occurs in the world, and so, the story manifested in the world, but only within the environment where Noah had lived by the sea.

THOU SHALL NOT KILL THE BODY OF LIGHT

Throughout the centuries, the body of Light would be killed as the light within one's own being is exterminated.

As the Light dims and finally is extinguished, the individual loses the awareness of his own light. He no longer feels the inner vibrations, nor the pulsations of a vibrating light. It is as though the individual has lost something within, of great value and now feels the utmost darkness within his spirit.

It is as though the individual is dead. But the death is of his own light and not the death of the physical body as man has long believed. When the physical body expires, the body no longer has any life in it, neither any awareness. Similarly when the body of light dies, there is no further awareness within the interior of one's spirit of this light.

Those who cater to their own physical appetites and indulgences of the physical body, with no thought or desire to follow any laws of discipline of any kind, will lose the awareness of their light. When individuals break the Laws of My Father repeatedly, whether these laws are known or not, that one loses the awareness of his own light.

Little children have an awareness of light but cannot define it. But as this light is not given life or expression in the world, and the child is constantly oppressed, the child builds up a negative reaction which would extinguish his own light after a period of time.

There are innumerable ways that one's own light is lost to one's own awareness. But when individuals reach a plateau in life, where they seek to understand themselves, their spirits and their lights, they are beginning to embark on the Path of Light. These begin a search to know how to resurrect their light. These desire to know how they can remain in the Pure Light of God.

The Light of God is given to all within the world. The soul is already with the spirit, but the individual is not consciously aware of his light shining in his spirit until that one gains the knowledge of his third body. Even though his light may be dim, he will seek ways to increase his light of God in various ways, such as through service to mankind; seeking spiritual knowledge and wisdom; searching to find one's own soul; or seeking to find the road to true love and happiness within the fulfillment of life.

2. THOU SHALT NOT STEAL

THIS Commandment is understood in the world as stealing possessions of others, no matter what they are. The higher meaning of stealing is taking from others that which is given by the soul, namely, taking the Light, the Life or the Love of God through force or deceit.

As one knowingly covets that which one desires and claims it as being his own, he is breaking the law. There are many of my own spiritual children who lose the awareness of their own light, as they take that which others have received and claim it as their own. These would have others believe they are the recipients of the Word of God. These individuals believe they will gain the recognition, esteem and love from others in this way, but just the reverse action takes place. They begin to be filled with resentment against others in not giving to them according to their own desires.

Some would sell books or booklets or even art works which others merited and labored to bring forth into the world. Some individuals would try to enrich themselves through the labors of others, caring not for the one who was the messenger who brought forth the inspiration into the world. They cared only for themselves. The light of these children now dims as they extort all they can from the productive one, but believe no one will know, and so they continue to plunder the writings or tapes or art work in a secret way. This practice has been occurring for centuries, especially within the churches. Often some women, as they received the Word of God, had to relinquish all they received to the authorities, who themselves would now claim to be the recipients of those Truths received by an obedient one who had served humbly and lovingly.

Others had purchased inspired books, and then copied them in such a way that they would claim them as their own.

It is my Father who inspires his children with fresh and original material as my children labor in his field. These would be honest children, willing to honor My Father even as He bestows upon them His enlightening words, filled with His Spirit of Divine Love. It is within the Spirit of Love in which He abides within each one.

3. THOU SHALT NOT COMMIT ADULTERY

FOR countless centuries the definition of this law has been: The husband and wife were to be true to one another and have naught to do with any other man or woman in a sexual involvement.

In a higher sense this Law is not understood within the realm of the body of Light. In truth, all Light belongs to the Father Mother God, the Source of All Light.

Within the marriage state, each is to love the Light of God in one another. When either the husband or wife excludes this Light, the union becomes adulterated with evil thoughts that each gives to the other. As light is excluded, the union becomes adulterated as the darkness formed by each one's thoughts cloud the light of each one and then flows into the spirit and soul.

All over the world over the years, man has judged woman in the same way that woman has judged man. As each judges the other within the union, the light is now filled with the perverted energy which flows with judgment, which in itself is darkness. This perverted energy is hurled against the Light of Life and the Light of Love that each one carries. Few people realize or understand this within their spirits. It is the most wonderful knowledge to have the husband and wife love the Light of God in each other. As they love with their Light, this purifies the union. To exclude the body of Light in the union, is to pervert the union in the darkness since the Light has been excluded from the soul.

My Father formulated the parable of Adam and Eve to show how Eve excluded the Light of God, the Life of the Father within Adam. Eve unknowingly shrouded the soul of Adam with her judgment against his life principle.

The same thing happens in a reverse way

as man judges the love in woman and shrouds her soul. It is this which is adultery. This judgment adulterates the Light of God with the perverted energy used to form thoughts of judgment against the other. To "adulterate" is to cause a substance to become clouded with impurities. The spirit of judgment sends the spiral of energy in a reversed downward motion within the negative, dark thought.

This dark cloud enters into the stream of Light, the Light of Love, and now discolors the spirit with the perverted energy of descending light.

The positive energy ascends but the negative energy descends and becomes cold instead of warm, heavy instead of light. Each feels this as a heaviness and coldness within their spirits but does not correlate it with their own negative creations. The uplifting is in loving the Love of God and Life of God which had flowed to each one in its Pure state.

Husbands and wives will consider this knowledge as a clue to their own happiness. The Love within the female is called the Mother; conversely, the Life within the soul is called the Father. Negative thoughts and emotions will adulterate the Light of God as it is being formed within the minds of the spirits of each one. Great will be each one's advancement in spiritual progress as individuals everywhere accept that each one uses the energy of life within his body to form a thought. The thought can be uplifting or it can be depressing to the spirit.

You have now been illumined in the reading of the higher meanings of the Laws of God. Meditate on God being your Light within your own being, centering your mind, heart, body, spirit and soul.

4. THOU SHALT HAVE NO OTHER GODS BEFORE ME

FROM the beginning of the creation of man, in all countries and all states of development in consciousness, man has worshipped gods in some form. Two thousand years ago when the great drama of the story of Jesus was enacted in the world, man began to accept the male as being the god in the world, despite who that male may have been. Great masters have appeared upon the earth throughout the ages. These beings could perform all manner of miracles and feats which were beyond the comprehension of the masses. Witnessing these demonstrations, the people accepted within their own credibility that this was a manifestation of the Spirit of God in the world. People would esteem and worship those who displayed supernatural powers. Nevertheless, the time has approached that the Truths will be flowing from many areas within the world.

ERRONEOUS CONCEPTS
SHALL NOW CRUMBLE

ALL erroneous concepts of worshipping any physical being upon the earth shall crumble to the dust from which physical man was made.

Since Light is now being discovered as being present in plants, animals, birds, the seas, within space, within the air, atmosphere, and in the sun moon and stars, man is presently perceiving the possibility that this Light is indeed all-encompassing.

These immortal words were spoken and recorded in the Bible: "I AM the **Light** of the world." Declared centuries ago, this was incomprehensible to the masses in their state of evolvement at the time. They were aware only of their physical bodies and did not understand even the spirit body.

THE TIME OF
ILLUMINATION
HAS ARRIVED!

THE Light of the Creator will be fathomed and acknowledged as it has never been affirmed before. There are currently vast numbers living upon the earth in numerous countries, who are now in contact with highly evolved beings. These highly intelligent, shining ones are teaching thousands about this Light, everywhere. The knowledge of Light is growing to such an extent that it will quicken great multitudes, and none will be able to block the electronic flow of spiritual knowledge. This is now taking place within the New Age.

So rapid will be the transition through spiritual acceleration of man, woman and child being transformed, that thousands will be astounded at the quickening occurring even now. Being sensitized within their own Etheric bodies, countless numbers are feeling the pulsations of rhythmic, energizing, flowing Light, which is being studied and analyzed interiorly.

Romance and love will be revived and renewed in a way unknown to the world in the past. The young women will be protected, cherished and nurtured by their own parents and others who are responsible for their care within the communities.

Men and women all over the world have experimented with sexual promiscuity and are aware within their own beings of what this has done to their own lights, spirits and minds. The Light of Life and Love has now been defined and the Source has been established. Scores of young people have admitted they have lost the awareness of their own light. As news spreads that they can be purified and restored to their soul presence, a great interest will well up in thousands of young men and women. Their amazement will be overwhelming, as they learn that the angelic host will assist all of those who desire to be purified.

The revelation is that this Light is the purer and brighter Light of the Angelic Beings, who represent the Light of the Creator, and they will now play a dominant role in the world.

MAN CANNOT
PURIFY HIMSELF!

A higher frequency of Light, purer and brighter, is required to flow through his being to purify him. Long have disciples accepted the beliefs of teachers in the world that they are purified through fasting or by eating specific foods. Although the physical body will release congestion through fasting, it is within the body of light that the negativity and density is stored. This negativity is removed and dissolved by the pure Light which flows through the Ascended Beings. Did not My Father say, it is He who doeth the works within the light body, even as the Higher Light is the Pure Light?

Meditate on the words which Jesus said, "I go to My Father and your Father to be purified within the self, spirit and soul."

These are the three stages of purification, or three days of darkness he referred to, before he would arise from the grave of his physical body. The hill upon which he stood as Mary recognized him, was a higher state of consciousness as she recognized the soul, at last. Jesus portrayed the role of the soul, the body of Light.

Great will be the joy of my children as they complete their own purification by coming to the Father and surrendering all that He shows them, in spirit, within their own beings.

WHAT ARE THE OTHER GODS BEFORE ME?

MAN at times felt compelled to worship something in some way. He would often worship that which was mysterious, where he at times felt an influence within himself. He would look into the skies and begin to worship the moon, sun, stars, wind, thunder, and the Light within the heavens. Looking into the world, he would worship the beauty in the world, in woman and nature. Woman would worship the strength of man, his talents, and wisdom which she admired. Man worshipped the love in woman. Men and women have worshipped personalities, various characters and all manner of admirable human traits.

THE CHRIST OF THE EARTH

FOR the past two thousand years, as my Father observed how his children turned to the one true Master who made the ascension, it was I, the Ancient of Days, who gave him the assignment of being the "Christ of the Earth for Two Thousand Years."

My children are now to know that Jesus has been appointed by the Creator to become the World Teacher for the Earth Planet. He will work with two other great ascended beings, who operate the same Rays of the Universal Light; the Ray of Wisdom, the Ray of Truth and the Ray of Love.

As an ascended being masters the first Universal Ray, he commences to learn the laws inherent within the second Universal Ray. There are twelve Universal Rays within the Great Central Sun, which my children have been learning to operate upon the earth with the ascended beings who are the administrators of each Ray.

Some ascended beings have been laboring within the inner planes for more than thirty thousand years. These ascended beings have mastered eleven Rays of the Great Central Sun.

Sanat Kumara, the Host of the Angelic Beings known as the Ancient of Days in the Bible, is One and the Same, who spoke to all of the prophets, to Moses and also to Jesus. He spoke through Lord Maitreya, who had long taught and trained disciples upon the earth. The Angelic Host were with all of the prophets, all of the masters, and even with Jesus himself. They appeared to him countless times, and particularly as he was in the grave. The Angelic Beings entered the grave, and removed the "grave cloths," which were the "beliefs of the world" preserved through his nation.

The ascended beings all serve the One Creator, the **Father Mother God** of the Great Central Sun, who is **not form**. He is the Pure Light of Life, Love and Light, with all of the virtues inherent within the Twelve Rays of the

Great Central Sun.

MAN IS TO WORSHIP
ONE GOD

THE time has come for the family of man, woman and child, to worship the One God, the Creator, who is the Pure Light which holds the entire earth within its orbit with His own Light. His all-pervasive Light holds all the spirits of all the children of the earth. Each one's spirit is as the atmosphere of the Earth which is within the Light of God. The inner body of each one's spirit is held by the Light of God, even as the Higher Light is in all and through all.

The Law of worshipping the One God will be obeyed at last! Man will acknowledge the Truth of God when he realizes that all the healing that takes place within the body, spirit and soul is done by the Divine Light of God, which flows within the spirit of man as energy in Light. It is the One Creator who is the Divine Physician, the **Father Mother God** of all upon the earth.

THE CREATOR CANNOT BE
CONFINED ANYWHERE

THERE is no church, institution, congregation, organization, country or race of people who can contain the Creator exclusively, as though the Creator could be confined or held in any given place or institution, no matter who or what it may be. **God is the Father of all, in all and through all.** As this great Truth will finally be accepted, **this will bring peace to the world.**

I reiterate, my children are to know that it is My Light that holds the spirits of every man, woman and child on the face of the Earth. As the spirit is within the body, so too is My Light shining in the darkness of the spirit. **The self has not understood this for two thousand years.**

Since thousands of my children are meditating, the Truth is flowing into the earth from many sources around the world. **None will be able to stop this flow!** Although many sincere laymen in all manner of churches in many countries, would hear the Truth of the Lord. (These laymen were not the sanctified of the church who obey their rules.) Therefore, these independent laymen were often excommunicated, or ordered to join the church, where they would be controlled by the authorities within their institution and land.

TEST ALL VOICES
HEARD INWARDLY

MAN, woman and child are not to accept all voices heard within. Each one is to learn how to test the voices with the message received. To ascertain if what has been received is the Truth within the Love of God, if any harm is directed to **anyone** within the message, the voice of God is not speaking.

Other spirits speak, and man is to know that under no circumstances would God harm any man, woman or child. Some individuals have a spiritual mind that would speak in the same way one hears through the still small voice, as he hears this voice inwardly. If there is any negativity prompted by some hidden motive, some secret desires of the self, which may be to retaliate against someone or harm someone for some grevious cause that brought suffering in the past, then these voices should be tested and verified.

Many sincere disciples, who have been prophets in the past, who were **not purified**, and whose messages were filled with doom and destruction, are bearing false witness in the world. These messages are not coming from God. The Creator loves all of His children and there is no destruction of any kind within His Being of Pure Light.

Desires, motives, secret ambitions and self-glorification are to be suspected. Some channels today, who have not yet gone through the full purification of the self, spirit and soul, would receive messages to cater to their own desire and will. Other unscrupulous individuals would attempt to gain vast sums of money or material possessions from others. These likewise are giving out false messages. My own children have not fully realized this. Often they cannot discern which voice is speaking. But it is My Father who trains his children, showing them how to ascertain how to discriminate between the self and the voice of the Father, through an ascended being. Some messengers who operate the Law of Love and love the Spirit of God within the words of the message, will feel the spirit of the self in the words. In this way, they will realize it is not from God.

Some of my children would pretend to love someone as they desire to marry, to serve their own motives, whatever they would be. As there is no true love, these are bearing false witness against one another.

When individuals hold marriage partners to the self and refuse to give the self to the soul in God, they are bearing false witness to true love. The human love that would possess the self, and bind the individual to the self, apart from the Love of God, is likewise bearing false witness.

It is My Father who brings true soulmates together, **at the right time.** Men who desire to meet the right woman, will see how I will guide them as they come to me in prayer and ask that I show them who their soulmate is.

Centuries ago, there were those fathers and grandfathers who had come to the Holy Spirit, to ask if the sons or daughters, who were of marriageable age, would be shown who their right partners would be. As the Father was consulted for His Wisdom and His Will, he answered and blessed those who would acknowledge His Wisdom for their children, in prayer.

5. THOU SHALT NOT BEAR FALSE WITNESS AGAINST THY NEIGHBOR.

To bear false witness is to prevaricate to serve one's own purpose. To bear false witness is to witness to the darkness and refuse the Light of God. Beliefs, conjectures, suppositions, false premises, misinterpretations, false opinions, distortions of any kind, are not to be accepted. Come to the Father for the Truth.

WHAT IS THE TRUTH?

IT was I who asked, "What is the Truth?"

As My disciples looked to one another and could not answer this question while they were with Jesus, My disciples did not perceive the silence of Jesus. It was My Son, Jesus, who stood silently and used the Law of Recognition: that I AM in all and through all.

The Truth is My Green Ray of the Great Central Sun. This Ray flows into the spirit as My children come to Me. As they recognize that I AM the **Truth** and ask for **My Truth** in prayer, they shall feel **My Truth** and realize who it is that released the **Truth**.

It was Jesus who turned inwardly and spoke to Me, declaring in spirit that I AM the Truth. As he did this, I released My Green Ray of Truth to flow into this spirit as Light in My Love which elevates My children even as the Ray flows into their spirits. But as Jesus recognized Me as being within my disciples also, Jesus operated My Law which gave to the disciples, and they felt the warmth of **My Love** in **My Truth** as it flowed into the soul.

The Truth is never given without Love. As **My Truth** flows, so likewise does My Love flow with My Truth. The Love of the Creator is with His own Truth.

As the disciples felt the Love flow into their spirits, they looked at one another in amazement and said, "Did we not feel the Flame of God, which warmed our hearts?" The disciples now recognized that the Truth flows in **silence**, into the soul, the body of Light. As man comes to the Creator and acknowledges Him as the Source of Truth, that one will receive the Truth according to His belief in the Creator.

Some of my learned sons teach young people to experiment with one another sexually to determine if each is compatible and can love one another. Some indulgent men find this as an excuse to experiment with many women, with no intention of marriage. This is bearing false witness against my gullible daughters, who trust what others lead them to believe. As My Father is consulted, He shows which man and which woman is of the same frequency of Light, even as My Father knows every frequency, which is each one's own light given to that one by My Father. Those couples who are of the same frequency, are complements of one another and balance each other. However, some husbands and wives have been married to one another in previous lifetimes. Each believes they belong to one another, not realizing that it is only My Father who knows the right woman for the right man who is ready for marriage.

Bearing false witness is being untrue to My Father, the Soul within each man and woman. It is the Soul which knows the Truth within the Father, the Light of God in all and through all. When He is invoked in prayer, one receives the Truth through the Soul. It is as the spirit of man or woman holds his own soul, his light, to his own beliefs that he will err. A man or woman will likewise err as he holds tenaciously to some mistaken belief.

Countless followers of My Father believed that as I spoke the words: "Unto thine own self be true," this was supposed to mean to be true to the desires of the self, whatever they may be. However, as these words were stated, it was the Higher Self, the Light of God within the Soul, to which one was to be true. It is this Light which is the Pure Light of the Creator, in all and through all. As He is the Whole Light and has all Knowledge, it is to this Light one is to be true. As one's own body of Light, his soul, is entrusted to the Whole Light, the all-encompassing Light, one's soul is called the **Over-soul**, or **Over-self**, the Greater Light. It is this which is the **Creator**. This Light has not been clearly defined to be comprehended.

6. THOU SHALT NOT COVET

TO covet is to desire that which belongs to another, no matter what it is. It may be talents, beauty, money, position, education, possessions of all kinds, popularity, the wife of another, or the husband of another, a child, or a baby belonging to others. Whatever each one has received in the world in a just way, meriting his gain through his own labors, his own education and talents, his own inheritance, or within his own family, belongs to the one to whom it has been awarded in the world.

It is My Father who is the giver of all possessions, all advantages, all inheritances, all property, all the blessings which come to the individual legally, which would bless that individual. This is the recompense of what that person has merited in numerous ways.

My Father holds the spirits of all his children and knows perfectly what will bless them. Those who desire and covet and take that which others have, while at the same time refusing to give to My Father in His Law of Balanced Interchange, will lose that which they have acquired through theft, devious means, deceit, or some illegality or loss in the world. These children are breaking the Law of God and will accrue debts within the soul, the body of Light, against My Father.

Although some people believe that there are those who have not earned that which they have received, no man knows the soul of any other man, woman or child. No one knows what each one has given to My Father in previous lifetimes. My Father stores all the gifts my children give, to alleviate suffering and help others. It is as though one would put his money into My Bank. Then, it is My Father who returns the money, **at the right time**, adding interest to the amount of money which had been given, and then it is returned to the one who gave to Me for my suffering children.

My Father is just and knows His children everywhere. He knows the perfect thing to do with each one. None can deceive My Father! His Light holds every spirit, and He sees the thoughts and beliefs of each one.

My children everywhere will become more honest as they realize that **I AM** so close to each one that their very thoughts register upon My Light. It is in all and through all, in every area of space. There is no place that My Father is absent. He is the Living Light which holds all life within His Light. But it is the son or daughter who would cloud his own light and pretend that I AM not with him. How can I be everywhere? No man can be everywhere. But **I AM** not the **form** of a man, woman or child.

My Body is Pure Light which is in all space, which holds all living things within my sea of Light as though my entire ocean is My Light and all living things in My ocean, are within My Light, which is the ocean. As the sun shines upon all, so too, does My Light shine in all. However,

My children become confused as they think of me as form, as they have for so many centuries. But as **I AM** accepted as being Pure Light, present everywhere, the mind can conceive how it is that **I AM PRESENT EVERYWHERE.**

7. THOU SHALT NOT USE MY NAME IN VAIN

MY beloved children, My Name is: "God is with you. God is Love. God is Peace." Those who profess to use My Name, and then perform some heinous act in My Name, are breaking My Law. Those individuals all over the world who believe they are at war with each other in My Name, are in truth breaking My Law of Love for all of My children. People who believe man is to be killed in My Name are breaking My Law. My Father does not break His own Laws. His Spirit is within the Law. He is the Law of Balanced Interchange.

Man will one day perceive that all that occurs within the environment, which commenced within his spirit, returns from the world which is within the Law: To give to you according to your belief. The world is like a reflective lake that receives all that is imaged upon the surface of the water. Men and women have now been given the insight to correlate their outer world with their inner envisioning light of creation.

Beliefs and thought patterns are created

from all manner of sources. Statistics, predictions from experts or psychics, seasonal predictions based on previous occurrences, droughts, cold waves, frosts: all these things occur, not only from images held within the spirit, but from the emotional perversions of energy which flow into the atmosphere upon the Light of God, existent everywhere. The majority of people hold within their consciousness that which they believe to be absolute truth. None can dispute their beliefs because they know it is going to happen. They believe in the source from which they obtained their information.

As man creates within his own spirit with the Light shining in the darkness, which he does not comprehend, the world confirms the reflections of his own spirit, just as a lake reflects what is mirrored into the clear water that acts as a mirror.

When man expects devastations to happen in the world, he believes in the power of darkness, and forms the image of what can happen before it happens. That person receives his own state of consciousness within his own visions in some way. It is not too unlike a spider spinning his own web and now he is enmeshed with his own creations of capturing whatever he can within his web. The spider feeds upon all those who likewise become entangled within his web. The insects and flies become the food of the spider; the food can be likened to his own thoughts which he created. The spider is given according to his own desires and images to provide his needs, which he receives within his own "energy web" that he himself has formed.

All are to realize and contemplate how My Father gave man a choice: "Choose whom you will believe." Man himself was given the freedom to choose what he would create within his own spirit, mind and energy. His energy flows from within his own spirit.

The parable of **Adam and Eve** illustrates how Adam was in the Garden of Eden with his own soul, Eve. As both were within the Light of God, they received all the blessings of Peace, Harmony, Love and Abundance.

But as man chose to give to the physical self and exclude God, he chose evil and gave his energy to holding to evil, and believing in the power of evil. Adam now attracted the evil to himself, as he left the Garden and walked alone with his own choice and as he separated himself from his soul and now followed the human creations of the world.

My children who curse, and use My Light as they curse, even as they use the Name, qualifying the Spirit of God, these now pervert their own soul-Lights. The soul now is filled with their own cursing. The tensions of perverted energy spiral around their own spirits. Their own energy returns like a boomerang and oppresses them with the tension and turmoil that was hurled into the atmosphere. But the atmosphere is held by the Light of God just as the spirit is held by the Light of God. As one uses this Light from the forcefield of his own mental chakra, the tensions return to plague the one who created the pollution in the atmosphere.

Oh My dear children, note how My Name is Love. God is Love. As this love, the Light in every man, is perverted, he suffers all manner of tightness, tension, cold and nervousness which become his turmoil.

When My children use their emotions against any man, woman or child, they have perverted the energy of Love, which is being used from the heart chakra and which governs the emotions within the body. It is here in the heart chakra that Love flows into the spirit. As this love is perverted to anger, hate, resentment, or all manner of negativity, he breaks the Law of Love and suffers all manner of tensions and illnesses within his own spirit. Finally, when the spirit has been saturated, the individual becomes ill.

This process may be compared to a plant which has received too many negativities in the air flowing from within the atmosphere where these misqualified energies have been created--and so the plant will wither and die. Conversely, in an atmosphere of the Love of God, plants will thrive. Individuals react to negativity even as plants. For the same light which is within plants is likewise within living beings. My Light is in all living things, including plants. It is the Light which gives life to the individual just as the Light gives life to the plants.

How many of My children have prayed to Me, while at the same time, continued to create turmoil and disharmony even within their spirits in silence. These children find that their prayers are not answered.

Did I not say: "Except you abide in Me," in My Love, which **I AM**. Now you can speak to Me and ask what you will, and I will hear your prayer in My Wisdom and perfect Knowledge of knowing the "Perfect Thing to Do" for each one. When My children obey My Law of Love in this, they will themselves see their prayers answered. However, as My children hold to their own spirits apart from Me, this is not My Name of Love which **I AM**. To abide in Me is to hold in Me the Light within your spirit, where **I AM**.

HE WHO LOVES GOD
WILL OBEY GOD

MY SONS, throughout the ages, have persisted in all manner of ways within their own wills, to imprison My Light as though I could be handcuffed to their ways and confined to their own control, not realizing that trying to use force in holding My Father in this way, they did not comprehend nor realize that they eliminated "Love" from My Father. He who loves My Father would strive to please Him and follow Him and trust Him. But he who denies and refuses this Love, would exert his own power in the world, to give to him according to his own desires and his own will and motives.

Deep within their souls, they held to the belief that the Light within their own beings was to be used to rule in the world.

These identified themselves with the "meek" who would inherit the earth. But the "meek" give this spirit to My Father, the Creator. Did I not say: "The Earth is the Lord's and the fullness thereof"?

The meek are the ones who recognize the Over-Soul, the all-encompassing Light of the **Father Mother God** of the **Great Central Sun.** All of My sons and daughters are to obey the Laws of My Father in the Love which He has for all of His children in the world.

8. THOU SHALT HONOR THY FATHER AND THY MOTHER

ALTHOUGH My sons and daughters have interpreted this commandment to signify that sons and daughters were to honor their own physical fathers and mothers, great are the rewards to My children as they would honor each one's Father and Mother, the Over-Soul. These are Celestial Parents, in whose image each was formed. My son, Moses, did not come to Me for this interpretation. Just as physical parents unite and the physical child is formed within the mother, so too is the body of Light formed within the Celestial Mother of each one.

My children will be overwhelmed to realize that as the Angelic Father and Mother are honored within the Heaven World, the life of My child would be extended upon the earth. As these Parents are accepted and followed, they are created within the image of their Divine Parents. As the child evolves to the place where he understands these teachings and is ready to surrender his own spirit to the **Father Mother God**, the Universal Mother who represents the Love of God, presents the third body of Light to the child to receive in conscious awareness. It is the Father now who teaches his own child how to follow the Universal Laws within his own environment, so that he can learn to live in harmony and peace within his own world.

How can a physical father and mother upon the earth lengthen the life span of any other individual, when the physical parents know not how to obey, nor honor their Celestial Parents, and would themselves dissipate their own life streams? Honoring your Father and Mother in Heaven, within the realm of the Universal Light of God would be to ask in prayer who they are within the Angelic Kingdom, and each will be shown. As the parents learn who they are and learn to obey them, these parents will discover how their own children will in turn obey them in the world. As parents disobey, so likewise the children disobey.

For the spirit of disobedience will be overcome as one learns the great joys and rewards which obedience to the Father Mother God will bring into their lives. Do not parents likewise give more to their own children, as the children obey their parents?

Honoring your father and mother has been ignored by thousands of young men and women. As the young gained new knowledge which had been refused by their parents, the parents would encase the spirits of their children within their own darkness, no matter what it was. The children would react against their parents and could not honor nor esteem them. Vast numbers would leave home at the earliest moment they are able to become self-supporting. Turmoil and tension brews as opposition is still rampant between children and parents. Frequently the child receives physical harm and punishment not commensurate with the misdeed. It may be a trivial offense for which one would receive severe punishment. All manner of discrepancies happen with the relationships between parents and children. Parents and children will travail in the world until they evolve to the place where they have gained sufficient knowledge to learn about respective Celestial Parents of their own souls.

Every man, woman and child has a Father and Mother made in the image of God.

As God is the Electronic Body of Light within mankind, so too do the Celestial Parents have an Electronic Body of Light made in the image of the Pure Light of God. The Celestial

Parents hold the souls of their own children until each child has matured spiritually enough to turn inwardly and learn about his body of Light.

As one gains the knowledge of the requirement of receiving one's own soul in conscious awareness, one is to permit his own Light to "go to the Father Mother God" by giving one's Light to them. One gives his light by giving his attention to the Celestial Parents daily. This is done in order to be trained to increase each one's light so that an extension of Life can be awarded to that one. Parents are honored as they are esteemed and respected, loved and followed. These Divine Parents follow the Spirit of God and know the Laws of God. Therefore, the Celestial Parents become the Teachers of their own children. All learn to obey the Universal Laws which the Celestial Parents have learned to obey; now the children of these Parents are enabled to come into the Eternal Light of Life. They receive more Pure Light and energy from their own Father and Mother whose bodies have become One with the Source of All Energy, Love and all the virtues of the Creator. Each child learns to receive more Divine Love which is abundant within the Celestial Parents, as they are One with the Source of Pure Love.

Each aspirant would re-enter the Garden of Eden in which his Celestial Parents dwell. Their progeny of Light, of the same frequency of Light as the Parents, would now abide within the higher spheres of flowing Light, Life and Love. These blessed children would now have access to all the virtues and **Rays** of the **Father Mother God**, which they would learn to utilize, to bless all of mankind.

The son or daughter now receives the knowledge that his or her own Celestial Parents overcome the darkness of the world. This knowledge is offered up to the Greater Light of the Parents, and the life of the son or daughter is increased in the world.

To honor one's Celestial Parents is to love them and follow their unique and marvelous ways which will provide stupendous rewards undreamed of by their own children.

Let these words be fulfilled by our children: "Seek ye first the Kingdom of Heaven, in which abides your Father Mother God, and all things shall be added to you."

In the Law of Balanced Interchange, he who gives his light of life and love to his Celestial Parents receives a Greater Light from the Celestial Father Mother God within the One Light of the Over-Soul, our Creator.

9. SIX DAYS SHALT THOU LABOR, BUT ON THE SEVENTH DAY, THOU SHALT REST

BASED on the creation of the earth, each day of labor signified a period of time, unknown to man. The significance of the "day" within the Biblical interpretation was "while the Light is upon the earth." Man would labor in the daylight but would rest during the night. The day that the Lord rested was the seventh day, called the "Sabbath." This day was the period of time one was to spend within the Light of the Lord. As man evolved to the place where he found the Light of God within his being, he would now learn to labor in this Light, the Light of his own soul. As the soul was surrendered to the over-Soul, the disciple would rest, and My Father would do the works in the world.

Man enters the seventh state of consciousness within the day or Light of the Lord.

Centuries ago, My children interpreted this Law for the physical body to have one day of rest within each week. Before this Law was inaugurated, the laborers and slaves and thousands of women would often become ill and pass away as they worked constantly. Often they were beaten, mistreated, and driven to work harder as though they were animals in the field.

The word "day" was used to denote a period of time, not necessarily a limited twenty-four-hour period. The Earth itself was created slowly, over a period of thousands of years. As the word "era" means a period of time, so the connotation of the word "day" was considered a period of time. But man comprehended not the length of time it required to create the planet Earth. Despite this discrepancy which my sons did not understand, God waited until his own sons would approach Him in prayer for the interpretation of the **Ten Commandments.**

Since Moses received them, it was Moses who interpreted these Laws, based on his limited human concepts. Moses did not comprehend at the time that man was to labor within six states of consciousness and development. Man was to use his own energy just as a child goes through a period of training and learning to become an expert in a chosen field. So too does a spiritual child go through a long period of training, within this state that he would labor until the seventh period, or seventh degree.

It was Jesus who depicted the progress of his own Light. He was sent to demonstrate the "soul progress." To be spiritually educated within the soul is to gain the knowledge of the Light of God, the Truth of God, and the Universal Laws of God.

In a similar way that a man became mature physically, he would now mature spiritually. Man would now reach the elevated state of progress where he begins to follow his Celestial Father and Mother. This is the period when he learns about his body of Light, his own soul. He experiments with his own light, not too unlike a teenager who would go his own way.

But as he matures in knowledge and understanding, he is ready to give his Light to his Celestial Parents, as though he were presenting them with a new musical instrument. His Celestial Parents are like concert artists and would teach him how to play harmonious music to the delight of all who heard him. But instead of a musical instrument, it is his own soul. He learns to use his own light in harmony and peace, love and good will to all. He learns to receive the abundance through his knowledge and training. At this point, the aspirant has progressed to the place where he is ready to relinquish his own light for a higher Light, flowing from his Celestial Parents.

During the first six periods of his spiritual progress, man is learning how to use his light. He begins to realize what he can and cannot do. Finally, as he is prepared to follow the Way of the Father within the Celestial Light, where the Father's Light flows in right action into the world, man at last learns to obey the Universal laws of God.

Note: He does not lose the use of his own light, but learns how to use it properly, to bring to him the greatest rewards in life.

As he surrenders his own earth light, the light which he had before controlled by his own hand with his own beliefs and creations, as Moses had done, he embarks on a more excellent way of higher laws. During this time he is amazed to discover there are higher Laws which are greater than his former ways. He is now prepared to accept the greater Wisdom from his own Father. He is now willing to exchange his lesser light for the Greater Light of the Creator: the all-pervasive Light within the higher dimensions of Light frequency.

All Ascended Beings have acquired the Wisdom of understanding why it is necessary to surrender their own ways, limitations and lack, as they witness the contact of the propitious ways of the Father. The aspirant becomes illuminated within his own mind as he envisions the Truth of the successful ways of the Creator in illustrating His Ways, as being true happiness and **right action in all things**. His way is truly the Way to Perfection. How sublime!

As the disciple reaches this point of illumination, now the disciple rests, and the Father continues the works. This is the Seventh Hour, the Seventh Day, the Seventh Degree, the Day of "Rest."

The disciple is taught what part he is to play and what he is to do. In his obedience, he receives the Wisdom of the Father who enters into his own environment, his own world, and gives to him the solutions to his perplexing problems. This is the dawning of a New Day as he learns the right thing to do as he trusts the Father.

Some disciples have a considerable number of erroneous concepts about what happens to a disciple as he willingly gives himself to the higher state of consciousness to direct him. Given time to experiment with the higher way, the disciple comprehends the great Wisdom of the Father and now his appreciation sky-rockets! He perceives at last his own higher **I AM** consciousness, which the Ascended Beings portrayed.

Now he can comprehend through their Divine Spirits what his divine spirit would likewise manifest within his world. He learns the great secret of how to blend with his own soul in obedience to the great Universal Laws, which enhance true peace of mind and soul. Multitudes have observed how, as the laws in the land are obeyed, there is peace, approval of others, and satisfaction with one's self. A great appreciation of the laws in the land accrue in his spirit as he senses how laws are necessary to protect others and bring justice, where justice is so necessary in the world.

Similarly, obedience to the Laws of the Father brings peace, contentment and approval of the obedient disciple. The neophyte experiences a new freedom from stress and unhappiness, a greater sense of well-being. This will be greater than he has ever known before!

All who reach God's Sphere of Love desire to remain where all the desires of one's heart are fulfilled. This is the Nirvana where the aspirant and all in his world are blessed. The thrilled disciple, who made the complete dedication, is now ready to become the living evidence of these living Truths of our Creator.

THE DESCRIPTION OF
THE HEAVEN WORLD

THE DIMENSION of the Heaven World can be described as a Palace filled with loving and understanding individuals, ready to assist one another in countless ways. All who abide therein have deciphered all the clues to the Keys which open the doors to the Kingdom of Heaven. The Ascended Beings have found the

Celestial Laws to harmonious and joyous living, where all that is provided is created to enhance each one's joy. Here there is no sickness, no turmoil, no tension, no darkness. All live productively in such a way that each one is continuously uplifted.

As My Father showed His children that on the seventh day they were to rest, he was illustrating that within the seventh degree, one finds the **Father Mother God One** with the "Ascended Host." Following this immense discovery of one's own Celestial Parents, the disciple grasps the knowledge and difference between their Lights, their great comprehension, their own ways, compared to the Way of the Father, which they now experience. How marvelous! Why would anyone want to resist surrendering to our Creator?

Would that all people everywhere could experiment long enough to prove these teachings to themselves.

10. THOU SHALT NOT MAKE ANY GRAVEN IMAGES BEFORE MY FATHER, NEITHER SHALT THOU SERVE ANY OTHER MASTER IN THE WORLD

As each one gives himself to the Father Mother God, and places the Creator first in all things, it is My Father who sets that one free to follow the Supreme Light of God. None can hold or control that one, even as the Father now claims his own son and daughter. He now lifts them up into His Own Light, which henceforth becomes the "All" of the disciple. It is the Light of the Creator who now supplies all the needs and provides abundance to His own child.

The graven images are all those in the world who hold all manner of positions of authority, no matter who they are in the world. Some would be the rulers over the souls of My children. However, as they follow My Father, it is He who shows them how they can be set free, peacefully, as His Ways are followed silently and obediently. It is the Father who overcomes all of the darkness of the appearances in the world. Their appearances would be the graven images, or the images which man himself has created. Often fear and power are used to hold My children to subservience to a master. Nevertheless, as the master is offered up to the Father, the disciple is shown what he is to do within his own spirit. In his obedience to My Father in the Law of Balanced Interchange, My Father makes all the changes in the world, without bloodshed, without wars, without pain and without suffering.

My Father is the reality and always has been the Eternal Truth. He is the ultimate destiny of all of my children. But all must go through their own creations and their own beliefs, before each one is ready to enter into My world of Peace and Love for all.

All who learn how to obey the **Ten**

Commandments as written in this book, will find the Spirit of God within their own beings.

The Creator, my dear ones, is this world of Light where true Justice, Love and Peace prevail within His Kingdom of Heaven, His own Spirit, the Pure Love of God for all. It is this that many of his disciples have now discovered and are learning to love.

Feel thou the Peace of His Love even within these Laws which were made to bring My children into the World of Light, where there is no darkness, no sin, no illness of any kind; neither is there any tension, nor turmoil in His World.

My Father bids all to come into His World of Light, which is His own Body, which encompasses the entire Earth. He nurtures all living things within His own Light of Love for all.

Innumerable children of the world desire to receive, but at the same time, they care not to give. As these children hoard their own light, their awareness dims and decreases.

Within the hidden spirit of man, woman and child, there are those who try to defraud the Father, unknowingly, not realizing that it was the Father who presented to them their wealth, their gifts and talents. These would refuse to share their gifts with others in the Law of Balanced Interchange. This situation is comparable to a river which clogs and stagnates, receiving no fresh water, just as a disciple receives no more illumination.

This river would signify the spirits of

those children who have not yet learned that My Father is within their beings, within their own spirit. Their own souls now becomes clouded because of their own hoarding.

My Father has since ancient times been recognized as having the All-Seeing Eye. He views all that occurs within the environment of every child. The day will ultimately dawn when My Father will be accepted as being in All and through All. When this awakening occurs, his children will discover that He does indeed permeate all space, in all places. It is true that there is no space, nor any place that does not harbor His Light which encircles, centers and pervades all within the earth as an All-Encompassing Light.

Great will be the day when My children finally learn to meditate and center within their own beings. Each one will come to the place where God will be acknowledged as the dispenser of all gifts and all things which bless the children upon the earth. Those who follow Him, will in due time give their attention to Him willingly, reverently and lovingly.

It is as the individual understands how to apply the Law of Love which Jesus taught, but which His own disciples could not practice even as they knew not Love, neither could they follow teachings which were utterly new.

Although his own disciples felt the Presence of God with Jesus, the Body of Light now ascended, and they still could not understand what this body was, nor how it operated. It would be centuries before such a body could be conceived within the spirit mind. Since the disciples refused to go through the necessary purification which Jesus completed, the disciples would teach the interpretation of the story and the immortalized words of the Father through their own human intellects. Therefore, it would be two thousand years before the Laws could be given to those individuals who were sincere seekers of the Kingdom of Heaven.

Once more, it is this disciple who picked up the threads within this lifetime to journey the Path of Light as the Ascended Beings approached her as she was an international prayer leader within the Protestant churches of the United States Army Religious Training Center. She was given the Wisdom of the Father which flowed in the Love of God.

It would be years before she would be trained sufficiently to teach the Universal Laws of Light. She was first to learn them, pass the tests and demonstrate to the Father that the power of Light given to her by her own Celestial Parents, would be used only under the Laws of Love.

All within this organization have seen how there was no force within these teachings. All have seen the calmness and quietness with which these teachings were being demonstrated by a woman. Others who experimented discovered that they, too, could apply the Laws which were taught and they, too, became channels of the Light of the Ascended Beings.

Feel thou this Light of Love even now, within these Words of our Creator. May all be blessed in the reading of His Words within His Love for All.

THE ETHERIC OPERATIONS

Darkness is changed into light within etheric operations. They simply dissolve the darkness and then raise the vibrations of an individual into a higher frequency of light. The Angelic Beings who perform this operation have themselves been highly purified by those cosmic beings who have a purer and higher frequency light to match the Pure Light of God. This pure light flows through the spirit body, where there are rotating spirals of light within the seven centers in the body. This etheric substance flows to the right for positive energy to bless one, or to the left in a perverted negative motion which brings the stress and turmoil to the nervous system. This happens as individuals react to all manner of conditions that depend on habitual patterns of the way one acts and reacts to all that occurs within one's environment.

The perverted invisible energy flows counterclockwise in a downward motion, and the positive energies flow in a rotating upward stream of light. The positive energies lift the spirit, and the perverted energies lower the vibrations and depress the spirit within. Often the natural flow of energy in the body is restricted or blocked when filled with the tensions and stress caused by mental turmoil.

In the higher purer light, cosmic beings offer the service to individuals who are willing to learn the laws of light, to be trained, enlivened and enlightened and are willing to assist in the improvement of life everywhere.

The invisible purifying light in its highest forms cannot be seen, but within the light itself, the essence of pure love is the magnetic quality in the higher light which purifies the etheric substance within the body. Thoughts themselves are formed by etheric substance. Emotions in conjunction with thoughts, likewise, form currents of light or darkness which are negative or positive, that flow through the body.

As water is imbibed, the water itself, if it is pure, acts as a cleaning agent within the human body; within yet a higher level, the water can be transformed into steam and yet, in a still higher form, the steam disappears into the atmosphere, but it has not been dissipated; neither does it disappear entirely. This is the same substance in the higher forms which contains the magnetic quality of love. The same essence is in the air one breathes and in the water one drinks.

It is the angelic beings who are able to purify a lower light or a lower frequency. It requires a higher frequency to purify a lower light frequency. This is the work of the Celestial Angelic Beings because they have achieved a

Oneness with the **One** light of the **Father Mother God,** the three in One Light of the **Great Central Sun.** This is the **Light** that flows through the entire planet Earth. It is the Great Central Sun Light which purifies the entire Earth including all the pollutions in the atmosphere through the Celestial Angelic Beings.

It is this Light flowing through the Angelic Beings that removes the tensions created by mankind in the world, in every country, city, and locality. Each one's own energies flow to each individual from God in the first place. These energies make up the life essence and the love and light throughout the entire atmosphere of the world in its purified state. Clean water has been stored and transported and flows through the pipes, coming through the faucets within the homes. This water is used to bathe and cleanse and refresh the physical body; likewise, in the highest realms and highest frequencies, the Body of Light of man and his energies are purified along with his spirit.

Ninety-two percent of the body is composed of water. All plants, all living things, and all animals and birds have need of water to some degree. Water carries the essence of love, just as love is within the air, in its magnetic quality.

Water is not just hydrogen and oxygen, but the added quality of love cannot be measured by any instrument in the world, for nothing has yet been discovered to measure the love in the atmosphere. The organ of the heart within the physical body can **feel** the magnetic quality of love. It is within this organ where the love essence resides as the Light encircles the entire heart.

Note how water is within the blood, within the entire body in all the cells and all the organs. The liquid itself is comprised of the essence of Light.

Over half of the earth's surface is covered by water. Note how air, water and light are essential to life. As plants are in darkness too long, plants will die. Likewise, as a human being is within his own darkness too long, he too, will die, from the various perversions and diseases that come upon the body, as the Light decreases more and more through the misuse of his own energies.

It is known by the Angelic Beings that the love essence in water flows from **God**. They also know that the essence of love can be extracted by their knowledge of recognizing God's Light and accepting this great truth, and **by their knowing and loving the essence of love in the water.** Therefore, these great Beings understand how to purify the body of the perverted mental and uncontrolled emotional energies. In their great wisdom, they can reverse the darkness into light.

Currently, there are thousands of spiritually enlightened individuals throughout the world who have been knowingly purified by the Angelic Beings. Millions in the Far East can attest to having been healed through the cleansing and purifying processes of the Etheric Operations.

All manner of mental illnesses have been normalized as individuals were willing to accept that truth which would set them free. One harbors numerous beliefs stored from the past, and they are continued into the present, where the energies, thoughts, and feelings have been perverted through the misuse of the Laws of God and the erroneous interpretations which have been propagated over the centuries.

Currently, it is known among the scientists that within our electromagnetic atmosphere, everything in the world vibrates. In the sensitizing of individuals through the purification process of the Etheric Operations, vibrations are now being felt of negative and positive low voltage emanations from the spirits of individuals. There is now a keener awareness of the flowing energies from the emotions of individuals where one can be repelled or attracted as the auras of individuals come into proximity with one another, and the vibrations are felt.

Thoughts are constantly flowing throughout one's own environment, along with the currents and low voltage from the individual's emotional body in all the various feelings of negativity constantly being charged and discharged within all that is happening in the world.

There are now mass aggregate feelings of the people within nations who are going through the battles, wars, and conflicts taking place all over the world. While millions feel the negativity, this still cannot be defined, nor associated with the mental and emotional state of individuals. Too long these have been defined as evil forces operating in the world. These are simply vibrations which offend individuals.

Often there will be a desire of the people in the land weary of all that had been happening to flee from such a place and go where there are warm and friendly, amiable and soothing vibrations. Even the plants and trees and all living things receive the vibrations that flow through the atmosphere. Little children will often be frightened and cry because of what they feel, but have not the vocabulary to define the painful element to their spirits.

Within the body, spirit and mind, there are centers of energy constantly rotating and throwing off negative or positive energy which has been used by the mind or heart to form thoughts of any kind. People form more currents of energy that are discharged even with speaking; the voice carries the spirit of the individual at the moment one is speaking.

As the spirit is critical or judgmental, or filled with anger, resentment and all the various negative feelings, that energy flows in a counterclockwise, downward-pulling motion.

Pure energy flows into the spirit as the body is asleep, but many people are filled with the rebounding energies that have been misused during the day. Instead of being able to sleep, they are often restless, anxious, and cannot feel the peace, nor can they relax so that the energies can flow. But as one falls asleep, after having had a day of blessing filled with constructive thoughts and feelings, as he has treated others in a harmonious way, that one will receive the rest and regeneration in his body as the energies flow and restore his body. These energies flow from the soul, through the spirit, and then into the body. All these energies are stored within various centers of the body and are used under the control of the individual himself. So as one is in a negative mood, the negative thoughts flow, and the individual at the end of a day becomes depressed, tired, and filled with animosity toward the world at large.

As individuals search to understand themselves and understand the operation of their minds and emotions, they become enlightened by the Angelic Beings who know the way to Peace, Harmony, Light, Love, and Happiness. They have the opportunity to have the stifling, restricting blocks of their reduced energy released from the interior areas of the body. These great Beings point the way for this enlightening process.

Countless individuals have discovered how to operate the Law of Love to God in prayer. They learn to love that pure essence of God in the highest, within the Angelic Beings who carry this essence and represent the Pure Light of God, as the Greatest Law of Love is learned. God's Love is loved through all within one's own being, within one's family, children, parents, relatives, friends, in the neighborhood, and the whole world. Now as each one has given this Love to all in the Law of Balanced Interchange, one receives the returning Light of the essence of God from the Light itself which holds the entire Earth and all within the Earth and blesses all those who obey this great law which generates good will.

PURE LOVE
BEGETS
PURE LOVE

As the Ascended Beings give this love in all that they would say or do or speak in the still small voice, these are the great Beings who beget Pure Love. It is as each one would learn to do as each sees our Father do. In the Pure Love of the feminine aspect of his Being, any son or any daughter who will love this love would receive again the same reciprocal love as pure as water flowing from a spring or from the top of a mountain.

It is from the higher vibrational levels of Light that one receives the necessary cleansing Light to remove the darkness accumulated from within his own spirit. It is permitting the higher Light to do the works as individuals are willing to submit from within their own spirits all that they have found to be erroneous, all that has been found to be perverted, all that is miscreated, all that has offended or harmed others in any way. As individuals receive the higher Light, even their own intelligence quotient will be lifted up as the spirit is lifted up. Within the medical profession, it is known that as the morale is lifted up, so too can the healing energies of Light flow through the body to facilitate the healing.

The Etheric Operation is a transforming of lower densities of darkness into a higher light by removing the densities which cloud the light. Clouding happens with stale or overcooked foods, or whenever alcoholic beverages are imbibed.

WHAT DO SPIRITS EAT?

Since, I, Tim at the present time am within my spirit body, I am in a position to answer this question. Even as Lilias, my wife is being strengthened within her physical body, I, too am being strengthened in my spirit body which my wife carries. Since her physical body and digestive system receives the food in the world, the food is not only solid, but it too, has its spirit counterpart.

In foods, there is indeed light in the form of energy. This light remains in fresh fruits and vegetables and can be taken into the body if the foods are eaten soon after ripening and harvesting. The sooner you can get the fruits and vegetables from the fields after they are ripe, the more light you will receive from them. Also preparation of the foods is vital to retain vitamins, minerals, enzymes, proteins and other food value. Cooking in the new ways to preserve the most food value is essential. This means cooking vegetables for a short time, and using the waters and juices from the vegetables themselves in soups and other dishes. In this way, the enzymes and other important freshness can be taken into the body and digested easily. In America, most of the foods are processed, canned, or frozen. By the time the food reaches the table, it has lost a portion of its vitality, and therefore the light received from it is decreased.

If my wife eats an apple, within the solid portion of the apple, the body receives the flesh of the apple or the substance of the apple. But within the apple fragrance, and within the liquid portion which would be the juice of the apple, called the essence of the apple. It is this portion, the fragrance of the apple in spirit form, that one smells. Within the spirit of the apple would be all the qualities of the apple itself. It is this portion of the apple which the spirit body receives from a higher dimensional level.

I am very much alive within my body of light or soul level, a dimension still higher than the spirit. I am now able to give the strength of my light to my wife, Lilias, which I knew not how to give as I was upon the earth. Although the physical body receives the food in the world, as a husband and wife are together in spirit, it is our spirit body that is nourished from the spirit portion of the food eaten.

All through our marriage, as she carried my spirit and I carried her spirit, and while I was still within my physical body, what I would eat and drink would be given to her spirit body. I did not know that as I would drink alcohol, the fumes were the spirit of the alcohol in the spirit essence, which flowed into the spirit body, not only within my wife but also into my own spirit body which she carried. Lilias often felt as though her head was in a fog. So many women have felt this but knew not why. But now they will know. But now, in the ascended state, we know what to do to remove all of this low density which shrouds the light of the soul and covers it in a similar way that a cloud in the sky covers the sunlight.

My wife and I will go through more than one layer of purification to remove the clouded density in our spirits to lift this heavy fog, which even clouds our vision and thinking processes. For the fumes themselves become cells in spirit of the spirit body composition. And then, these same alcohol cells desire to multiply in the spirit and so there is an inner craving for alcohol. In order for the fumes to continue to exist and remain in spirit, these cells must receive more alcohol. This is the vague craving one receives in the beginning, and so the desire for alcohol increases as the alcohol cells increase in the spirit body.

Whatever one drinks does indeed affect the body depending upon whether the drink is nourishing, such as fruit drinks, vegetable drinks, milk, or water--all have degrees of energy or light to lift and bless the body. Conversely, liquids can also lower the vibrations of the body within the density of the liquid's effect upon the body and spirit of each one. There are all manner of drinks which can nauseate one especially when some drinks are fermented or spoiled. Such drinks do have a negative effect on the body and spirit. It will be comprehended how food and drink does indeed strengthen and uplift the spirit in our body. The adage many nutritionists have accepted is indeed true that "We are what we eat and drink."

Lilias and I will go through releasing the spirit of alcohol which includes the wines which we would serve with our meals. But not only will we give up our love for alcohol, but also the smoking of cigarettes which I had done for so many years, since I now see how the smoke has lodged all through my spirit body and also clouded the light of my soul. In those who still have their physical bodies, the spirit body is now being seen as spirit which permeates and extends around the entire physical body.

If you were to see smoke pouring out of a building, this is comparing the building with the body and spirit as one smokes, and this smoke pours out of the spirit body, since smoke is spirit.

Smoke cells also form within the spirit body and affect the skin, especially the hands, lips, and even the mouth. Smoke permeates the taste buds, and enters all of the organs, even the mucous of the body and the blood also receives the smoke fumes. At times one can smell the smoke in one's hair, and even the eyes will cloud and blur.

Yes, dear readers, the entire body respires, not just within the expiration or inhalation through the nose with the ingoing and outgoing breath, but the cells in the body throw off smoke just as one sees wood burning and the smoke will continue to flow out of a log after the fire has been extinguished.

Within the ascended state (for my soul is within the level of light to the degree of my own frequency), we see this pollution flow out of the body. Each one within his light body can smell the residue still flowing from the pores of the skin. Even when the residue dissipates and becomes invisible, it is still smoke.

We now understand how the flesh of animals when eaten as food, does indeed lower one's own faculties within the denser vibrations and lowered frequencies inherent within the flesh of the animal. The solid cells within the physical body receive the solid form of the meat **and the spirit of the animal** flows into the cellular structure of one's spirit body. The animals have their own lower frequency level within their own kind, in their own species.

Oh my dear disciples, and all those who have followed these teachings: Never have I been so filled with remorse in what I have done to my physical body, to my mind, to my heart and to my spirit body, and to the spirit body of my wife. I weep with shame. But even in weeping, the One known as the Universal Mother has comforted me, as a mother comforts a little child who has burned his hand in what he has done as he played with fire and smoke. What I have done is a way of playing with fire as I was present in my physical body in the world.

I now understand how the residue of the

smoke fills the lungs, my heart and the entire chest. It is here that I suffered so many pains and my wife, too felt these pains in her own chest. But here in the spirit world, we believed we would be punished. O My God! All who read this book are to **know that there is No Punishment in God.** I now see how we do indeed punish ourselves in all that we do in our own beings and with others, but **God** cleanses our spirit bodies. He removes all of the infections, and He repairs, rebuilds and renews us in an astounding way that we are so humbled. I can understand why Mary Magdalene kissed the feet of Jesus, for I too would do likewise as I have seen how His Pure Love washes away the grime.

So illiterate have we been in the world, so unknowing, so unrealizing, so uncaring for our own bodies, and spirits.I have, at last understood the two greatest laws in the Bible: "Thou shalt love the Lord thy God, with thy whole heart, thy whole mind, thy whole body and spirit, thy whole will and strength."

For as one loves the higher light within one's own soul, now the second great Law will likewise be understood: "Thou shalt love the Light of the Purity of God within thine own self, spirit and soul within your own being," and then one will learn how to love God in thy neighbor.

Having gone through the blessed Etheric operations which have removed the dross and the grime and the filth we have given to ourselves, the purification was done with the Pure Love of God. Just as a toddler has played in the mud and soiled himself and all of his clothes, all the soil and muddy water was washed away, but the child was in no way harmed any more than a babe is washed by his own mother lovingly.

This Love is also within clean water, the pure water that flows from the mountain into fresh clean falling water, so delicious to drink from a spring. This is analogous to the Love of God (the mountain) flowing from a higher level. It could be compared to an Angel Mother who also has gone through the complete purification within the ascended state, which would be the top of the mountain.

The Angel Mother has the Pure Love in its highest frequency of the electromagnetic light in the Spirit of God which permeates the atmosphere and entire world, and is in all and through all.

Instead of being whipped with a lash, we in the spirit state are enveloped within the Love of God. In this way, we are transformed, and understand the teachings of the Christ Light as we have never understood them before. But many who do not understand these advanced teachings, have suffered from what each one has done to himself from one's own perversions which settle in the body, spirit and soul. But at the time they know not what they were doing. I, too, had no knowledge of these higher teachings as I was in the world. Just as Jesus said on the cross: "Forgive them, Father, for they know not what they are doing."

What great comprehension has come into

my own spirit mind since my wife gave me to the Universal Pure Light of the Father Mother God when I made my transition just a year ago. But during that whole year, her dearest friend worked to operate the Laws of Love to God to assist the Universal Mother with purification through the clearings of Etheric operations in my being.

So profound, so deep, so grateful am I that all that I have, all that I have earned in the world, will go to promote these teachings. This will be my love and gratitude to God in all of mankind.

SO BE IT!

The Great Second Coming

There are those of My children who have believed that space ships will lift off thousands and take them to other planets, and that life as it is now upon the earth will be no more.

Oh, Mary, note how there are those who are constantly leaving the earth. These now become spirit and enter the spirit world. The time will soon be here when the atmosphere itself will part and My Light, which is as a thousand suns, will appear upon the earth. It will be known that **I AM the Creator**. As this takes place, there will be thousands who will not be able to stand the great, powerful Light that will appear upon the earth.

And so, My children who will know who **I AM will rejoice**. For it is My own Light that is the Second Coming. The old beliefs will pass away and life as it is known and has been known upon the planet will go through a great change. All will see how it is that **My Father is forever creating that which is new**. And the newness is always with the **Creator**.

The knowledge now will spread over the face of the earth. Those who will not be able to accept the new way will not be able to stand the higher vibrations upon the earth. The lower forms upon the earth will be removed from this planet.

But as they are removed they will go through the change from the physical to the spirit body, and in this way, be taken to other planets to continue their evolvement. This is written in the book, **My Truth.**

The time is coming for it will take place within this century, and you will see this, My child.

When this happens, My children all over the earth will be ready and news will spread everywhere of these teachings, since the Angelic Host will be working within the atmosphere in great numbers. None will be able to stop the spiritual progress upon the earth which will be the **quickening period** of which I spoke through My sons and daughters who are following Me. Untold numbers have learned to hear Me speak to them just as I always have throughout the ages from within their own soul. This is the higher light body, which in this Age, is being resurrected through a special dispensation of rapid acceleration.

All who are willing to serve the Ascended Beings throughout the Earth, need only pray to God and declare their willingness to follow the higher teachings to the best of each one's ability. The sincere ones will be guided to find the place where these teachings can be received in various countries throughout the world.

These are the ones in their Light bodies, where the Teachers are the higher ones known as the Celestial Soul, Ascended Beings.

TRUTH WITHHELD
ON THE CROSS

Although my Father selected the scribes who were to write the Truth of the words which Jesus spoke upon the cross, I was testing those of my own disciples to see if the Truth would be given to the world. I have spoken within the souls of many of my own disciples and messengers who would give portions of the Truth, but would withhold the "Key" for themselves. They believed they would, in this way, retain My Power. All knew: Knowledge is Power.

My sons had memorized the caption: "Cast not thy pearls before swine." It is this which would justify their deletions and withholding from my children. The scribes in the past often became the spiritual leaders and teachers since they had absorbed that which they had written and which others had written. The scribes would copy what had already been compiled as being former messages from Me.

A FORMER PRINCE
OF THE CHURCH

We in the Spirit World have surrounded your home and have been within observing how beautiful everything is. The two of you women are becoming so purified and enlightened that you are learning how to love within the Light of the Purity of the Celestial Soul. Each one of you has now received the Universal Soul, and are learning the laws inherent within this Light.

It has been written in Sacred Writ that the Lord is the Husband within the Universal Soul. This was illustrated as the Angel Gabriel was with the Pure Light of the Father and this Light united with the Universal Soul of Mary. This is the Light of the True Husband whom Jesus, the Body of Light represented as the Father was with him. He came into the world with the awareness of His Father in Heaven. But we have never heard of anything like this before.

As we were serving within the church, we were taught to abstain from union and become celibate, but we would demonstrate our love to God through our service and by carrying the cross of suffering. But while we carried the heavy cross of abstaining from earthly pleasures, the physical body would clammer.

The cross was believed to be that we were to remain pure in the world, and while we would remain in purity, we would still be within the sinful world. Therefore, we condemned the whole world. But in our thinking we were not of the sinful world because we were sanctified with the Light of God.

The sanctified were to abstain from cursing anyone, using Christ's name, as a layman would damn even his own brother. We were not to speak hatefully, for if we did, this was an indication that we were not of the higher World. One was to learn to love his brother since Jesus commanded us to love one another.

We had forsaken our families and our friends in order to remain with the church and so we separated ourselves from the way of life in the world. Simultaneously, we were to bring children into the world and receive from the world all of the unwanted children who were brought to the church as babies, and we were to bring them up in our orphanages. The male babies would become priests and the female babies would become nuns. The children born within the orphanages knew no other life than the one they were taught within the church in which they were associated and lived.

These were the babies who were so conditioned and so filled with self-righteousness that they would now carry this superiority throughout their entire lifetimes. Each male who would impregnate the virgin nuns were giving to the church the purity, and therefore, propagated the way of the church with its own kind.

There were many women among the nuns who rebelled and judged every one of us. In their minds, they held us to the darkness of evil or Satan. As they saw what we were doing they especially resented the priests and others who had no responsibility of their own children and kept it a secret. The women denounced us again and again. These were the women who were often put away and far removed from the rest of us as they were secluded in cloisters, so that they would remain silent and serve the church in prayer. Nevertheless, the pregnant women would be living among these other judging women within the cloisters. There are so many nuns who knew the truth. Not only my wife, but also her best friend had been former nuns and both had lost their lives. Henceforth they would have nothing to do with the church.

Countless numbers of impregnated women turned against the church. Many married but some went out into the world and would defiantly sin and do as they now pleased, for they had lost their faith in such a God who would deny who the parents were to his own children.

The women who married often suffered in their marriages and lost their husbands to other younger women less judgmental who would accept the ways of the men. These women will see what is written and recorded upon their own souls.

So many in the spirit world do not realize

what they have done. My wife and her best friend realize not what all of this revelation and new knowledge has done for all of us.

Within the organization as it is known what to do with the spirit of the past, we are now asking for others to assist us in operating the laws of light in the spirit world, to remove this spirit of the church from our souls.

There are now purified women who are with their own divine immortal souls, and they know what to do to help us. Thus, we would be able to return to the earth much sooner. Our lives would be so greatly changed, for now we are walking through the valley of the shadow within the spirit world, but have no fear of evil, for we now understand the flame of the Love of God, and we perceive the light and what God's Light can do in redeeming all of us.

Then we too one day will restore the spirits of others just as our spirit is being restored. We thank God everyday for the two of you who have indeed assisted us in our new understanding. For oh, dear ones, we have all been weeping, not sadness, but the joy of such revelations and now we know why you have remained with the Angelic Beings within the Light World, restoring so many in silence.

But we are the ones in the spirit world who have been seeing our own darkness which is the shadow which each one of us has created within the world. But we knew not what to do. How great were those words of Jesus upon the cross when he uttered the words, "Forgive them,

Father, for they know not what they are doing."

We are so gratified to know that there are those disciples in the world who follow the Spirit of God and it is He who knows what to do. Our love now has increased exceedingly to God.

JESUS OPERATES
THE GREAT UNIVERSAL LAW

As Jesus was on the cross, in the Law of Balanced Interchange, he surrendered his own light to his own Father when he said, "Unto thee, Father Mother God, I return that Light which thou hast given to me. Forgive me and forgive all those who have likewise usurped thine own Power. Henceforth, I pray that Thy Will may be done on Earth as it is in Heaven."

As these words were pronounced, his opposition to the Father Mother God was finished.

Jesus fully realized that even as he had received the Light of his own Father Mother God, that he was to be the "King" in the world. But he confronted the great Truth that the Father Mother God within the Creator were to reign over the entire Earth. He knew that the Earth belonged to the Lord and the fullness thereof. He now conceded his own power to the Father Mother God whose Light had been given to him to dramatize "the Path of Light" each disciple was to follow. Jesus was assigned to become the "Wayshower to Ascension."

KEY TO ILLUMINATION

Love to the Creator in His Words will illuminate the minds of my sons and daughters everywhere.

There are those of my members within this organization who have now grown so sensitive to feeling My Spirit within My own Words that they can discern the self within the messages of the writers. Some of my daughters are able to discern the self within the messages of channels themselves. They have not yet learned to discern which is the self and which is the ascended being speaking through the soul.

Scores of my sons have refused Me in woman and would turn away from these teachings. These would seek other organizations where their own beliefs are fortified. It is as though these children were ascending on an escalator, when suddenly the power was cut off. All upon the escalator would remain at each one's elevation until their own blocks could be removed. As this takes place, the power to propel the motor in the escalator is restored, and they begin to ascend once more in spiritual progress.

It is I who divulge the "clue" to my children as their progress becomes retarded. Each one who comes to Me in prayer, would now ask the question: "Father, what belief is the stone that needs to be rolled away?"

Note how it is My Father who rolls away

the stone with His own Light. Then, when it is rolled away, it is dissolved on Monday night, within the Etheric operations which I perform with my disciple who has learned how to operate My Laws. She is my vessel within this organization. She is also My own daughter, now recording My Messages for each one's edification.

Did I not say that she has completed the Path of Light? I told my own disciples that she is true but they believed in Me not, as being with this disciple. Was it not Mary who gave her son to Me to serve My Purpose? Likewise, this disciple has given her light to Me to serve My Purpose.

Thousands of my sons and daughters will make the ascension as each one follows the Path of Light within his own being. Illumination on his own path will be given by the Celestial Parents of each disciple. It is within this organization that my sincere disciples who follow these teachings will be cleared. They will go through the Etheric operations which erase the spirit of the past. My sons and daughters will progress rapidly. As they perceive the elevation of their spirits, all will herald these teachings. These are the disciples who will become the forerunners of the New Age Teachings.

The great truths and revelations will now be offered through the University which has currently been established within this organization. All the students who have enrolled will be prepared to become the teachers, leaders, counselors, writers and speakers in the world in the near future. Because of the vast knowledge each will accumulate through the quickening of their sensitivity, these individuals will become the leaders in the world. Countless numbers will usher in the Knowledge and Truth of the Universal Light of the Creator.

The third body, which will now develop and evolve within the individuals upon the earth, will be the soul, the body of Light. There has been evanescent information conveyed about this body as books have been compiled, gathering the information from the four corners of the globe. However, the understanding of this miraculous body belongs to the ascended beings who have acquired their electronic bodies and are expertly qualified to disseminate this knowledge in the world. It will be within the University that the great quickening will take place in the spiritual progress of the family of man upon the earth. Instead of having to go through years of research, experimenting laboriously, the laws inherent within the body, will be so taught that trial and error attempts will not be necessary. It is the Creator Himself who has assigned the task of teaching about this mysterious invisible body to the ascended beings. As pioneering disciples have ventured courageously into the spirit realms, there are myriads of explorers all over the world who are having supernatural experiences to support these teachings.

It is as the information is being gathered together and studied that glimpses of the enormity of these discoveries are shedding light into inter-dimensional levels of our own auras and atmosphere of our earth. It has been ascertained by sensitive individuals that before they could see invisible beings, they could feel their presence by the vibrations which would be detected.

The eyes within the physical body are held to function within a lower vibratory light frequency, but the soul eyes are constructed of higher frequencies. Throughout the world, vibrations emanating from various beings are not only being sensed, but countless numbers are receiving telepathic messages from them. How are telepathic messages received and what are the laws governing such communications? These questions have baffled many scientists world-wide.

The brain waves flowing through electrodes attached to the head, record the intensity of the vibrations of energy. But how this is transmitted to form thought patterns or images is not yet fathomed. It must somehow be proven in the laboratory so the scientists can see the operation. Theories have not satisfied the honest seekers.

A concerted search is being made to try to discover what it is in the brain which translates the vibrations and telepathic thoughts which are received by individuals from the interior of one's mind. There are sincere seekers who have become volunteer subjects who would permit electrodes to be attached to portions of their heads, to ascertain what part of the brain in man continues to be active during the sleeping state. With all the probing, the researchers are still working with the physical body. They are trying to find the answers within the four lower vibratory vehicles, which is still within the physical body. It is known that before one expires, the spirit is still with the body. But as the spirit passes out of the body with the last expiring breath, what occurs within the spirit is still so incomprehensible. It is not perceptible to the human vision but has been seen by sensitive individuals who have spirit vision.

Those members who have enrolled in the University will begin to feel the growth of their sensitivity as time elapses. Submitting all the negativities which are being pointed out through what is being revealed and printed within these booklets, gives each one clues in what is to be eliminated to remove the veil within the spirit body.

The nightly clearance will gradually lift the lower vibratory energy spirit of the past so that the veil which has long covered the soul, can be lifted. When this occurs, the members, and especially the new students, will begin to perceive a subtle, inner vibration.

With each Etheric operation, note that the more that is submitted to be erased every night, the quicker the spirit body will be released from the hold of the "self." All that has been programmed into the Etheric body can be removed and it is this which will set my children free. No amount of experimentation on the physical body will remove what has already been set into the spirit. It is as though concrete has been poured over a road surface and now the vehicle travels upon that concrete path.

As you know, concrete is formed by the mixture of sand, water and cement. Man likewise would form concrete with his own spirit, within his being in an analogous way. The sand would be compared to all that is formed by the human light within one's own thought processes, images and creations. The water would be compared to the human love one had for one's own way of thinking. The cement would be one's own holding power, or one's own will and desire to retain one's own spirit just the way it is.

As one releases the love for his own spirit which each one creates within himself, easily and willingly, especially as one gains the understanding of the basis for one's suffering, now the tenacity to that spirit is dissolved. Sanat Kumara's Essence dissolves the cement so that it now disintegrates and returns to the soil. The cement is the hold to a negative habit. But His Pure Love now nourishes the spirit with new light and raises the spirit into an elevated plateau, especially as His new creations are incorporated into the spirit. This is done by the acceptance of God, by the belief in God, and by the love to God. God's Spirit in his words now become the building blocks for His Temple within the self, spirit and soul. **And the word became living flesh.**

As His pure Light flows into the spirit, now "the Lord is in His Holy Temple. Let all the world keep silent." The world is one's own environment which reflects all thoughts, beliefs and images flowing with the electromagnetic energies into one's own gravitational force field. This will be the evidence to these teachings of the soul light as it will be understood in this New Age.

The scientist himself would discover his soul as he would follow these teachings. It would not be necessary for him to use other subjects. It would not be necessary for him to search among the ancient books. It would not be necessary for him to seek for these truths in churches, temples, institutions, or in some distant area where ancient cities have been found.

"ONE INVISIBLE, ALL-PERVASIVE GOD."

CHAPTER VII

THE ALL-PERVASIVE GOD SPEAKS

"And God so loved the world that He gave His only begotten Son, the Lord of the World, that whosoever should believe in Him, shall not perish but will have Everlasting Life."

This is the **One Light** in all and through all: the Light within mankind; the Light in all living things that have life. And His own **Light** was within all of His creations within the oceans, the seas, and all that live in the seas; all that live in the atmosphere of the sky; and all that live within the earth below; all plants, all trees, all flowers; all nourishing foods in growing fruits and nuts and all that is edible; including the plants and herbs for the healing of My children from all manner of diseases and illnesses to restore My children to health. All the minerals and jewels and brilliant stones, yes, even the sand in the earth and all the elements of the ground were created within the Light of **God**.

There is no place where His Light is absent. Within the fresh air is the healing Light of Life and Love. Within the rivers and seas are the healing waters of **Light**. Within the pure earth are the wells of healing water. The springs that flow from mountains likewise are healing waters. Above and below, within the encircling of the whole Earth, is **My Light forever flowing into the planet earth**.

All things have **My Light** to some degree. The power of energy flowing as electromagnetic energy is **My Light** on all levels and dimensions, within all frequencies of light from the lowest to the highest. For in time, the lowest will become the highest; and then the highest will become the most humble in **Me**. When each one becomes as humble as a little child in **Me**, these children begin to rise within a higher dimensional level within a higher light.

Every man, woman and child belongs to the **Creator**. As each one returns to **Me**, all that I give to each one of **My Spirit, now these become My Sons and Daughters within their own light. These sons and daughters have My Intelligence to think, see, know and realize who is the Source of their own being.**

I AM the **CREATOR** on every level. But man knows this not. For every new thought and innovative, original creation flows from **My own Creative Wisdom** to give to My children as they have been prepared to use that which I have, so that all may share in the improvement of each one's life.

Six days does the family of man labor to give to himself. But on the seventh day, he learns how to come to **Me**. And then man rests; and My Father in his body, spirit and soul does all of the works with **His own Light**. Then **My own Light**, which I have given to him, is to reflect **My own Light of purity** in all that is imbibed and in all that is assimilated into the body.

I am not the body purified by man's own standards and beliefs just by thinking that whatever is desired, is pure. But **I am that Purity** which flows from **My own body and from My own Creations.**

It is as man learns to love My All-Encompassing Body of **Light in the Purity of the Purified Love of the Universal Light** called, 'the Holy Ghost' which is **M y own invisible Light** that he will feel **M y Light** and learn to differentiate between his light and **My Light.** A ghost is a spirit, invisible to the physical eyes of the majority of people. The mortal eyes are within the earth frequency light of the physical light, within the physical eyes of man, woman and child. The light of man without the Pure Light of God could be compared to the daylight without the sun shining. But **God's Light** would be the sun shining into the daylight of the Earth. Thus man's light would be the daylight and God's Light would be the sunlight.

I AM seen through the eyes of the purified soul with the purified body of Light. All of My purified sons and daughters are within the realms of **Light within My Heaven World** which is each one's own **Light blended** with the **Oneness of My Light.**

When My children are purified within their own aggregate light of the world--the son of man in the world--these children will arise in their own spirits and recognize the difference of their own light and the Pure Light of the Father Mother God within their ascended Teachers. For all men are sons and all women are daughters of the light in the world which is each one's own light. But these do not yet have the awareness of the Pure Light of God.

It is when each one learns of **Me** from his own Father and Mother within the Celestial Soul from the Heaven World, the Master, Teacher and Lord speaking to the son or daughter from the inner higher dimensional world, it is then that the disciple is on the right Path of Light. Enlightenment and understanding dawns as the "higher **One** teaches about the **Creator**, The **Father Mother God** of all of mankind." These are the teachers who have merged with the **One Light**. They are also known as the saints of the Angel Brotherhood who have ascended **into the One Light**, the Infinite, Limitless **Light of the Universe**.

These are the ones who are the brothers and sisters of Jesus now following the **Will of God** in their assignment to assist all others on the Path of Light, just as Jesus assisted them to understand the great immortal teachings of the **Christ Light**. These are the Fathers and Mothers to My sons and daughters in the world. But their Light flows into each one's own light, and into the soul within the frequency of light which matches the light of one's own mortal parents.

As My sons and daughters in the world accept their "Soul Parents" these are the children who receive the **Universal Light**. It will be clarified to the sons and daughters that after complete purification, each one's own light is lifted up into the higher Universal Light and matches the higher frequency. The Celestial Parents teach from the Heaven World as though a sunbeam surrounds and touches the light within the follower. Thought waves of light filled with higher knowledge enter the disciple's mind in meditation and prayer to uplift each one.

The purified Light of the Celestial Parents has merged with the Celestial Light of the Universe. This is the **"Only Begotten Son of the Creator."**

The Earth Planet was created with the **Pure Light of the Universe** known as "the **Great Central Sun which ever was and ever shall be."** This **Light** would be the **Father Light.** But the Earth Planet would be "**the Only Begotten Son created in the image of the Father** for our Earth." In a similar way, a father may have a son in the world while he is still living with his own father.

This **One Light of the Great Central Sun operates through all of the Celestial Sons.** These are the **Sons** who have mastered the "Light of the world"--Jesus--whom they followed. His disciples learned to hear His voice as **He** taught them. It is known that Jesus became the **Way-shower, as** he **became One with the Father. It is the Father who overcame the "Light of the world" as Jesus ascended. (The Father is the Over-comer.)** Jesus taught those who would henceforth follow the higher teachings He had gained from his own

Celestial Father Mother God.

Millions all over the world are following the **Only Begotten Son, the Pure Light of the Great Central Sun and are serving the One known as the Ancient of Days** and the **I AM that I AM.** My children are to perceive the orderly progression of their own elevation of Light.

Know that the **Celestial Light is limitless,boundless, invisible** and **soundless.** Indeed it is **endless, all-encompassing and all-pervasive.**

All Light comes from the One Source: the Great Central Sun. This is the Lord of the Universe. This is the Light that All Light originates **from out of the One Source.** All stars and all planets and all comets, receive the **Light** that is and ever was from the beginning of time. **God's** time is endless. **All Light** is within the **One Light. The One Light** is the origin of all creation **in the Universe which is called, GOD.**

My children are to grow perpetually as the stars that shine. For even the **stars are lights of MY LIGHT.** Each one of My children is to evolve steadily and continuously to the magnitude of each one's own **Celestial Parents** who continuously give of their **Pure Light** to their own children so that they may reach the higher frequency which the **Ascended Being Parents** have achieved.

All of My Divine Sons and Daughters are within My Heaven World. Their Light

is LIGHT OF MY OWN LIGHT, living in My own intelligence of my own magnitude of wisdom within each one's respective, evolving growth.

My own Pure Light flows from the lowest levels to the highest frequency of light. I AM ON ALL LEVELS IN ALL.

All wars shall cease as the Family of Man know ME and learn to love MY WAYS OF PEACE. All eventually learn that it is the **Celestial Light in My Being that is good and loves all.**

I do not harm any of My Creation. Harm comes from each one's own creation in each one's own unknowing of himself or of **Me.** All see in the darkness, create in one's own darkness in one's own mind, in one's own inner spirit according to each one's state of evolvement in what has been learned in the world.

But I AM the knowing one and I harm none. How can it be otherwise? Know that **I Am** the **Pure Light in which is My Pure Love for All.** He or she who would **love Me** in **My own purity in all, shall arise in Me!**

THE IMAGES OF MAN

Within all the images of what man sees, studies, and believes, man reasons in his own light and forms his own beliefs from his own thinking. This is the light of one 's own light within his own consciousness or evolved state of knowing. This aggregate light is the "self using his own light." All such lights would be "the light of the world." **But I Am in the Heaven World of the purest frequency.**

The one who comes to **Me** is he who gives his own light and his own creations of his own ways and plans to **Me.**

When the Mother of Jesus obeyed My Law of Balanced Interchange, she surrendered the soul light to **Me,** which Jesus portrayed as he said, "I am the light of the world." It was this light which was composed of all that he had learned in the world. This was the knowledge he had gained as a small child while he was in the world. But as his Mother gave him to the will of the **Divine Father in the Heaven World, he was now being taught by his Celestial Father** who spoke to him within the still small voice of his soul.

He was to depict to his followers, the **Way to come into the Heaven World.** When he said, "Believe not in me but believe in the Works of My Father" which he demonstrated in all of the

305

miracles, his disciples were to turn to **the Purer Light of the Christ and permit this Light to purify them of their own beliefs of the past, their own opposition and judgment** in which they believed, and their own human interpretations of what he would say.

All of his disciples were to do as they saw him do. Jesus would pray to the Christ Light before any miracle was performed. He knew it was this Light, the Father of all of mankind, which did all of the works. Did he not teach others to pray saying, "Our Father which art in Heaven;" this was the Pure Light which was good. This was the Light which knew the perfect thing to do in the world. To this day, the words are still being repeated: "HEAR OH ISRAEL, THE LORD THY GOD IS ONE!"

But the **"Only Begotten Son"** was in the **One** within the "light of the world." The light in the world is one's own intelligent knowing of what one has learned in the world about God. Jesus portrayed this light and came to demonstrate the "**son** of man," which is the "light of the world." Look at the inner light of a candle and you will see one light within the other. **I am the inner flame of Light.**

This is just an illustration of two lights. But instead of a light that burns, **My innermost Light is the invisible Light of Love in My Truth.**

It was the inner spirit which received and

stored the light of the world just as a computer stores all that is encapsulated into the memory of the computer disks. It is one's knowledge which is used and controlled to serve one's purpose in the world. This is the same knowledge that is stored as it is accepted in the world as being each one's own truth. The son of man is the physical, mortal, solid body which is taught in the world by other mortals, even the parents in the world. But when one's light is given to God, one exchanges his own light for the **Christ Light, the all-inclusive Light of the Heaven World.**

Jesus turned to the innermost **Light flowing from the Heaven World** when he was on the cross. He was now to repeat the immortal words of the Father: **"Not My will but thine be done."**

Jesus, at that moment, was showing that henceforth he was to obey the will of the Father in all that he was to do. The cross would now symbolize the Way to the Father was through purification of the spirit body. The Way to the **Higher Light of the Father Mother God was the purification of the lower frequency light, the "light of the world, or the light of the self"** or his own light, of his own nation which held the Law of Moses within man's own interpretation, by man's own intelligent reasoning and his own conclusions.

The son of man, Jesus, died to the rule in the world of his own light. For it was his own **Mother** who gave this light to the **Father,** the light of the soul which Jesus portrayed. **This is** the light which was the son, now surrendered to the Supreme Father, the Lord of the Earth and Father of all of mankind. This is the One Light and Source of all light which created the Planet Earth. This is the Light that ever was and ever shall be. This is God. And now it is called the Christ Light, whose Will the Son will obey in all that he will do as his Father is the Lord of the World.

For the Christ Light is the indivisible Trinity of the Father Mother God within the all-pervasive invisible Light.

The Fathers and Mothers who are the Elite, Shining Ones have come into the atmosphere of the World once more, to show the Way into the Christ Light. These are the Angelic Beings who become the Celestial Parents of every sincere disciple seeking the Way to his own higher soul.

CELESTIAL PARENTS

All the Divine Sons and Daughters within the Ascended State are Parents to the children upon the earth. These are the Divine Parents already within the Heaven World who know the Way, and have the divine Wisdom to impart to all who are willing to follow the Will and Way of the Christ Light. These Celestial Parents know exactly what knowledge each disciple has gained in the world, and know the perfect way to lead each disciple upon the Path of Light. The ascended Light Beings are assigned by the Lord of the World to act as parents who now inherit the children of the Earth.

These Elite Ones become the Teachers who take the children of the earth to the **Christ Light--the Light that permeates the entire Earth**. This Light is the **Begotten Son of the World who is the Father to all of the divine Sons and Daughters within the Ascended State.**

This will be comprehended within this Age only as one accepts **the Only Begotten Son as** the **Limitless Light for our Earth within our galaxy.** This **"Only Begotten Son" is the One Light of all of the Rays of God** known as the "Lord of our Planet Earth." It is this which was **known as the Nameless One, the Illimitable One,** the **I AM that I AM.** This is the **All-knowing One. It is from this Source that the Pure Light of the Rays flow to all within the Planet Earth.**

CATASTROPHIC OCCURRENCES

Whenever there is any catastrophe within any country, silent thoughts of people all over the world begin to circulate in the atmosphere about all that happens. There is a great deal of subjective thinking to determine why such catastrophes have happened. Each one has his own beliefs on all levels of each one's development, according to one's knowledge based on observations and what has been heard from so many different sources, about what has happened. Someone or something will be blamed but this will not be expressed outwardly.

People will speculate about punishment being given in some way to all the people involved in an area where the earthquake or hurricane or volcano takes place. Those who do not know how or why this happens, will think about evil forces in the world being to blame, or that the masses of people have sinned in some way and are being punished. The authorities in the land who are purported to be knowledgeable rulers, will express their own views in a reasoning way, based on what has been gathered as current knowledge in the world where mysterious forces are operating within the earth, or within the atmosphere in some strange or unknown way.

At times, information will be sought from spiritual leaders in the land or from the scientists, or from those who have the most knowledge of the earth's magnetic fields and can give some plausible explanation to all that happens.

When answers are not known, people will revert to what they have learned from books, from higher authorities, or wherever the information can be obtained to satisfy the curiosity of millions. So often one will hear that sinners are to blame, that God is slow to anger and will punish the people for their great sins continuing over a long period of time, unabated. When floods or earthquakes, tornadoes or hurricanes take place, the people within the respective areas may believe they are being punished.

All who suffer react as children who have been spanked and harmed by their own parents. They turn away for awhile, reject them, avoid them and wherever possible, such children will often refuse to obey, no matter how they may have been punished. What they will do afterwards, would be in retaliation against their own parents for having been hurt by them.

It is known that force used on children begets force; since the children will do even as they have seen their parents do. Abused children become abusive parents. The future behavior of a child often becomes established in their early formative years of development.

It has long been believed that all children should be disciplined by the parents so that they will not continue to behave in the way which brought to them the rapid punishment. Still, these same children will show their parents that they will avoid the obnoxious behavior only in their presence where they have learned that their parents nearby will take quick action against them, and the children learn to obey and will know what irks their parents.

Millions of parents are not aware that the child's spirit being reflected to the parents, is the same spirit within the parents themselves. The child carries the spirit inherent in the parents, often unrecognized. Many do not realize that the children do even as they have seen their parents.

Great will be the day when the knowledge of the angelic beings will spread to the extent that each one learns that parents have higher Celestial Parents who have perfect knowledge. They would teach the parents how to raise their children successfully. These great Ones would show the way for parents to have their own reflected traits erased as though they had never existed. And the children would be lifted to improved ways of behavior.

The Celestial Parents are known as the God Fathers and God Mothers. These Celestial Parents will overshadow their own children of light, and guide them to those places where they will gain a higher knowledge of themselves as they mature. While physical mothers will teach their physical children, there are knowledgeable women in the world who would act as spiritual mothers and teach children in a spiritual sense.

The Celestial Parents are those in the past who have made the ascension, learned from their own higher Celestial Parents within the Heaven world, and now these Parents are trained to know the way to teach others as they have learned.

The Celestial Parents know the Laws inherent within the higher Light and teach their children about each one's own light. These understanding parents assist their children as they are ready to be purified. They also assist them in their own resurrection into one's own higher Light within their conscious awareness. This knowing and accepting is what enlivens each one. Generation after generation the light is passed on to the children from their own parents in the world. But it is as each one is cleared of his own past states of consciousness that one is redeemed and raised into a higher state of consciousness. Continuing to repeat the past is like repeating the same grades in school and retards the individual from progressing forward into the New Age of Light consciousness.

Astounding and marvelous would be the enlightenment and spiritual growth given to each woman, and child, if the women knew they carried not only their husband's spirits, but also their parents' spirits. These women would learn the truth in the way to bring the Light into the inner awareness of each one. To accept the Father Mother God Light within the inner light of each one, would transform the world in such a wondrous, peaceful way that has never been known before.

The understanding of the spirit body within would show the parents how to have any objectionable spirit they see in their children removed in a miraculous way. The purification is like erasing a blackboard in a loving way, given by the angelic parents. These angelic parents lift the spirit with their pure love essence and then erase the darkness of the past, not too unlike an eraser obliterates the errors that have been made.

Today within the magic of magnetic electronic keys on a computer, not only letters, but words, paragraphs and whole pages can be wiped out with the pressing of one key. That Key within the Celestial state would be the Pure Love of the feminine aspect of God in His Love. This Pure Love of God sweeps over the darkness and transforms it into Light. And then, the Universal Mother of the Earth steps down the highest frequency to the Angelic Beings who are assigned to assist in the purification process.

It is this Love which has been unknown for centuries, and has been reintroduced within this New Aquarian Age when the great Convergence took place. The Earth itself was lifted into a higher Light where thousands upon the Earth are feeling these new vibrations and frequencies.

Hundreds have learned how to become purified. And now, from the spirit world, Colonel Fred Timmerman has completed the 360 Etheric operations. He is now giving the evidence of his being very much alive within a higher dimensional level, and is now in communication with the angelic beings. He has received his Celestial Parents who have been teaching him, purifying him and lifting him up into a new state of consciousness. What he has experienced he can clearly define, explain and give the evidence of what is within these higher inner dimensional levels, not only for his wife and her best friend, but also to members within his own immediate family. All that is being written within this book, has been taught by the Angelic Beings who have so accelerated his spiritual progress, that he has come into the Christ Light.

It will be incredible to the readers of this book. But it will be refuted and disputed by spiritual authorities who will refuse what has been written, that it is not God who punishes anyone. Each one himself creates his own punishment according to his acceptance of all that he has learned in the world from the time of the pharaohs to this day. Since the laws of the pharaohs were first formed and have been handed down through the centuries, these same laws still exist today and were believed to have come from God because the pharaohs believed they represented God in the world. Many spiritual authorities still believe in the age-old, man-made law of retribution of the pharaohs, that one is severely punished in the spirit world.

But in this world on earth, each one is encased within his own spirit. All that he himself has given to others, no matter who they are, will be returned to him. Now it is the law of retribution in which each one believes, that brings one his own belief in punishment in what happens in the spirit world.

The one great Law, "Be it done according to your belief," is recorded in the lights of millions. This is the Law which was taught by Jesus. He saw the beliefs of those who followed him, and showed them that they were not to believe in the mortal, but believe in the "Works of God" which he had displayed to the unbelieving, spiritually illiterate people.

The pharaohs and kings of the past were supposed to have represented God for thousands of years as though the rulers were god. But the rulers themselves hired scribes to declare that the laws made by the pharaohs had come from God.

And so the people believed that the pharaoh received the words of God, and they thought these laws were true. The laws of retaliation brought great fear to the masses who could not differentiate between what came from God and what came from the rulers.

The old law of retribution was believed to be the law of God for generations. Therefore, millions have held to this law even as this law was recorded within their spirits. All the wars which continued throughout the ages followed this law in some measure. This same law is still being propagated in the world. This law was so written that even the reading of the law became stamped upon the spirits of the people.

In the Celestial Light bodies among the Saints, the angelic beings, the Great White Brotherhood, and the illumined ones are still serving a beneficent, loving God. The One God remains silent just as Jesus demonstrated silence and judged not. Neither did he use a sword or any type of ammunition against anyone, even on the cross. How true His Words: "Forgive them, for they know not what they are doing (to themselves)."

"For whosoever shall do the will of my Father which is in heaven, the same is my brother, and sister, and mother."

Those who follow and obey the Christ Light flowing from the ascended beings, are the brothers and sisters of Jesus within the Heaven World. All of the saints work together to perform God's Will. Within His Will is also the

Love of God, in knowing the perfect thing to do with each one. As His Laws of LOVE are obeyed, as taught by the ascended beings who are the Celestial Fathers and Mothers, the Divine Parents of the sons and daughters within the world, others shall see the blessings from His every action.

If each Celestial Parent would be accepted and followed, the parents would learn that "God does not punish His children." He knows they know not what they are doing.

The Angelic Beings have taught that although man can change his ways in his physical body, and affect the spirit body, the assignment given to the Angelic Beings is to transform the soul. For it is God who wipes out that trait which the disciple releases willingly as he has been taught first in how to operate the higher way. As the offensive trait is dissolved, the follower can demonstrate the new way.

As the children reflect the spirit of the past of the parents, it is the Celestial Father and Mother who remove and dissolve the spirit of the past in children when the father or mother recognizes his or her own spirit in the child. Unfortunately the way of the world is that the parent will attribute some offensive streak not to himself, but to his mate.

The father sees any offensive streak as being the mother's fault and the mother believes any fault comes from her own husband. Each blames the other. As soon as judgment takes place, each one covers the other with that which is still within his own spirit. But before God would obliterate the offensive spirit completely, the parent is first to come to his altar and release this spirit from within his own being. Then God will hear his prayer to transform the spirit in his child.

God is constantly transforming His children and renewing them. But the Angelic Beings can show the way that this is done. For they too, have offered up all the negativity and perversion from their own spirits.

Has it not been written that the Truth shall make one free? But it is the Truth of God which the Angelic Beings give that sets one free of all negativity, and all that is darkness. The Power of the Light of God in its purity and Love dissolves the errors, misunderstandings, old beliefs and perversions. God's Power wipes away all that is released to Him in prayer.

The parents are taught the Law of Love to God by their immortal, Celestial Parents. It is the greatest Law in the Bible. Once this law is learned, great will be the spiritual progress as it is operated within all and through all. But one begins with himself and his own family and then learns how the Light expands and includes all within each one's country. This is the Law to be operated within each prayer. This is the service each son or daughter in the world is to do, to receive the higher light of one's own Celestial Soul. And then, eventually the whole world will be included within this Loving Light of God who blesses all. And then one will know how to know one's own self and be set free of the darkness.

As the parents know not themselves that the children are reflecting that which has not yet been redeemed or released, the children would continue to do as they have seen their parents do. This has been going on all over the world for centuries. It is as though the scenes have been repeating themselves all over the world. But the populace is not aware and the leaders themselves know not what to do to extricate the offensive spirit from within one's own environment. But it is now recognized inwardly within one's own spirit because the eyes see outwardly into the environment or world, and understand not what their own spirit is carrying, or is even composed of from the past states of consciousness.

Although it was written that all manner of diseases take place as a result of the issues of what comes from the "heart," this is the emotional upheaval and "stress" created by everybody, everywhere. Emotional and mental stress is used to stir others to do what must be done. The stress would be like a rider who would beat his horse to run faster, jump higher, and at times, extend his energy beyond his own endurance in times of danger or during a race.

The perverted force of stress is the anger displayed, which is used by the mind to direct it upon the one who receives the stress, to accomplish his own purpose, whatever it may be. But this force now returns upon the one who had given out the stress from his own heart. The love principle inherent in the heart, flows and becomes

319

anger, and is now perverted to a negative emotion which disturbs the peace of the Light of God. The mind first gives the forceful command and this energy is now defined within the emotion of anger which oppresses the spirit, filling the one with tension upon whom the emotion has been directed.

The spirit world permeates and surrounds the entire world. So too, does the spirit of an individual permeate his entire being. The spirit extends beyond his body and surrounds it.

The spirit world is superimposed upon the electromagnetic atmosphere of the entire world. Although the spirit world has its own current of a low voltage,each individual is constantly expelling his own spirit in his breath. Bloodhounds can detect the spirit of an individual in their sensitivity of the spirit in everything, as they smell the peculiar spirits of individuals.

"Out of the heart (or the emotional body) are the issues of life." The life of the individual is also one's own light. As one uses his light to create the emotion of anger, the individual perverts his own life principle which flows through the nerves. This perverted energy can be monitored today as a perverted current flowing in a counter-clockwise, downward motion **which oppresses the spirit.** In a great rage, individuals have had heart attacks. This rage within the current flows with an enormous power of perverted energy from within to without, and then returns or rebounds from the reflective electromagnetic atmosphere back to the originator. As the spirit was created by the mind and within the emotional body from the heart area within an individual, so too does that same spirit flow as darkness into the atmosphere. Therefore, the law, "As it is within, so it is without."

All have felt this rebound of their own emotional turmoil, and parents have suffered within their own spirits as the children are punished in a state of anger.

This perverted energy that flows out of a man, woman, or child, may not be returned immediately, but the force will return as "stress" to the nervous system. It is often at night that the swirling currents will be felt in spirit as the angry words are heard repeated in one's own spirit. So often parents and children are involved in the turmoil each one gives to the other. It is as though the emotional explosion backfires, with the words and thoughts heard and registered within each one who has been involved in the problem.

As this happens, the individuals are entrapped within their own turmoil inwardly. Many have often felt headaches or pain within areas of their own body which was not associated with the stress one had received. Too long thoughts or feelings were believed to be of no substance. Therefore, the belief turned the individuals away from the occurrence that brought on the pain, and each one would now wonder what had been eaten or why was one filled with the vague pains felt in various parts of the body.

So well is all of this understood by the

saints or the ascended beings also called, "Celestial Parents." There are many names given to the angels, who are the purified ones in higher dimensional levels, just as Jesus has also been called Sananda or Jesu or Jesias within the Heaven World.

With the Christ Light, He sees what is happening in everyone's spirit and has such perfect understanding of each one, that there is no judgment in him. He has overcome the "judgment of the world" because he knows so many have not yet learned to know what they are doing to themselves.

All within the Heaven World of the innermost and higher dimensional levels see what is taking place within the encircling "chakras" known as whirling miniature focal points of light.

THE KEYS TO ANSWERED PRAYERS WITHIN THE CHRIST LIGHT

Keep Silent
1. Go into the closet of your spirit and shut the door to the thoughts of the world.

Keep Your Mind on God
2. Pray in the silence of your soul with your complete attention and mind on God.

Release Negativity
3. Give to God in prayer, all negative thoughts, emotions, human ways, and

preconceived plans which have been created by the human mind against any man, woman or child. All this God will dissolve as it has been released to His Pure Light.

Use the Law of Recognition

4. Recognize within your being and within your mind that God is Omnipresent in all living things.

Rely Not on Your Own Understanding

5. Ask in prayer and earnestly seek His understanding of every situation and event that is disturbing to the soul.

Listen

6. Be still and let Him speak as you listen. Pray that He hold your mind still.

Rely on the Christ Light

7. Pray within the Law of Reliance on His Omnipotent Light to do the works. Pray that He hold your conscious mind, subconscious, and unconscious mind still from all turmoil. Go ye apart and love God's peace in the Temple of your Soul.

The Christ Light is Pure Love

8. Enter His Pure Love which is God in

your soul by loving His Pure Love as you breathe slowly, deeply, and in reverence within the silence of your soul.

Let Go and Let God

9. Be patient and let God do the works by letting go of the problem and trying to do the works with your own mind. Memorize: "It is the Father who doeth the works in the Love of the Mother."

Serve God

10. Spend a half hour in prayer daily, loving the Pure Spirit of God within the Universal Christ Light. Remember this as part of your service to God within the Law of Balanced Interchange.

How to Pray

11. Let your prayers be in the Pure Light of God and in His Love for all concerned so you can abide within His Light. Ask for His Will, His Way, and wait for His Perfect Timing within His Supreme Wisdom through His Love for all mankind.

Recognize His Presence

12. Recognize His Universal Light in your being first, and then with all in your family, country and the entire world. Give thanks and acknowledge God when your prayers have been answered in His Love. For God is Love.

THE SOURCE OF ALL LIFE

The source of all life, all love and all of the virtues inherent within the Body of Mankind flows from the **Great Central Sun, the Creator of our Universe.** It is our Creator, God, within His highest frequency, appointed the Lord of our Planet Earth, known as the Ancient of Days or Sanat Kumara as He revealed His Name. His Divine Complement, the Universal Mother Kumara, represented the feminine principle of Pure Love with the Lord of the World, also known as the "**I AM THAT I AM.**"

Sanat Kumara's Eternal Light is formless, endless and limitless. But even so, the Father Mother God principle in His being is perfectly balanced.

The Celestial Fathers and Mothers who are the Angelic Beings have become One with the Lord of the World.

All of these highly evolved divine beings in their **Oneness** speak the words of God. They receive the highest frequency of Light from the Lord of the World, the Only Begotten Son. This One has been chosen by the Creator to be the Christ Light, the **Father Mother God** of all of mankind.

Among all of the sons and daughters in the world who have dedicated their lives to serve God--all are under the guidance of the Angelic Host.

Although all of the mortals are guided by

those whom they choose to follow, still, in every field of endeavor, no matter what it is, the highest Master and Teacher in his field is often guided, but not always.

Did not My Father give the Freedom to all "to choose whom each one will follow." Nevertheless, it is as My children dedicate themselves to God and choose to follow the One--these are the sons and daughters in the world who receive My Spirit as they dedicate themselves to Me. These are the ones whom My Father accepts as His own children, and now they receive His own Light.

But even so, the Light of the One gives to All. And then, in each one's own timing, one by one eventually comes to the Father Mother God through an ascended being. These are the individuals who receive the guidance of the ascended beings who often work through leaders and teachers. Not all in the world follow the guidance of the Father Mother God, represented by ascended ones.

THE DIFFERENCE BETWEEN A HUMAN SPIRIT AND THE GLORIFIED BODY OF LIGHT OF AN ASCENDED BEING

By The *HOLY COSMIC BEING, AEOLUS*

(Dedication prayer of the vessel:)
Father Mother God, the Holy Light of the great Central Sun, I now give myself wholly

to thy will and to thy purpose, and to thy desire, dedicating my whole being: conscious, subconscious and spiritual mind, and my soul all to thee in the Law of Balanced Interchange. I pray that no thought or desire of my own, no premeditated plan or motive of the self may come through. I surrender all to thee for thy message. Beloved **Father Mother Fire Flame Light**, recognizing your presence in the being of the Holy Spirit, I give thanks to you for the privilege of being thy vessel for thy Light to flow through my being. Amen!

I am here, Mary. I have been observing your first attempts, dear, of becoming a recording technician, inasmuch as you will now be alone to do your work for awhile during the time your husband is in My service overseas.

And now, My beloved child, the message that I give to My children this day is to show each one that through the years as you have been assisting Me as a vessel, it is I who have been teaching My children how to hear My voice. My children have not yet learned to discern between the conscious mind, the subconscious mind, or the spiritual mind thoughts. These children have been writing down the thoughts which have been flowing, for the first portion of the instructions which I have been giving them.

My beloved children: as ye follow My instructions diligently, believing that you will know how to receive and how to hear My voice, as you follow Me and follow the instructions that I give to you, even though you will err in the beginning, it is in this way that you will learn what has taken place as you have erred.

For you will also begin to understand the thoughts which flow from the self and to recognize previously held thoughts which were repetitions of that which you were at one time dwelling and thinking upon.

For deep within the consciousness of My children, as their thoughts flow, many times they are but vaguely discerned. These thoughts flow as though a conversation is being listened to; the individual is listening *inwardly* to the thoughts.

He knows not in the beginning which thoughts he himself has formulated. Daily practice is important. Set a time each day, and come to Me, and be ready to receive. Surrender all as you have read what My disciple has surrendered to the **I AM Presence**.

Oh My beloved children, some of you may have believed that My vessel was possessed by a spirit, and this spirit would take control of her. You are now to learn the difference between spirit control, and the willing dedication to the **Father Mother Fire Flame Light**.

For, as you begin to pray and dedicate yourselves to My Father, this prayer will hold you to the Light of the Father.

My Father **is** the Light of the Central Sun, the Light which flows into thy being. As thine own energy flows through you in the form of the Light, you have dedicated yourselves to the Father and Mother, the **I AM Presence**, the Pure Light within the Central Sun.

For My Father hears these prayers. A child need only say, "Father," and turn inwardly, and recognize that the Father is the Light in all and through all.

Some of you recognize that the Light of the Father is the Light which encompasses all of mankind. This is the Light that surrounds the earth, and is in all and through all.

As ye, My children, turn to this Light in prayer, and address this Light as "Father," ye, My children, shall see that it is this Light which now comes upon you. It is this Light which now surrounds you. It is this Light which comes forward.

Ye, My children, are to recognize that it is this Light which now flows. And My disciple, at this very moment, is in her complete consciousness. There is no part of her being which is being controlled by a spirit as my children understand spirit control where one gives himself to a spirit.

The By-Laws

Inherent within the one Law of Love are all the By-Laws, which are now given below. By studying these By-Laws, you will gain a deeper understanding of the one Law, just as these Laws will teach you how to apply the Law of Love in each situation.

The Law of Balanced Interchange

You have seen how, in order to receive the whole Light of God, flowing with his Wisdom, Will and Love, plus all the divine attributes, it is first necessary to love with your whole being. This, my beloved ones, is the Law of Balanced Interchange, which operates in such a way that you receive in direct proportion to that which you give. Therefore, if you give but a portion of your being, you receive but a portion of the Light, but it is only as you give your whole being unreservedly, lovingly and reverently that you now receive the whole Light of Love for all.

The Law of Sacrifice

Members of the **University of the Christ Light with the 12 Rays** who have completed 360 Etheric operations are now receiving their Celestial Body of Light known as the Universal Soul. It is through the knowledge and practice of the Laws that you redeem your own earth light, for all the knowledge and beliefs and attitudes you have gained in the world throughout your many lifetimes are stored within your own spirit, which is the light of the world. In the Law of Sacrifice, you gradually give up all of the beliefs, which you have accumulated over many centuries within your own spirit, so that the pure Light of God may flow into your being.

For centuries, man has not recognised his own spirit of darkness, blocking the flow of Light from within his soul and thus causing all manner of sickness to his body, as the Light of Life and Love could not penetrate the negativity causing all manner of adverse reactions and turmoil within his being. All of his beliefs, which have been recorded on his own light, are like the grime and dirt which sully a window pane and it is only as the sunlight shines through the window, that the grime and dirt become visible.

Likewise, in order to recognize the negativity stored within your spirit, you need to activate the flow of God's pure Light to shine into your spirit from within the soul, exposing all the erroneous beliefs and concepts, which cause you to react in the world the way you do.

This is done by operating the Law of Love in the manner described, loving with your whole being the all-encompassing Love of God in some individual or situation that has stirred negative reactions within you. For half an hour, as you love the Love of God in all of mankind, as well as within the individual or situation that has stirred negative reactions, the Light of God now exposes negative reactions, the Light of God now exposes all manner of beliefs and conditions within your spirit, unknown to you before. It is in this way that you will gain an understanding of your own spirit and begin to feel compassion towards others. All of my children pass through the same states of consciousness at one time or another, interpreting all that they see in the world according to their own limited understanding. Now, you will see and feel all of these beliefs released within your being. Those who know these laws write them down in a notebook. The members of the University know how to operate this Law of Sacrifice and have learned precisely what to do to prepare for the etheric operations.

It is during the etheric operations, that these beliefs all pass away, being replaced by the pure Light of God, which is stepped down into your being, filling you with new understanding.

Thus, you understand how it is necessary for the members to operate the Law of Sacrifice for half an hour each day; for it is in this way that they will be able to ascertain what is to be surrendered. At the same time, students will have obeyed the Law of Balanced Interchange, inherent within the Law of Love. In order to receive the higher radiations of pure Light and Love stepped down into your being to dissolve away all that you surrender, you must first give of your own love to God. As you are loving his all-encompassing Light of Love in one whom you rejected in the past, that the debt is paid. All of the beliefs that caused you to reject that one are now revealed to you and uprooted one by one as you recognise them and write them down. It is this which will set you free, my beloved ones, so that your own earth light is redeemed and the Spirit of God may now fill your whole being, as all of the darkness is removed, so that his Kingdom can now come upon the earth and dwell among men.

Note how rapid this process of purification is, dear ones, so that you no longer have to be taken through each one of your beliefs painfully and slowly over a period of many lifetimes, until you finally perceive the greater Wisdom of the Father and renounce the old ways. This is a great privilege and a gift from the Father Mother God, which cannot be received, unless you first give. It is the giving through love, which opens the door and sets you free.

The Law of Precipitation

After you have followed the requirements for the etheric operation at night, the old spirit begins to pass out of your being. You will need to come to the Father Mother God in meditation the following morning and ask what new spirit is to replace the old one. Once more, as you are loving the Love of God in all and through all with your whole being, so that your attention is not focused on the self, but on God alone, now God's new creation for you will flow into your mind in the form of a thought, which you are to write down in a notebook, kept specially for this purpose. You will now need to bring the Father's creation into being by loving each word and believing in what the Father has given to you concerning his Creations and Plans. This, dear ones, is the Law of Precipitation, which you will need to repeat once each day lovingly for seven days until they come to pass. It is in this way, my dear children, that you co-create with the Father so that his Will can be realized on earth.

The Law of Reliance

This Law amounts to putting your complete faith in the Love of God, trusting in him to do the works, according to his Will and his Way in his perfect Timing.

These teachings bring man into that elevated state of consciousness, which is the seventh degree, whereby he has already passed through six stages where he has learned all that he could about his own power and his own light. Formerly he believed his own power was to do the works in the world. But he finally learns to recognise the limitations of his own power and his inability to control his environment and solve all of his problems. Now he is ready to relinquish his own power and control over his own being and his environment. He is ready to lay down his life in exchange for the greater Life of the Father, who now comes in to do the works. Thus, you see how it is that *he who loses his life, shall gain it and he who seeks to save his life shall lose it.* As you put aside your own will and your own habitual way of thinking, believing instead in the

Father's perfect Wisdom in all things, now you have "laid down your own life for his sake" or his upliftment. You no longer rely on the self to do the works in the world. When you are laying down your life for your friend, you are laying down the negativities, beliefs and worldly images. Thus, you are indeed laying down your life for your friend. The disciple is ready to follow the guidance and greater Wisdom of the Father all the way.

Some of my children believe they have given the Father complete control of a situation and yet still worry in their minds as to what should be done. These are the ones who pay lip service to the Law but believe not in the Power of God's Love within all things to do the works in his magnificent perfection. As you learn to love the Father Mother God in all and through all, relying on God in all things and coming to God alone for his Will, now my children shall see his Works and they will be astounded.

The Law of Recognition

The Law of Recognition consists of recognizing the Presence of God within you and within each person and situation in order to activate that Love, which will now perform the works. Since God is Love, it is necessary to love God, as you recognise him within your being and within the person or circumstance concerned. Now, as you do this, it is the pure Love of God which comes forward and does the works. Thus, as you are confronted by any situation or person, it is only as my children cease to believe that I am separate from all and recognise my Love within all of creation, that this Love now brings the right action, the understanding and the perfection in all things.

As you dwell on the self, or on the selves of others, now you receive all that is of the self, which are the perversions and the misunderstanding. But the moment you recognise my Presence, flowing as Love within each one, now you receive in direct proportion to that which you have given. Note how the one Law of Love operates in all things and how the By-Laws are the properties of this Law. They are not separate from each other, although they have been described to you separately for the sake of clarity and convenience. In truth, these By-Laws flow simultaneously with the one Law of Love to all, even as they are the very workings of this Law.

These Laws are also referred to as the Laws of Light, for God is Light, even as he is Love. The two are not separate, even as God is both Father and Mother to your soul, flowing as Light and Love and cannot be separated, the one from the other. And now you know.

THE FOUR MARYS

This message from Tim will be about the four Marys:

THE FIRST MARY is the Mary who is fully aware of the power of her physical beauty and the pleasure she receives through her five senses.

THE SECOND MARY becomes aware of her spirit and her emotions, which she tries to control in endless obstacles confronted in her way of life.

The THIRD MARY now realizes she is responsible for all her thoughts and her actions and that she must learn how to control them. She seeks a higher degree of awareness and learns that she is responsible for all the actions which seem to abound back to her self. She learns there is a higher form that she begins to follow as she sits at the feet of Jesus and is taught by him. She learns how her problems can be solved, and her life becomes more peaceful, harmonious and silent.

THE FOURTH MARY now has learned to follow the higher beings. She is able to hear them speak to her and learns to follow all the instructions that are being given to her. She is aware of how to overcome the self and the spirit in the world. Now she learns that she has four lower bodies and three higher ones. Each one is to be understood and she will learn to know herself and come into the presence of the Divine Mother.

The three higher bodies are in a higher dimension. It is the Divine Mother who lifts her spirit into her soul body. Now she learns how to become one with her FATHER MOTHER GOD who has been with her always.

I know the reader desires to read about the Fourth Mary. The Fourth Mary is the Mary that has overcome the world and is now in the dimension of the soul, where she is to learn the higher laws of the Great Central Sun. She will meet her divine soul who has waited many centuries for her duality. Ultimately, she learns to work with the Celestial Mother and Father of the Great Central Sun in the One. She is taught that the Ascended Beings first love the One in whom they live and breathe and have their being. The One is therefore within her Divine Soul.

They are together now in their duality and henceforth will work to serve the One. She will be trained by the Divine Mother whose Pure Love is everywhere and in all space, and so she will understand how to become a Divine Mother in the Pink Ray while she is still serving in the world.

It was I who sent the Mother Mary into the world within an environment of such abject conditions that she would have to go through every state of consciousness while she was a very young woman. Overshadowed by the Holy Spirit who guided her as though her own light was sleeping, her own awareness was clouded within the density of her environment. This state of being would be likened to the physical body having no awareness of the finer atmosphere.

These New Age teachings could not be given until the right time, until the Harmonic Convergence took place within the New Age. The new knowledge would come through a pioneering organization from which advanced revelations would flow to a dedicated disciple, trained throughout her lifetime for the role she was to dramatize within the silence destined for her own self, the physical aspect of her being. She would bring forth the advanced interpretations of the angelic beings to the extent that none had ever heard of such teachings.

"I come as you call, my child. I AM She whom you call 'Universal Mother.' I AM in all and through all. All are my children. I AM in all of my children. Truly I AM in your experience. Hold not judgment against yourself for the exposure of the children. It is all in spiritual agreement but not on a conscious level. This experience was created to teach your human family that I have many different types of children, but they are indeed all of my family, and I love them as I love you."

I AM Lady Master Venus Kumara

The Universal Mother is Glorified
by Her Mortal Daughter, Mary.

Mother, My darling, you are such a treasure,
A loving sunrise that one cannot measure.
In your infinite knowing omniscient mind,
So calm and so peaceful, and always so kind.

I love and adore all the Rays that are thine.
Each one filled with treasures that are so divine.
You fill me with wisdom, my head is now glowing,
You have this great gift of perfection and knowing.

My daughter, for you I've waited for eons of time,
To follow right action in His Will so divine.
How long I've yearned to be known and then loved;
But My Pure Love you knew not which flowed from above.

Many lifetimes you had borrowed
My Pure Love and then sorrowed.
Confined to the self, you limited me in all,
And fear of My spirit closed your ears to my call.

This new Love, My True Love, for Me you were yearning,
Then for so many years, you'd spend in new learning,
To clear all the dross and you made a new start.
In joy you found me and I entered your heart.

I AM your Mother spinning your heart in a whirl.
What a price you have paid for My Lustrous Pearl!
I am raising your spirit to a Universal new birth.
With Me, you'll vibrate in God's Love for our Earth.

THE ASCENDED MOTHERS

Great has been the silence of the ascended Mothers who have been assisting mankind throughout the ages, unrecognized, unknown and disbelieved. Few of the churches in the world have given place to the divine Mothers as the Pure Love of God. Few understood the great roles they have played to elevate men, women and children upon the earth. These are the women who had turned away from the ways of man in the world and turned to God for sustenance, Truth, Knowledge and Understanding.

Although some women have served within institutions, they had believed that it was here they would receive the spiritual enlightenment each would be seeking through service, study and the things they were taught by the authorities within the institutions. Little did most of them realize that within the church itself, the men too, desired to be enlightened by those who had scaled the heights within the positions of the church.

Some men, but mostly the women, discovered that true spiritual knowledge was highly coveted and jealously guarded. It was within the policy of the church to give to all the atmosphere, the opportunity, the time and the materials available for each one to make his own effort. It was believed that each one was to seek the Kingdom of Heaven for himself. No other could do this for one. All were to strive as each would be guided from within his own being.

There were those who would work diligently and industriously to gain the favor of the more knowledgeable. But spiritual ambition in competition prevailed within the circles of the sanctified. As the women began to turn away from trying to obtain their knowledge from the men, those who had now turned to God in prayer, seeking His Knowledge, found that in the silence as they knelt in prayer and were dwelling on God, there were thoughts which would flow.

Many of these women were not aware that these thoughts were flowing from the Body of Light, their own soul. Even so, the knowledge would be noted but not written down. Some of the women would ponder over that which flowed into their minds. But they knew not the source of this Knowledge. They presumed these were lofty thoughts flowing through their minds just as a silent wisp of air passes through their spirits.

Some women received poetry and would write down the lines filled with rhythmic music within the sounds of words. One disciple loved poetry and first began to receive from us as a young woman but realized not that we were giving the lines to her in the silence of her meditation. Often as she would be resting, the lines would begin to flow and she would arise and write them down. One day she received a poem filled with strange thoughts. It was in a vocabulary unfamiliar to her.

Through this poem she suddenly realized someone was reaching her telepathically, but she still did not know the source. As she became a prayer leader, timely words flowed from her to the audience in such a way that all felt the Truth in what was said in such a loving way.

As the Chief of Chaplains in the United States Army heard her, she became accepted as an International Prayer Leader. She was invited to become a minister. Each year for eight years, she served on a Conference level, teaching prayer technique, and problem-solving. She worked with women with all manner of problems. In some cases, women knew not where to go. Nothing could be done for them in the medical world, because their cases seemed hopeless. These women appealed to her for help. Those who were cooperative in prayer were healed; but those who did not believe in her nor her prayers drew a wall of despair around themselves.

They continued to seek help, going from place to place in the world, searching for someone who could perform a miracle without their having to lift a hand or cooperate in any way. Those who experimented with her were restored to health.

As she became fully aware of our Presence and saw the marvels which occurred, she knew that we were the Angelic Host. She has been serving us in the various assignments ever since, and will continue throughout this lifetime upon earth.

My children are now to know that she will henceforth operate as an Ascended Mother, working with her Mother who is now Lady

Master Venus Kumara. As this disciple entered into the elevated Light of the Divine Father with the Divine Mother, she became body of their body.

Throughout the many incarnations each one would receive parents in the world of the same frequency of the earthly parents at the time of birth. However, it is as the child progresses in receiving a higher education that one's light becomes more elevated. As one receives more knowledge spiritually and expands within his service to God, one likewise receives a higher frequency.

This disciple, who had followed the Cosmic Holy Spirit and His Divine Complement for countless lifetimes, was not aware of their Presence within herself. It was an evanescent awareness, and she was not able to define nor express her inner experiences.

As she studied what happened within her spirit and soul, she was able to formulate a clear terminology through her early years. Her spiritual progress became exceedingly rapid, beyond our expectations in how she persevered within the severe tests we had given to her.

Her indomitable spirit persisted and overcame the obstacles placed in her Path of Light.

Undaunted, she would stay close to us, believing that we had all the answers and clues to all that happened in the world. As she attuned to us, she trusted so implicitly that we gave to her the victories. Then her great trials were finished.

Within the understanding of this disciple, the resistance of the spirit, self, and environment is overcome. Each disciple will likewise be aware of the flow of Light in a continuous pattern.

As this is accomplished, now the soul is receiving the guidance and direction for whatever is to be accomplished at that moment. In the beginning, daily communion is exceedingly important so that verbal instructions can be given inwardly. Gradually as the disciple persists, one learns how to obey us in our Way in God's Will and Wisdom, to **bring forth the perfection within the environment.**

The importance of being constantly attuned cannot be overemphasized. A visual impression of this can be gained as one visualizes using an electrical appliance such as a sweeper. While the power is flowing through the appliance, the work is being accomplished with carpets. As the power is disconnected, the energy flow ceases and the motor is now cut off from the source of its power and now is not able to perform its function--as the spirit is cut off from the soul. The self would be under its own power, as if using a hand sweeper. The self would be doing the works with one's own hands, using his own power and strength.

Now, although the power would be controlled in the world by the ability of man to turn on the switch of the electrical sweeper, so, too, would the disciple understand how to turn on his own power within the attunement of his own soul, through which flows the energy.

Within these teachings, however, a higher energy is used where one does not rely on his own battery of Light which supplies the energy, until the battery has discharged all the available power within the limitation of the amount of current that has been stored.

Permitting the higher limitless energy to flow, according to the laws inherent within this Universal Light, would be comparable to having the Light purify the entire atmosphere within the home. The home is cleansed and the dust would be eliminated without the disciple having to do the work in a physical way with his own hands.

The power within the hands would be surrendered to the Father. The disciple within his enlightened attunement would now love the Way of the Father and desire His Wisdom to prevail in the operation of the task, no matter what it is. This is the meaning of "My Father doeth the works."

The lesser light is relinquished willingly within the understanding of the disciple. He has observed the Way of the Father and sees the great superiority of His Supreme Knowledge. Where man would apply his power to cleanse his own home, the all-encompassing Light of God would flow through the entire earth and cleanse the entire atmosphere of the globe. So vast is His all-encompassing Light.

All things work together within His own Light to accomplish His Way of doing what needs to be done.

The resistance throughout the ages has been

the belief that man himself is to do all the works with his own power, his own set pattern which he has learned, as though his way is the best way.

It is easier for woman to give up her way to the Father inasmuch as she has been taught to follow and obey for so many centuries. Nevertheless, women too, are now experiencing the mental resistance to their own souls as they have gained a measure of expertise in the training and education which so many are now receiving. Some women have had all the advantages to excel in their chosen fields. They too are now enjoying the success of their own accomplishments.

The Oversoul

To be willing to cooperate with the Oversoul--the Light of the Universe which flows into the entire earth--is Wisdom itself. The Elite of the Earth, the Angelic Host, the Shining Ones, the White Brotherhood, the Ascended Ones are all those who have inherited their perfected Light bodies, and are obeying the Universal Laws of God. These great beings are as loving Fathers and Mothers who desire their children upon the earth to arise in consciousness and learn all that they are presently illuminating to accept and follow.

Known by many names, these beings will show each one how to arise into the higher radiations and receive the higher knowledge for a way of Life that will bring the utopia of a Heaven-world into reality.

Embellishments, such as one has never dreamed could be possible, are obtainable with their loving assistance.

These beings are now revealing the Way for all travellers upon the Path of Light. The only obstacles to be removed are the traits that are limiting, doubting, refusing, blocking and negating. It is as though the individual would not want any motorist to pass him on the road. Each would try to block the other from forging ahead. But this spirit becomes reversed within the Love of God. For the higher beings strive to make the road easier, and point the way to smoother travelling in an orderly fashion.

Miracles take place on the road with the vehicle itself. Slowly a transformation takes place. The vehicle changes from a bulky, heavy, noisy, ugly vehicle to a lighter, more flexible, smoother-operating car with a luxurious interior and pleasing exterior. The vehicle glides with a flowing automation that removes the drudgery of operation.

Of course, these are mere comparisons of the transformation which takes place within the physical body which is the exterior; the spirit body is the interior body, and the soul would be the mechanism which receives the power.

The three bodies would all be raised to higher vibrations, receiving the Universal Rays of God which bring the great beauty and flexibility into the soul of the individual.

Women the world over have followed those whom they admired, those who had high positions, those who were deemed to be wise and trustworthy, those who were their own parents, teachers and ministers.

For a woman, to break away from the worldly way of following the world of illusion, where appearances were created to obtain the desires of one's own heart, was exceedingly difficult. It was as if she were to turn to something she could not see.

She did not realize that each woman had a Father in Heaven who would give in to her deepest desires as she would accept Him.

She had previously followed others. Too often she had been filled with fear-engendering obstacles which would prohibit her from seeking, experimenting, believing and trusting something intangible, mysterious, and unobtainable. Women had long been taught to trust those who were teachers and preachers of the most high God. But even these women who learned to trust such men, became disillusioned in the realities of life as they found that they were often betrayed in their own innocence. Scores of women had turned to God for consolation, for comfort, for assistance in solving problems beyond their own abilities to cope with unsolvable circumstances. In the very inadequacies which they felt within their own spirits, they did indeed find solace and answers to their perplexing difficulties.

Women turned to God in prayer, silently,

where none knew that God was listening and heard their prayers. Their faith abounded. They were the silent ones who sustained the waning faith of men in the world.

The men did not realize that women appealed to God in His Wisdom to help them. And He answered their prayers.

But as the men directed God in their prayers, and would tell Him what He was to do, their prayers were heard but not answered by the Lord. The men did not realize that as God saw the commands which were given to Him, it was as though a child, three years old, was commanding his own physical father to do what he desired to have done.

Children soon learn that they are the ones who are to obey their parents. Likewise, sooner or later the demanding son learns that it is an affront to the Father to have the child command what He is to do.

Men in high places were accustomed to directing women in what they were supposed to do. As such a man came to this disciple, demanding that the organization lend him a sum of money that was preposterous, my daughter came to me for My Will for this man. He had never seen a woman consult the Father openly in prayer. When she was given the Truth, he was caught in his fictitious story.

As women learn how to come to the Father for His Will in any problem, none shall be deceived. None shall be betrayed. All will be given the Truth as my daughters declare that their heavenly Father is the Truth.

As women learn to rely on the Wisdom of the Father and learn to love His Wisdom, there will be great respect given these women. They will not be the pawns of the unscrupulous.

There are those women whose husbands protected them, cared for them, and attended to all of the affairs of the family in the world.

As these women became widows, where it was known that they had inherited a sizable fortune, there were all manner of schemes which were used to divest them of their wealth. Such women would be given the Wisdom of the Father in what they were to do with their inheritance. The Father will bless these women in such a way that they will find greater happiness in following His Way and Will than they have ever known before.

So much heartache among women could be averted if women were to come to their own Father in prayer to guide them in His Wisdom. Scores of women have seen how, as they surrendered each day to His Light within His greater Wisdom and Care, so many mistakes could be avoided.

Raphael Speaks: My Father would so protect his daughters that he would not have them go where their presence would be endangered. It is this disciple who has cancelled her engagements as I guided her to avoid going into those places where I knew the plans and states of mind of those of my sons who tried to discredit her. As my daughters realize that My Father knows the spirits of his children everywhere, it is He who knows the perfect thing to do for each one as He is trusted and obeyed.

Many times, as I would begin to contact my daughters through some member of the family or friend, as these women followed Me, recognizing My Presence within the one who would protect them, they learned how to discern when I was speaking.

Yet at times, a woman was so intent on going her own way that she refused to recognize God's Spirit in those who were blocking her and resented their interference. She discovered that her own desires were now denied by others.

Whenever there is doubt within the spirit and turmoil over what should or should not be done, as my daughters will **remain silent** and give the turmoil and problems in prayer to Me, they shall see how I will solve the problem to the delight of their hearts.

Some of my daughters have learned to operate the Law of Sacrifice. Within the midst of their families and friends, where turmoil was brewing and family members would congregate to discuss the immediate problems within the family, my daughters offered these teachings to others, only to be ignored. The teachings were rejected. As my daughters had successful solutions to their own problems which they had seen in the past, they believed in these teachings. But others reacted with indifference. My daughter likewise experienced negative reactions to these teachings within her own environment as she would visit with relatives and friends.

Having observed the remarkable changes which I would do, she would speak of me openly. No matter how many times problems had been solved, it was done in such a way that all seemed to fall into a natural solution. My Father's Light flowed into all of His children involved with the problem and guided each one in what was to be done. This is so incredible to my daughters.

How can His Light flow into those who do not follow these teachings or operate these laws which they have been practicing?

My daughters were stymied. Unaware that their beliefs were still holding them, they found it puzzling that I was with those who followed not these teachings. These are the beliefs set within the stones of the **past**, namely that:

I AM only with those who believe in Me.

I AM only with those who go to church.

I AM only with those who are the chosen, the prophets, the authorities, the sanctified.

These are the beliefs so deeply embedded that they continue to affect the thinking processes of my children.

Unearth these stones that cling so tenaciously to the binding soil. Release them from the tight hold of the spirit. It is my Father who will dissolve these stones with His own Pure Love.

Have my children not seen how water will eventually crack the biggest rocks? Does not water descend as rain, dripping gently or falling vigorously from above? So too, does the Love of

God flow gently or vigorously from the Light of God.

Be not concerned about the beliefs of others, or about the reactions of the world to these teachings. Be concerned about your own advancement in having discovered the way to the solution of problems. Be still in the midst of discussion.

Be still where there is turmoil, arguments, hostility, or retaliation being demonstrated by those who are being blamed. Enter not into the volcanic vortex which would spew out ashes of the past.

Turn instantly to Me inwardly, and I will calm the swirling currents. When your chakras have become peaceful, now give all within the environment who are involved to me. Centering peacefully, now let my flow of Love encircle all within your midst. It is as though you have taken hold of a lariat of Light and now are lassoing all within the area with the same rope of Light. Suddenly, a calmness will come upon all. The transformation is taking place. My Light of Love has stilled the stormy sea. At this point, begin to love My Wisdom Ray in My Being. Note how **My Being is in all and through all, those who believe or those who do not believe in Me.**

My Love enters into all, as the rain falls on everything, the stones, trees and grass, and all the people who are outdoors unsheltered in any way. Let this vision be held for your edification. Meditating on this scene will be the evidence to my children that **I AM** indeed in all and through all.

The concepts of the past will be willingly unearthed and released as you contemplate what occurs in your many tumultuous experiences.

My children will soon learn how to avoid these disturbances. Members of the family will begin to grow sensitive and realize that you have something which they do not comprehend.

Many will observe your peace and then, themselves begin to turn inwardly to Me within their own beings, turning away from all others. These will now be thinking of me in their own ways.

Nothing will be said about what they are doing within their spirits. They will simply be quieter and know that they feel their own light and are immersed within their own spirits. These children know not the laws of how to bring Me into their midst. They are just within My light, and for the moment that is sufficient.

How much easier it will be to turn over all the darkness to Me and know that **I AM** Light. How much more peaceful it is to bask within the light than the stormy emotional seas which are created by my unknowing children. But one by one, each disciple will become illumined just as you have learned about My Light.

My Father has placed one such child within the midst of many who comprehend not the Light which you have been awakened to feel and recognize. My Father brings his dear children into the environments where they are to practice unceasingly, to grow strong in their knowing.

Often as the tumultuous emotional wind is blowing, my own children will forget these teachings and suddenly enter into the darkness. Their light has fallen asleep and the self is tossed upon the same waves others have created.

It is My Father who knows that His own children are to have countless such experiences before others can no longer use their own lariats upon them.

Being alert to My Light, the victorious Light in all things, will convince my own children after they have experienced the victories under all manner of situations.

My daughters especially need to cling to My Father's Light, the Light in all and through all. This is My Greater Light known as the Father's Light. It is not enough to just hold to the Light within, but find your center within and then arise within the Love of God to His Light in all. This is the Light which is victorious.

Those of my children who will direct their own light to do the works, will find that they will meet with resistance as others feel the force and control. But it is in loving My Father's Light that the spirit of my children will arise into His Peace. As each one himself has learned how to do this, now there is no force, no control. Love prevails! This is the Spirit that is irresistible. This is the Spirit that calms the stormy waters of perverted emotions.

Say thou inwardly to thine own spirit: "My Father is the Alchemist who converts the darkness into Light." Memorize this lovingly, so that as you detect the resentment in the spirits of others as the vibrations are flowing in anger, disagreement and malevolent incriminations --start immediately before any words are spoken, to turn to the Light of the Father. Call on the name of your own Celestial Father or Mother. Let your thoughts be upon their all-encompassing Light.

With your own thoughts raised to your Celestial Parents, silently say in spirit inwardly: "Beloved **Father Mother God** within (name the ascended being), I give this situation to you. Your higher Light is in control."

Your own belief in us parts the clouds and brings our Sun into the entire area. Feel this warm, loving Light enter into your spirit first. Love our brighter Light as you feel it descend into your being. Your Love to the Love of God, the brighter Light, causes the clouds to disappear. It is the Pure Love of God that disperses the clouds and melts the ice within the darkness.

Long have my children misunderstood the words: "Command ye, me." My children are to command the spirit within their own beings to "Be still!" Speak firmly to thine own spirit with the knowledge the self has now gained.

My beloved children have learned that the spirit is not the body made in the image of God, but it is the body of Light, which is the soul, made in the image of God. The self is not to command the soul. The soul is to be given to God by loving the **Father Mother God**.

Remember, dear ones, it is your love--your soul is composed of this love--it is this love flowing from the interior of your being that is directed to the Pure Love of the **Father Mother God**, that draws their Love into the scene as a magnet. You are to use your magnet to bring the higher Love into the area. As you learn how to do this, you will see the miracle before your eyes.

But do not make an issue of this before others. KEEP SILENT! All will feel this and know, in some way, a wonderful thing has occurred.

No one will be praised or applauded when this happens. Note how the Father has done the works. Since He is Spirit, one is to turn inwardly and acknowledge His Spirit. Each one gives thanks by acknowledging Him silently, loving what He has done.

So many of my children desire to be acknowledged as having been instrumental in doing the works. It is this love to the self which is to be overcome. Give thou the Love to the Mother and the Father, the Celestial Oversoul. As you praise them more and more, the self remains humble and is accepted by your family, friends and neighbors and all who are involved within the controversy. This is the higher way of solving problems.

Although my children have received instructions about how to solve problems, lurking deep within the spirit are still beliefs of the past which hamper the continued practice of the higher way which brings peace to all.

It is as my children come to My Father and Mother and ask what these hampering beliefs are, that they are successful in having them eliminated from their own spirits. There are layers which one does not suspect within the spirit. Are we not ready to assist each one to a higher consciousness as one learns the higher way?

Once more, repeat inwardly, "The Great Alchemist changes all darkness into Light." Attune to His Loving Light by loving His Light.

All of the members have had need of absorbing these lessons which need to be reviewed and practiced until the habit pattern is established in what each is to do within any environment which my children enter from time to time.

Once more, My Light of Love will encompass you throughout the day and night as this disciple continues to operate these Laws of Love for all.

I AM THAT I AM.

UNIVERSAL POETRY

THE HOLY SPIRIT over forty years ago contacted Mary through her love for poetry, especially when she read Walt Whitman's Leaves of Grass. This book fascinated her to such an extent that she believed the author was divinely inspired. She recognized Walt Whitman's love for humanity which was so beautifully illustrated in his poetry. She understood why every nation claimed him as one of their own, so universal were his feelings within his rhythmic lines in expressing his own recognition of the all-inclusive love for the **ONE GOD** in mankind.

It was through poetry that this disciple was willing to listen to the still small voice that she heard within her own spirit. She felt the soothing, calming vibrations in the very beginning of receiving the inspiring verses which she had heard.

The college within the small town where her family lived beckoned Mary to take classes in journalism. Her college teacher encouraged her to submit the poetry she had read in class to the editor of the college newspaper. The editor accepted not only this poem, but all that she would write in the future. After this recognition, the following poem was printed during the Christmas season.

OH, HOLY NIGHT

The Light of God is with thee,
Ever was and ever shall be.
But it is for thee
To remove the scales from thine eyes,
And see with My Light of Love for all.

My Own Body, Mankind AM I
Pulsating and throbbing,
Out of the Holy Night I AM calling
Come to Me within thee
HERE AM I.

Bend thy ear to Me and listen;
I AM the Voice in the air,
Where Pure Love is flowing,
And My Joy, you'll be knowing
As you give thy Light to My Pure Love.
Say thou, "God in the highest,
Thou art with Me,
Within My soul.
I come to Thee in humility,
And bow before Thy Majesty."

Holy Christ Light
Within the Pure Love of God.
Born on that Holy Night,
When I gave myself and My Light to Thee
To love the Love in my bosom.

That Holy Christ child,
Who will the whole world save,
Even as the world is God's creation,
Created in His Love for mankind
In the Light of His own Creation.

Meditating and praying
Looking inward and not swaying
From the narrow road of the Light
Which is leading the Way
Out of the darkness, out of the world of night.

Silently walking through beliefs and creations
In mental observations,
The traveler seeks the Truth

Directly from God,
In His own Light of Love.

Long hidden in the stable,
The dark cave of judgments and perversions
Of evil imaginings and pollutions.
God holds the traveler
In the stillness of the night.

His Love illumines him,
And beckons him to follow
The Path of Love
In His Harmony and Peace,
In Life Everlasting, it will not cease.

Round and round he travels
Up the spiral staircase,
Releasing the darkness of the night,
Gathered up in the stillness,
Away from man's sight.

Slowly, ever so slowly,
The soul is purified
By the Holy Flame of Pure Love,
Dissolving all the darkness and density,
Known as the "dust of the world."

Oh, Holy Night
With the Star shining so bright;
Lead us once more,
All the way to Thee,
From early darkness to morning Light.

Hold us tenderly
In thy Loving Light,
Until from all darkness
We have been set free,
And the veil has been removed.

In the Glory of God,
His Pure Love
Now arisen in you and me.
Oh, Holy Night! Oh, Holy Night!
Awakened we are, at last, in Thee.

Within the self, spirit, soul and world,
All now awakened
Within Thy Pure Love.
In Thy Spirit set free!
Oh, Holy Night! Oh, Holy Night!

Light of Pure Love in thee.
Through the long night of waiting,
In the darkness of one's unknowing,
Is born the Pure Light of God
Known as LOVE.

Held in the stable,
Until man and woman are able
To discern between what is Light,
and what is darkness.
None knows the way,
but the Christ Child in God.

Picked up by the Light of God,
And lifted into the Flame of His Love

And as the dross and chaff is eliminated,
Lo, the Light of God
Flows into the Soul.

God now Lights the Way on the Path
To hear the Voice of God
Speaking and teaching Truth,
And understanding giving,
As His Love brings Joy into the heart.

Laws of Light in Balanced Interchange,
Lived and practiced
Brings the disciple
Into the Presence of the Father Mother God,
The Universal Christ Light which flows to all.

The night light of darkness is now discerned
In the self, the spirit, soul and world.
And the Light of God,
The Pure Love of the Christ Light
Has now arisen in the world.

Filled with Illumination,
As He is found everywhere,
In the air flowing as Love.
Oh, Holy Night and Holy Day,
Oh, Holy man, woman and child.

By THE COSMIC HOLY SPIRIT through Mary

Soon ministers from churches contacted
Mary and gained permission to use her universal
poetry in sermons. So beautifully presented were

these poems that at times, the verses sounded as if they had been biblically inspired.

Having already been a Sunday school teacher for over twenty years, this disciple was familiar with the Bible to such an extent that now some of the ministers invited her to give sermons within their churches.

In one instance, where a church was in the process of being constructed by many of the men in the congregation who assisted the professional builders, a service was called to be held outdoors near the construction site on the lawn of the church. Members brought folding chairs and some brought blankets to sit on the ground. But on the Saturday before the services were to take place, Mary was telephoned and asked if she would give a sermon to the people inasmuch as the minister was ill. "Of course," she replied.

She arrived an hour early to oversee what was to be done to assist in the preparation of the seating arrangements. Volunteers transported the altar from the old church and decorated it with fresh flowers.

After Mary arrived, some women were scurrying around putting everything in order, so that she would have time to listen to what they would say. Since some of the elders in the congregation had been ill, Mary changed the topic of her prepared sermon to "How to Pray for Healing."

This was the apparent need for there had been illnesses also among many children within the families. Mary elaborated on the importance of loving care for the sick ones during their convalescence.

So thrilled were the women and especially the older children that they kept so silent. The men too thought it was so innovative to hear a woman minister speak, knowing that she had three children and knew just what to do in times of illness. The men were smiling and showed delight in what was being said.

All listened with rapt attention as they heard the story of a patient who did not respond to any medication the doctor had prescribed. Finally, the doctor ordered one of his nurses to sit beside the bed and hold the patient's hand lovingly. This was to be done twice a day after taking the temperature of the patient. After awhile, the patient unfolded his story of how his sweetheart had rejected him for another, and he was so heartsick that he didn't care whether he lived or died.

But now, as he felt the love of the nurse, who in the beginning pretended to show a loving interest in him, now he noted her caring ways and looked into her loving eyes, and soon fell in love with her. It was amazing how rapid his improvement accelerated. Although he was dismissed from the hospital, the dates began with this nurse and the two now fell in love with each other for real.

Love was the healing medication which lifted the morale of the patient. And now the healing energies which had been blocked by the mental attitude of the patient, began to flow through the body so that the healing could take place.

Following the sermon based on the importance that Love played in healing, Mary explained how Jesus commanded his disciples to Love God, the True Healer, in the patient, while any one of the members in the family was ill.

At this point the men pulled off their hats for donations to be given to this lady who gave such a timely sermon. But as Mary received the hat filled to the brim with dollar bills and change, she was so overwhelmed that she held the hat in her hand and prayed silently. Then she told the congregation that she was returning the hat full of money to them toward the building of their church. She said she enjoyed the people so much that it was more fun talking to them than going on a picnic. So many embraced her as they had seen what she had done, that stories within the small town circulated everywhere.

The women declared that there should be more women ministers, so touched were they by her humility and love displayed to all.

Protected by the Blue Ray

On one of Mary's second travels around the world, she flew to Nigeria, Africa to visit a 400-acre compound owned by the Chief whose son was an educated minister, also a devout member of this organization. The compound was 80 miles from the Lagos airport, where the plane had landed, and the two travelers, Clayton and Sylvia, members of the organization were travelling with her.

The only address Mary had was a box number from the nearest small city, Abak, 40 miles from Lagos.

Therefore, she turned inwardly and asked the Holy Spirit in prayer what she was to do to find the compound.

Her question was quickly answered and she was directed to go to a nearby lot where scores of taxis were parked. She approached the drivers while operating the Law of Recognition that she would be guided by the right one.

Holding the written address in her hand, she discovered that there were those drivers who could speak English.

Encouraged to talk to more than one, she was overjoyed to learn that one young man knew Udoete, a member of our organization, and could go directly to him to deliver a written message. Mary gave this driver five dollars not realizing that it was like giving the taxi driver fifty dollars in the exchange value in African money.

Thus the young lad was thrilled to drive directly to the compound and deliver the note giving the address and telephone number of the hotel in Lagos where the three would be staying until Udoete could contact them personally.

At five o'clock the following morning, there was a loud knock on the door. Upon opening it, there stood Udoete and the same taxi driver whom Mary had trusted. The taxi driver was so impressed with her generosity that he was ready to serve her wherever she would go.   So it was Udoete who now guided this taxi driver to return to his compound with the three travelers, who hastily prepared themselves to make the trip.

The taxi driver drove his old car through the bumpy unpaved roads filled with potholes for the eighty-mile drive.   The road continued through meadows and woodlands in the country and the road seemed to be deserted of any traffic, save an occasional truck driving slowly around the deeper potholes in the road.

Finally the car was driven into a forest where there were no visible tracks, only a pathway that led deeper into the woods. Undaunted, the driver followed the right spaces between the trees as though he were familiar with the turns and curves to the location of Udoete's dwelling place. But all this seemed mysterious, that they were able to find exactly where to go through the woods,   since there were several miles yet to drive.

Mary wondered how the young black driver ever found the compound.   One would have to become familiar with the differences in the trees to find the way, and especially to know the empty spaces where one could pass through the forest.

The Chief was there to greet the three travelers who had come from America so far away. A score of little children gathered around the white visitors and silently stared at them.

But all were polite and bowed and shook Mary's hand and reached out to shake the hands of the other white guests as they were taught to do. What a strange-looking house the chief lived in! It was the only house visible. But it seemed obvious that they had no tools to work with, for one could still see some of the hand prints on the mortar where iron rods visibly stuck out from the walls, holding them together. Chicken wire protruded on the inner sides of the walls, and the floors were covered with small stones over which was poured concrete.

Window spaces were formed, but there were no frames nor glass, just an opening in the wall for a window, as well as a door, but no door existed to close the entrance to the home. The floors inside were not level, following the contour of the ground. On the second floor the porch leaned to a dangerous degree without a railing from where one could easily fall. There were so many little children that needed protection.

Nearby one could see a few goats and chickens, and several dogs and cats roamed around near the people, who approached and silently stared. They wanted to see what was going on with the three white guests who had come to their compound for the first time.

As the Chief waved his hands, indicating all were to leave, he seemed very proud to have these guests come into his own newly-constructed home. The roof over the house was made of galvanized tin which seemed to fit loosely into place. There were two bedrooms available, one for Mary and one for the couple accompanying her. But there was no furniture in the rooms, except for a wooden plank which served for the bedstead on the floor. An old mattress had been provided for each bed, but there were no pillows, sheets, nor blankets. To have a mattress was considered a luxury. It appeared, however, that it was the type of a mattress that one would see on the side of the road in the United States that someone had discarded, too old and torn to be used anymore. But nothing was said by the three of us. We would be kind and make no comments of any kind. We understood, and simply thanked the Chief for his hospitality.

Mary observed that the older children were given large curved knives to protect the three guests from wild animals in the forest.

Whenever any one of us would leave the house, even for a short walk, these older children with their knives followed us closely to protect us. We were told there were about four hundred families who lived in their hand-hewn native huts.

Shortly after becoming settled, one of the young women brought a pail of water to be used as drinking water. She carried the pail on the top of her head, balanced upon a padded scarf wrapped around her head. She walked with such grace, with such a balanced posture that not a drop of water was spilled as she transported it from the river a mile away through the field and forest. The young black woman wore only a short skirt wrapped around the lower part of her body.

Mary noted that not only were all the children very lean, but also they were as firm and muscular as the adults appeared to be.

It was obvious that the bathing took place in the same river which was used for their drinking water and also washing the few clothes worn by the people.

The three of us were always accompanied by at least six of the older children who carried the curved knives. Walking to the river site one day, the children gathered around Mary, believing she would remove her garment before going swimming in the water.

Mary saw how the children scratched their heads and looked at each other as though they were thinking, "What a strange thing it is to go into the river with clothes on!"

They kept staring at her bathing suit. Mary intuitively understood their thoughts as she looked them in the eyes and saw their amusement. She could not join the children and be naked in front of them.   They gave her some soap and showed Mary what she was to do with the soap as though she had never seen soap before. It was uncanny how as Mary used the Law of Recognition with the children how perceptive she was and felt the thoughts of the children without needing to speak, and they too seemed to read her thoughts.

The children became very solicitous to Mary as she observed how one of the smaller girls not more than seven years old, held her little baby brother in her arms and began to wash his face in such a way that the soap would get into his eyes, and the baby would cry. When Mary saw this, she extended her arms and asked in silent communication, to hold the baby. The child understood and handed the baby to her. Now Mary cradled the baby in her left arm and held the head in such a way that she could wash the head with soap without getting any soap in the baby's eyes.

At this point all the children gathered around to observe this technique. She slowly put a little soap on her hand, and washed the baby in such a way that the baby stopped crying and trusted Mary. This endeared all the children to Mary, as they thought how their parents had washed them when they were very small and the soap would sting their eyes, and they too would cry.

Now they learned a new way to protect the baby from the sting of the soap. The demonstration was understood without having said a word as they instinctively felt her love for all of them. Mary realized that she was able to communicate very easily with children, as the love principle of God was within their spirits and she attuned to this all-encompassing Light which they sensed but could not understand nor vocalize. The children simply felt a oneness with her spirit and were attracted to her as though she were a member of their own family. From that time on, the children followed Mary as "little lambs" wherever she would go.

Early the next morning, Mary arose at dawn to go, alone, to the river to have a good swim without the children.

She looked around everywhere nearby and

in the distance and not seeing any animals or snakes, Mary started to walk to the river anticipating joyfully a good swim.

Midway on the same path, in the distance, she glimpsed a black man carrying a huge curved knife.

Instinctively, panic gripped her, and she imagined now what could happen to her as she approached him. If she would run in any direction, he would chase her and could run faster than she could.

Momentarily she stood silently praying to the ascended being, Orion and asked that he protect her with His Blue Ray. Instantaneously she felt the Light as if it were a canopy over her entire body which extended throughout the area, encompassing the black man on the path as he was coming closer.

She could see there was a strange look in his eyes, as though he were walking in his sleep. Very quietly and slowly, Mary continued on, holding to her concept, which to her is the Truth. She felt the magnetic peaceful Ray enshroud her nervous system which calmed her as the man walked toward her in the wilderness.

It was now as though she were within another dimensional level blanketed by an invisible magnetic light. So quiet were her footsteps that she passed him upon the path within inches of his being and saw his glazed eyes looking straight ahead as though he did not see her, as if he may have been hallucinating. She noted how matted his hair was, and how lean and shiny his body appeared. He wore only a grimy black loin cloth tied by a string around his hips. He continued on his way and did not molest her, for it seemed to her as though his eyes were not seeing anything around him

Within moments, she heard the screams of the children running after her on the path with their own curved knives. As a young black girl approached her, Mary put her arms around her and hugged her, thinking she would never again go to the river alone, for now she realized the many dangers. And she saw the relief on the faces of the other children that no harm had come upon this white woman.

SANAT KUMARA SPEAKS:

I am here with you and heard Tim give you the Fourth Mary, and how each Mary must first learn to love the Divine Mother, loving all mankind and seeing no darkness.   This is the training that you are to undergo. As you love me more and more, I will instruct you how to love as a Divine Mother.

You will love me with your higher soul, although you forgot to include him in all your prayers. I will now help you. I will give you the Pink Ray which you will love in me with your divine soul. You are to love the Pink Ray within your Celestial Soul and then you receive this higher Light of Love. The divine soul has the Pink Ray. You are to learn to love the Pink Ray and then recognize it as the all-encompassing

Love of God in the whole world. As you do this, the darkness and turmoil within the spirit disappears. Love this Pink Ray which is the Love of God, and your spirit light will grow stronger and stronger.

Our lesson will begin today about the Love of the Divine Mother. Her Pure Love flows throughout the earth to all of mankind, no matter to what depths a man or woman may fall, her Love lifts them up as they pray and call to the Universal Mother for help. Her Love for all is the Glory within the bosom of the Christ Light in Jesus. This Love transforms the soul and obliterates the darkness or negativity in mankind and within the atmosphere and in all the kingdoms of the world. Her Pink Ray within its highest frequency flows through the higher realms and then is stepped down to the lower frequencies through the soul. But it is the Fathers and Mothers who are the Angelic Beings, through whom this Love flows to all upon the Earth. It is this Love which reverses disharmony and brings into the environment the harmony and peace.

Her Love is the most healing and soothing energy in the world, and opens the doors to Right Action. Love is the invisible soft magnetic flow of Light from the soul which flows into the heart. For the heart is the seat of Love, and the more Love you give to God in silent prayer, the more each one will receive within.

Her Pink Ray is with each one of the Twelve Ray Administrators, and each Ray now becomes visible to all. While the Pink Ray is

376

visible in the skies, especially at sunrise and sunset, it flows as an invisible Light and can be felt by all who operate the Law of Love.

SANAT KUMARA speaks through Tim to Lilias.

To follow **The Path of Light** is to follow the higher Light inwardly. The path in the world is the path of the self or the ego. When the Laws of God are understood and obeyed, the disciple feels the Wisdom and desires to exchange his spirit for God's Light. The aspirant remains within his own created world until he has experimented with his higher teachers, the ascended beings. His experiences will lead him to learn to love their Wisdom, Peace and Harmony. But to the resisting disciple, the path is delayed. Often one is attracted to many strong leaders who have the appearance of great success in the world, and all the embellishments and enticements lure the traveller to the path still in the world.

As long as an individual follows worldly leaders, his spiritual progress is sidetracked or delayed until the disciples learn that only the Ascended Beings have the knowledge of the soul, the Body of Light. These are the great teachers and masters who guide the aspiring ones to overcome the outer gravitational pull of the world.

The suffering associated with the cross has been eliminated. Since a special dispensation has been introduced by Sanat Kumara, the Etheric operations have accelerated the Path to such an extent that Colonel Frederick Timmerman at the Eleventh Hour has completed the Path in one year with 360 Etheric clearings.

This is the path that has been illustrated within this book in the way to overcome the past. For the disciple learns that **God is the Overcomer of all difficulties.** This can be slow, or accelerated by setting your own pace. Choose the Path you will follow. You may now receive the acceleration with Me (**Sanat Kumara**).

Come to Me for the Easy Way

I have heard the teachings that have been given with the examples of true stories. How easy it would be if people could understand how to be at peace and harmony within their souls which reflect in the world. The reflections within the mind will later return to us. But now we learn how to change the inner creation first.

Sometimes we make wrong decisions which bring turmoil to the soul as we go our own way. As man understands how to follow "Right Action" he will be at peace and in harmony within his soul. Through the ascended beings one learns how to release resentments, judgments, and criticisms of himself and others. Great will be his gratitude as he learns the higher ways.

Now is the time that great understanding will be given to mankind. **Sanat Kumara**

MAN NEED ONLY SEEK WITHIN
HIS OWN SPIRIT AND SOUL

Did I not say, "The Kingdom of Heaven is within one's own being?" It cannot be found in outer space, nor within hidden libraries or hidden tombs. Wherever one would search, as he finds the Truth, it leads to the same place, "within." It is not with others that man is to experiment, it is within himself that he is to probe.

It is My Father, the Creator, who proves Himself to man. No man can prove the Spirit of God to another man. The evidence can only be received within one's own being. For God, and God alone, proves Himself to His own Children.

LOVE WITHOUT WISDOM

For millenniums in the world, the Love Principle of God had been separated from the Wisdom of God upon the earth. Long had man known that those who desired the Wisdom of God above all other virtues and desires within their own environment, which is each one's own world, receive His Wisdom. This is especially true as any disciple would serve the Lord in some way with the Wisdom which would flow as a Golden Ray.

For thousands of years man has recorded the story of King Solomon. He was so favored by the Lord that as King Solomon sought the Wisdom of God more than wealth, it was the Lord who showed His children that as one receives the Wisdom of God and follows it, one would likewise receive wealth. Solomon was a great example of this.

The Creator was showing man through this great king that Wisdom was rewarded in the world. All who displayed the signs of having great wisdom would often be placed with those learned men who were already in service to the ruler in the land. Gifted young males were assisted in their preparation for service to the king. Emissaries were often sent forth throughout the land to seek out those young, promising men who showed signs of being sensitive, highly talented and highly intelligent.

These young men were frequently trained to assume responsible positions. As they proved themselves to be loyal and dedicated to the king, these intelligent men would be handsomely rewarded with titles and often awarded land and wealth. In turn, they would obey the king in assisting him to govern his kingdom.

Although it was accepted in the distant past that Wisdom was bestowed upon the favored of God, a God of Love was yet unknown upon the earth. Life from God in its pure state would be resurrected from the depths of one's hidden spirit long before Love could be resurrected.

Since ancient times, Wisdom was attributed to be bestowed upon males. Kings had ruled in the world for countless centuries. Love was neither understood, nor did man know the Source of Love. It was simply a tender emotion displayed by the mother for her child, or for a coveted object.

It would be centuries before Love could be comprehended or penetrated. It would take years before this Love could be so loved that a disciple could demonstrate this Love as the ascended beings operated the Laws of the Love of God.

Centuries have had to pass before a disciple could be found among the women, to become a prophet of God in the ways the ascended beings would teach her. Woman would have to wait until this disciple gained enough education, experience and knowledge in the world before learning how to turn to God through the angelic beings for her Wisdom. It would require years of study and application before the Universal Mother would be recognized for **Her Wisdom**, which would be the 'clue' to a woman's receptivity of **God's Wisdom** in the World.

Great was the revelation that the **Universal Mother** opens the 'spirit door' to the **Wisdom of the Father** in man. So too, does the **Universal Mother** open the 'spirit door' to the **Wisdom of the Father** in woman.

Often women who dared in the past to obtain the Truth knew not how to give Truth in the Love and Wisdom of God. Women were often declared mentally and emotionally unstable as they made any proclamations of Truth to man in the world. Centuries of the tenacious hold in the beliefs were propagated from generation to generation, that only man was the recipient of the Truth of God.

This repeated barrier was like an iron wall separating the divine Mother from blending with the spirit of woman. Women the world over were refused as being vessels of the Truth and Wisdom of God, despite the fact that the women had been receiving messages even within the churches for centuries. As these women were silenced within the institutions, they were ignored in the world. It was believed by this treatment that sooner or later, the women would turn away from hearing the still small voice, and eventually turn to other fields in the world. Man firmly believed that the religious field belonged to man, even as he held the concept that God is a man and He is male.

Oh, My daughters everywhere, meditate on these great **revelations**. Feel thou the **great love** which **My Father** has had for the **Mother within His own being in the Trinity.**

As His Life of Light is in all and through all, so too, is Her Love within His Light in all and through all. It is the Love of God which has been held in the mire for eons of time.

In holding the Love of God to darkness, the soul of man was covered with his own darkness, with his own refusal to permit woman **to have equal place in the Spirit of God**, with him.

Man is now to meditate on his **own duality** and the **Trinity** of the **Godhead**, the **Oversoul**, the **Creator of Heaven and Earth.**

Man is to meditate on the immortal words of God: "That God so loved the entire world that **He** gave **His Own Light** to the Earth." He gave **His Own Light of Life to all living things.** For the atmosphere itself now contained the **Light of Life** which all living things breathed.

AFTER PURIFICATION — SOUL UNION.

SPIRITUAL DARKNESS
COVERED THE EARTH

From the very beginning of Life upon the Earth, the Love of God was within man's own life, but man would travail in the world for eons of time before he would comprehend the Love of God within the wisdom of man's creation.

The time has come for the **Great Revelation** that within God's every Creation is His own Love for His every child. **All are His children upon the Earth.**

Now My own dearly beloved sons and daughters in this International Organization, My own Light Extensions, man has been bereft of the Love and Wisdom of God throughout the ages. **The Universal Mother** has been disregarded, disbelieved, rejected and refused by man as though She were created to be a **lesser portion** of man's body, spirit and soul. The virtue of worldly wisdom in man was believed to be given to him for the purpose of the **control** of woman--to direct her, teach her, hold her and mold her into the beliefs he has held throughout the ages.

He acted as though woman had no Divine Mother, no Universal Feminine Principle of the same Triune God of which he was created. He acted as though he were the very creator who gave life in the first place to his own daughters.

He was totally unaware that as he was given the 'seed of Life,' so too, was woman given the 'seed of Life.' As man contained within his 'seed of Life' the seed of Love; so too, did woman contain the 'seed of Love within her seed of Life.' It was this which was the basis for the belief that man was the creator of life in the world and woman was the recipient of his Life.

But *man was the recipient of the Love in woman which contained the life in God.* This is the great Truth hidden from woman so that his beliefs would prevail upon the earth to keep the religious dominancy in the male principle uppermost within the global male consciousness. It was in this way that the superiority of the male would continue to be maintained. It was in this way that woman would be held to serve man in the world and continue to be his helpmate.

But contrary to man's logic and reasoning, contrary to man's resolute control in *his way, he imprisoned his own higher consciousness* which would bring to him the true Wisdom of the Father to reign upon the Earth within the Pure Love of the divine Universal Mother. **She is** within the Consciousness of the Creator Himself, whom the son was to follow. It was as though man himself drew a dark curtain over the Love of God which would now shroud his mental faculties from receiving true understanding of his own duality.

It will be woman who will learn how to raise his consciousness within this Love that man will awaken from his self-imposed spiritual drowsiness of sleeping through the ages. His soul has not matured spiritually beyond the sixth state of consciousness of the "John the Baptist spirituality." He could not understand the spiritual mysteries of the ages because he could not accept the Omnipresence of God since he had not gone through his own purification of his own light. John refused to follow Jesus, even though Jesus showed him the Way of being silent and forgiving to those who knew not what they were doing.

That is all, my seeking children of Light. Feel thou this Light in My Love for All.

HOW TO COME INTO MY PRESENCE AND HEAR ME THE CHRIST IN JESUS

Beloved holy Father Mother God, the Trinity in One of the **GREAT CENTRAL SUN within the CHRIST LIGHT IN JESUS,**

As all has been dedicated and consecrated within my being to serve your will, and receive your message, in the Law of Reliance, I pray that the Christ in Jesus will hold all within my self and soul to listen only to thee so that no other voice may intrude to serve your Purpose. Love the Love of God within your Celestial Soul within every word that proceeds from the One. I count it a great privilege to receive this Message in humility and in your Knowledge and Truth through the Love of God. Amen.

My child, I AM here, ready to teach my own children who have long followed Me throughout many lifetimes. Multitudes have served Me in different capacities. Thousands of My children have loved Me and believed in Me. It is I who have come to be the Teacher to show the Way to hear Me speak as they love that Love which is in God, while listening attentively, humbly, joyfully and expectantly in reverence as though one is bowed and in prayer, now dwelling on Me.

My own children within this organization know **I am the World Teacher.** It is I who will teach My own children how to receive Me and how to hear My still, small voice. My voice is as still as a clear lake that resembles a mirror. Let thy mind be as unruffled as a calm sea where the sun is shining and glistening but there are no waves.

My voice is a small voice because it flows in the Love and stillness of the **One Light**, invisible, flowing silently throughout the world. But My Father would be the vast Light encompassing the entire ocean. But in His Love, the waves are still. Just as the emotions within the spirit are to be still but the heart of the individual is loving that Love of God in His Light.

Stretch forth thy light as though it were reaching upward above thine own self. As your thoughts are on Me and not on thine own self, it is in this way that My Light descends as a beam of Light which will now shine as the light of the sun would shine. But My Light shines inwardly into the inner spirit body, into the depths of your own soul. Although you have a solid body, you also have a spirit body which is even as the wind which you feel in the outer atmosphere, blowing from the sky.

My dearly beloved children, you have prayed the Prayer of Dedication. Now recognize the Universal Light in My Being which is the **Christ Light** with which **I am One. You will love this Light which is so peaceful and magnetic.** It is I who open the door to My own Spirit as you do this. It is the Love of God as a Pure Light that flows into the spirit of your spirit, as you dwell on My being One with the Universal Light. This brings you into your own light body, your soul.

When you feel this rhythmic, vibrating Light flow as a sunbeam into your soul, now be very still and give to Me your complete attention. Look at the teacher while you are listening quietly to what she is saying. Think of your being in a classroom; give your undivided attention and look at the teacher. While you are listening quietly to what she is saying, no thoughts of your own are to intrude. **Keep centered on Me as Light.** Let your own thoughts be still and know that **I am with you. "Be still and know that I AM God."**

Condition your mind to hold steady on the Light of the Christ. While you are in a state of joyous love, listen enraptured within the Light. Remain expectant, and believe that you will hear Me speak to you. Any doubts will shut out the Light, since they are like clouds that obstruct the sunlight.

Let your spirit be as though you have shut out the thoughts of the world and you have closed the door and are now within your closet, but you are within an elevated state within the Light of God. You raise your own elevation to the frequency of the Light as you are dwelling on God in His Wave Length of Love. Your mind is uplifted in your own peace and calm as you pray in this reverent and loving state.

Breathe in the Love within the air itself. Now as you love the higher Light, hold steady while you practice loving the Love in the air itself which is flowing from My sunbeam to your light. You are now as one who is attuned to the station of My Love as you are worshiping God as Pure Light.

It is easy to speak to such a loving child. Is it not easy for you to speak to others as they are in an amiable state?

The Light will flow freely into the soul as the disciple is in this peaceful, humble and relaxed state. If it is not peaceful where you are, find a place in your home where it is quiet and peaceful and you can be alone for awhile.

There should be no effort, no strain, no tightening up of the spirit. There is no need for you to form a single thought, not a ripple. The Light waves flow easily without resistance when you become passive and are not even wondering what I will say, or whether I will speak. Just be still with your own thoughts and be in a neutral state so that you are receptive. You receive as you are listening quietly and loving the Light with your own heart. It is in this way that the peaceful thoughts of God enter, oh so quietly.

Note how it has been written: **"Be still and know that I Am God."** In your stillness, you are recognizing **My Presence and My Light.** At this point, if you find that your mind persists in mental activity in forming thoughts, **stop thinking and pray**: "Father, of myself I cannot hold my mind still; neither can I stop the thoughts flowing into my mind from the world. But you have the power in your Light to still my mind in your Peace. I surrender my whole spirit, body and mind and emotions to your stillness. You can do all things in the **Christ Light** and I believe in you."

This is the Law of Reliance which will bring success and insure your peace and stillness. My Father never fails for it is the **Christ Light** who overcomes the tumultuous mind in the world. Now permit the **Christ Light** to do the overcoming as the thoughts of the spiritual mind oppose the higher Light and would hold the attention and control of the individual.

Remember how Jesus said: **"Lo I have overcome the world,"** which are your own thoughts in your environment, within the world in which you live and breathe and move and have your being. Each one's spirit permeates each one. And this spirit would be your own force-field within your own aura, or atmosphere of your own being controlled by the mind.

As one would tense up, the spirit is now like a wall which refuses the entrance of the light. Just as tension blocks the circulation of the blood, so too does tightening up of the spirit bring a tension that shuts out the light. No matter how you strain to hear, this in itself defeats the listener who is trying too hard. And then, as the human mind tries to control the thinking processes, this is like the busy telephone signals are operating so that you cannot reach your party with whom you desire to hear what is to be said.

Control not your head. Remember to be at peace and **strive not**. Let these words prevail: Let go and let God speak to you. Peace, be still and you will achieve a sense of peace which will soothe you as **His divine Spirit** enters silently.

Think of God's atmosphere the way it is in the Springtime when the flowers are exuding their perfume in the air. His perfume is this **Pure Love** flowing in the air. Be in a state of listening **grace**.

Now study your own mind. Are you meditating on one thing? Thinking only on God brings you into an expectant state of mind. What are you seeing with your inner mind? Is your mind only on light?

My disciples are not to try to guess what will happen, nor conjecture what may be said. It is like listening to the telephone; you are not aware of what is going to be said. Just listen quietly. There are those disciples who will realize that I speak lovingly. You will in time become familiar with this flowing Love within the Light accompanying the words which I will speak.

Practice daily learning how to breathe in the Light of the Love of God. As you persist, suddenly you will hear My voice so softly as though it is a thought flowing. Catch the thought with your conscious mind and write down what flowed through your mind. This will happen while simultaneously a magnetic quality will be felt within the heart area. The air is exhilarating as though you were on top of a mountain and had climbed it in spirit in an elated mood.

It is within a rarefied pure Light that the angelic beings live and breathe and move and have their beings. You too will learn how to come into this atmosphere in spirit. This would be called the Heaven World because the frequency of Light is very high. But even so, this Light is Omnipresent as you have heard. But that is true. It is everywhere. It is present where you are. It is even within your own mind but you have been so conditioned by the erroneous beliefs that you cannot enter this atmosphere.

But you will learn how, as you operate the most important Law in the Bible: "Thou shalt love the Lord thy God..." And in time, you will learn how to love the Lord thy God in your own home, in the garden, in the office, at work within any area, no matter where you are. Am I not with you always?

The Light of God is Peace. You have heard that I have been called the "Prince of Peace," and so I AM. However, when My children are tense or worried, troubled or depressed and are within a perverted state of mind or spirit, come to Me in prayer and give all this to Me knowing that I can restore you to peace. Start loving Me in all within the environment where there was all the turmoil and you felt it all around you. Now use **the Law of Recognition** that **I Am** with all who disturbed you. Keep silent and remain peaceful while thinking of Me. **LOVE MY SPIRIT IN ALL.**

This will diffuse the storm and clouds swirling all around your being in your spirit. As soon as you love My Spirit of Peace in all, I will restore you to My Peace.

I use many different avenues and ways to speak to My children. My ways vary with each disciple. To some, I will speak in pictures and visualize scenes in their spirits which they will see inwardly. I know the contents of each one's knowing and I will use symbols which my follower will understand.

To some I will give revelations, interpreting their spirits, minds and beliefs as though I am reading their mind.

I may give one a riddle or a poem, lyrics for a song, or I will sing a tune which will be heard. And then, I await to see the reaction of My disciple in what I have given. Oftentimes, a disciple will analyze what I have said and recognize that I have answered a problem which was an enigma to the individual. But I await to see if My listener will recognize My Wisdom and Truth which he hears, but knows not the source of what he receives from within his own mind.

I will pictorialize visions, to some, in color. Some of My disciples have experienced the Green Ray in color which is My Truth Ray. These sensitive ones will describe what they have experienced. They will feel the radiations of My Love and be overjoyed in the experience. But should the human mind begin to interpret and analyze his own experiences unknowingly, then one has lost the golden opportunity for enlightenment by not coming to Me inwardly. And for awhile he will remain in his own human mind and spirit until he can think of Me and let Me interpret what he has heard.

Ask questions, dear ones, and in your humility and love, you will see how answers will be given to you. My words flow upon the Pink Ray of Love which you will receive as you are loving instead of analyzing what has taken place. In Me, your spirit will be escalated as though My Power propelled an electronic chair in which you were seated. It is I who lift you higher and higher within My Light of the Pink Ray.

It is the Love Principle which awakens My disciples from their sleeping state. You are in this state as long as you are not aware of the Light flowing within your own spirit. But as I sprinkle My Ray of Love which flows with the energy of Pure Life within My Pure Love, you are awakened by this New Life and Love flowing to you as though a Ray of sunshine filled the room of your spirit body inwardly.

Note, just as the sun is the supporting system of Life for the Earth, I sprinkle My Ray of sunshine within My Perfect Love portraying the role of your soul which I AM in the supporting system of the energizing essence which is uplifting and warming. This is the energy which flows from the interior of the Great Central Sun, from the Spirit of God. As God's children pray to Him and ask for the Light, it flows into your body of Light which is your soul. You will recognize the magnetic quality of this **All-pervasive light** in the sense of feeling a tingling in your spirit.

There will be a deep impression of Peace flowing as a quiet stream of fresh air almost undetected. It is for you to enter this subtle flow which is the Love of God, as you learn how to love in spirit and your mind is on this holy Light. You may hear the words: "**I AM HE.**" If you do, repeat the words, think of Me speaking, and dwell on God being the "**I AM HE.**"

Some people speak to themselves in spirit and believe this is the way they hear the still small voice, but it is still the self in the spirit speaking. Some people will even speak to themselves in dreams and mutter out loud as they are dreaming and speaking.

The spirit itself can speak silently and form words. Many will visualize objects such as an apple and then they will speak about the apple. Within the ascended state, we too form visions and speak as an inner voice. I, too, speak softly so that only you can hear Me because I flow as a beam of Light. As I speak to you, pay attention to those thoughts softly flowing so silently. Become receptive and reach for the nearest pencil or pen and write down what I have said. It is when I see you write it down that I know you are following My instructions and believing in My being with you.

Fresh and original are My words. But as you receive something that is wonderful to you, do not be tempted to run and tell somebody in the beginning. Others who know not how to commune, may ridicule or doubt or discourage you in your attempts. They may be filled with the beliefs of my having lived two thousand years ago, but I cannot possibly be alive today. Therefore you will understand how these are the sleeping children who are not aware of My Presence and have not heard of others hearing My voice except highly privileged and sanctified individuals. Thus they may think you are imagining and will not believe you.

Review step by step all that has been written, and recognize that I give biblical verses and then reveal the Truth in them to many of My followers.

My dear ones, know that Jesus' Light can be everywhere and indeed within your own soul. I **AM the all-encompassing Light that is everywhere at once.**

Feel thou My Love as you attune to Me while this Omnipresent light is flowing during the Christmas Season.

I love each one of you and will give this Love to you as you open my door by obeying the Law of Love. This is the Law which commanded my children to love the Lord thy God with thy whole heart. This unlocks the door. **Love to Me** unfastens the door of your spirit within. Haven't you opened the door to one whom you loved, joyfully, swinging the door wide open, with a joyous welcome to a dear friend? I will be your dear friend as you open the door to the light within your own being, to the Father of all of his children. I love you, each one, my own blessed children.

Great will be My gifts to My children as each one learns to hear My soft and soothing, loving voice.

I AM JESUS.

My Perfect Timing

The time has arrived for My children to understand and realize why all are to follow My Perfect Timing. Long have my children believed that as I dictated a message, predicting a future event, many of My children would sit on the side of the road like wandering travellers, waiting for my words to come to pass. It was as though they were waiting for Me to transport them in the world by lifting them up upon a magic carpet where they would sit on this carpet of Light. Then I would do all the works in the way they desired and take them to the place where in their own visions, they were determined to go.

When nothing happened, these same disciples began to run ahead of me as they grew weary of waiting for me to keep my promise as predicted. Since nothing was done, they will now do whatever they had planned themselves. But the timing was their own scheduled arrangement. As they continued to perform the works in their own excellence and experience,disappointment was felt. Something wasn't right. Others would not cooperate or do what they were commanded to do. Dissatisfaction in their own performance ensued in whatever they would try to do. Since they searched outwardly in the "appearance world" they began to blame others for having blocked their ways.

They reasoned that they had done the best they could under the circumstances. In retrospect, they really felt disgruntled and then began to suspect the truth.

This was the self operating in the world, not the Father. Vague thoughts repeating the passages of these teachings coursed through their minds: "The Father never fails." Another truth welled up from the depths of the consciousness:

"No man knows what My Will is unless he comes to Me and asks in prayer."

The angelic beings spoke further truths which crept into the spirit minds, but were so fleeting that they did not remember them. Finally the disciples decided to experiment with what had been written and repeated to see if these Laws of Light really work. Many believers will now turn inwardly and attune to the Light and will try to use the Law of Recognition with all who are within their immediate families. A little stream of love will be directed to the Universal Mother. Her name is sounded silently within.

While practicing loving this Love, many have asked in a reverent attitude, "What is your will, Father? I am now seeking your Way in your timing and Wisdom. What would you have me do? I have observed my own self-centered actions and now place them upon your altar in humility." As this prayer is cited, the disciples are following these teachings.

The angelic beings formed scenes from the Bible that entered their minds. For example, the sheep are following a shepherd, but their shepherd is the Lord. Then they felt sheepish and recognized why it is necessary to be humble and love their Shepherd because He leads them in the "right Path where they will not stumble, and will be protected; and where each one will reach the destination in the timing of the Shepherd and the perfect knowing of what to do for each one of his lambs."

My own disciple believed that in order to have something done right, she would have to do it herself. In the past, she had learned from others that one was not to bother God with little things. He was too busy with important issues in the world to have the time to guide individuals with their little personal problems. Each one should do whatever work needed to be done himself that the individual was capable of doing.

But what one could not do in a particular task, now the Father should be consulted for His Wisdom and assistance.

These teachings are contrary to what has been taught. They are puzzling. There is no precedent of such teachings. But she would experiment with them and realized that it is necessary to release and empty one's own spirit of all former ways in trying to be self-sufficient. She had always had confidence in herself in "going her own way."

Always in a hurry, she would now have to slow down, relax and release the syndrome in her psyche: "Whatever you have to do, do it now and do it quickly. Do not postpone until tomorrow what you can do today." These beliefs were incorporated in her mind and now she became aware of her own impatience because she had learned to time everything she would do and measure how long it would take her to complete each task.

What a blessing those Etheric operations are in the rapid transformation that is needed to enable one to follow the way of the Father.

Children at times are impatient and demanding. But in observing the parents, the children will likewise command others and expect them to do immediately what is to be done.

When news circulates that a circus is coming to town, the children often run excitedly to their parents and command their parents to go to the circus instantly. Such children often do not realize all the preparations that are first to be made. Neither are they aware of all the advertising necessary to inform the people when and where the circus performance will take place.

Such children will often refuse to listen to any explanations about any circus delays. As their instant demands are refused or ignored, so frustrated will these children become that they will have temper tantrums. This type of behavior labeled the "demanding spirit of asserting the self" has been programmed into the child's spirit, and is often handed down through the generations.

Children will try their own parents just as adults will try My Father. All manner of ways have been used by disciples to force My Father to obey their own inferior ways.

Students who have the same spirits as their parents will experiment by refusing to serve the Father unless He gives to them first. Such individuals were trying to subjugate the Father in their own impatience to have done what is desired **in their own timing** as though the Father is a servant to the selves.

Nevertheless, in **His** non-judgmental, silent ways, He observes the actions of His own child who now will try to withhold his love from the **Father Mother God.**

Many will retaliate by refusing to operate the Law of Love to all, daily. Some have gone so far in trying to force the angelic beings that they will go on a self-imposed hunger strike. A few of My demanding children have threatened suicide if God did not obey them and give to them in their own timing, and in their own plans and ways.

Some members of the organization resigned because the leader would not give to them and obey their ways. A few of the members would send in their messages showing what the leader was to give to them. "The message came from God," the members would declare. Therefore, the leader was to obey their message unquestioningly without challenging them or seeking any confirmation.

When messages are challenged by this leader, she knows that what is repeated from the mind of the self is given to the disciple. All were taught that the ascended beings are under the law to give to each disciple whatever belief is held within the human mind.

Our Father repeats to the disciple each one's desires, plans and timing, as though He were telling them what should be done. This is the procedure given to all aspiring spiritual students so that each disciple will "know himself" and see his own ways in his own created thoughts and formed images.

At this point, these young adults who are still as children within their souls, will resign and want not such teachings. Neither are they interested in admitting to anyone anything that is hidden in their spirits. Their own spiritual mind would often intrude while the Father is speaking.

They believed that their will is also God's will. But such disciples are not willing to seek and follow God's will since they believe their own light is the **Christ Light.** Isn't man supposed to inherit the earth and subdue all within the earth? These are the strong truths their own parents have followed and they will not give in. No! not even to the ascended beings, these disciples will declare.

It is true that My Father centers his children and sees all of their thoughts, beliefs, ways and habits. In some serious cases where strong-willed individuals will attempt suicide to force their wills upon My Father, He shows his compassion to those disciples whom He knows are planning to annihilate themselves and who intend to carry out their threats of self-destruction, if God does not relent and give to them in their way and their timing. He shows them in a clear vision what will happen if they carry out their plans.

So horrified will these children, at times become, that they now plead to be forgiven for using such drastic methods to force the Father. Finally, after all manner of force has failed, these children will give up their own creations, images and self-destructive attempts which they envisioned within their own spirits, and finally release all such behavior to be wiped out within the Etheric operations.

What a revelation these children discover as the resistance to God's own Will and Ways has been overcome. What a relief they feel in their spirit and soul. The great turmoil has been erased and they can now become peaceful as they feel their own subdued spirit.

These are the children who had learned how to force others to give to them first within their own environments. They would be elated in their own sense of having achieved a victory over others, and tried every method upon God to see if He could likewise be subdued. But God never fails because He knows His children. It is believed that the act of subduing others increases one's own strength and power over others. But it is usually the weaker ones who are subdued.

Eventually My children gain sufficient understanding of these teachings. Just as teenagers have outgrown their own immaturity, so too do My spiritual children gain the insights and knowledge to recognize the wise ways of My Father as He knows the perfect thing to do in **His own Timing.**

Children have not had sufficient experience to gain the knowledge that their parents have through their maturing years. And the parents realize that their children do not have the understanding of what their own desires can do to them when received prematurely.

This disciple completed her training and acquired the ability to assist each one on any level of consciousness. Leaders who have known her for many years, were astounded to find a woman who had become so advanced. They noted that she learned the way to find and know the Will of God before she would envision her own plan.

She learned to recognize how her mind was thinking and in envisioning what she would do, she caught those thoughts which were her own. She did this before she would pray and ask what was God's will. Her own thoughts were cleared frequently.

She had been taken through so many experiences in this that she now studied her reactions, and learned to eliminate her emotional turmoil daily. As a result, she quickly saw through her own inferior, human ways and wearied of them. By this time, she was able to compare her ways with the magnificent and brilliant ways of the **Father Mother God, where there was no opposition and all things worked together.**

She desired to have erased all that she recognized as needing to be eliminated in herself, and now in humility and love to God, she sought His Way in His Will and Wisdom, which she now desired with all of her heart. And **He** taught her to **"let come what may in My Timing." He showed her His Will for her environment.**

Few of My children are aware that as this disciple served Me with My children for so many years, and assisted them to receive rapid elevations, it was in this way that **W**e elevated her. When the mind is open and the disciple is willing to share these teachings with others--this is the magnet that brings **Our Light to help them** to remove their own blocks.

When in the heat of arguments and strong resistance along with the pressures placed upon individuals in stressful problems, it is as though one has been bound and held in the vortex of a whirling oppressive spirit. Asserting one's own independent actions and ways within a retaliatory anger does not solve problems, and will alienate family members, relatives or associates.

Members of this organization have accepted mentally the truth that the Light of God is all-pervasive. But during great turmoil, one is unable to practice these teachings. But the arguments persist until each individual begins to experiment in the way problems can be solved. Those who have learned to hear the voice of Our Father, are to come to Him for the underlying purpose of what continues to happen.

All are given experiences in life to give each one an opportunity to learn how to operate these teachings, to have a change take place within the environment itself.

Each one has read that all that takes place outwardly, first is formed in images, thoughts and emotional reactions to given situations. In the beginning, the disciple is to become aware of problems created by one's own ways and thinking patterns which are to be changed. Unless a transformation first takes place within the subconscious mind, one cannot accept that God is indeed within those members of his own family who show no interest in these teachings.

How can one use the Law of Recognition with his friends, family and associates, unless the negative thoughts and emotions have been cleared away? The negativities must be eliminated and cleared away. Although it will take time to learn how to overcome all manner of opposition and remain at peace, the experiences one encounters and confronts are necessary so that the aspiring individual will follow the teachings of resisting not, keeping silent when turmoil exists and turning to God to rely on Him to solve the problem. Ultimately, raging storms will be calmed and a transformation will take place as one learns to do his own part first of keeping silent. During this time, center and silently pray to God and say, "Have thine own way, Lord," and now love His Spirit first within, and then in all who are involved in the turmoil.

In the mystery of keeping silent and loving God, He will shine His own Light into the tumultuous spirits of all and bring His Wisdom in His Peace in knowing the perfect thing to do. He can solve any problem where all will be satisfied.

Eventually, My followers will learn how to keep silent in turmoil and turn to the Father so that He can show them how He succeeds and does the works as the **Law of Love and Recognition of His Presence is performed within the silence in the midst of the turmoil.**

Many members just think of Me and do nothing more. But that is not enough. **Each one is to surrender the problem silently in prayer, and then center within his being, knowing that I AM Present with all, and he is to love My Presence.**

Each one will remove his spirit and mind out of the darkness of turmoil the moment one centers in the higher Light that pervades all space and all of mankind. Know that My Love is to prevail and flow to All from My All-Encompassing Light. Think of this Light.

All of My disciples are to learn to calm the waves with the Love of God by loving God in all involved. This is to be done **first. You have to know what to do and do your part.**

Be vigilant when predictions are made of any dangerous happenings. Oftentimes negative thoughts and fears will accumulate where sensitive psychics will sense these thoughts and make predictions, giving a specified time and place. Their own beliefs of events emerge as facts and a date is predicted as to when the event will occur. The news media at times will print the predictions and then the people discover that what was supposed to happen, did not happen.

What is not known is that there are now great numbers of prayerful individuals who reject predictions and will counteract the negativity by recognizing God and praying for the protection of people in the predicted environments. My own disciples have learned how to pray for the Blue Ray of God to protect them. And those who believe in God's Light have seen how they were protected and no harm came upon them.

My disciples have experienced how the mind and spirit will form numerous images and have learned that God does not create images that will harm individuals. **He is forever saving those who call to Him for help in times of danger.**

It is as My children persevere in the teachings of the ascended beings that they will learn the Laws inherent within God's Universal Pure Light. They will gain the insight of how all the angelic beings work together **His Wonders to perform in His own timing, in His higher Wisdom in knowing the perfect thing to do in every instance.**

The time will come when the disciples will so love these teachings that they will be willing to do as they see the Shining Ones of the Father Mother God do.

THE SUPREME DEITY

For centuries, in every country and every nation, each one followed a deity proclaimed to be the One and Only, the True God, and all others were false. All others were pagan gods.

Within these teachings, we have been shown that there are Planetary, highly evolved beings, who were, at one time, deities upon the Earth. But after centuries of serving the One God, they were promoted to higher and still higher positions within the Celestial Hierarchy, or within the Heaven World.

Within this organization, as you know, at one time only **7 Rays and States of Consciousness** were known. Through the revelations given through this disciple, it was shown that there were 12 Rays of the Great Central Sun, the Source of All Light, Life and Love and all the Rays and virtues likewise came from the Great Central Sun, known as the **Nameless One**, the **Illimitable One**, the **I AM THAT I AM**. And many names were given in each country for each deity who represented the One. And within this nation, the Christ was the acceptable Name as being the One.

The **One is Omnipresent with all**, in All and through All, not only within mankind, but also the Light of Life is in all living things, above and below, within and without.

The **One God was in existence before the Earth was created** approximately four billion years ago, the scientists tell us. Before the planet Earth or man was created within the world, **God was and ever shall be.**

Now **God** does not have just one attribute such as prosperity. Neither is there only one God who represents prosperity. But this attribute of Wealth and Prosperity is God's Spirit inasmuch as **He is the all of prosperity.** "The Earth is the Lord's and the fullness thereof" is His Prosperity.

All the virtues in the world belong to His Light which **He is in the purest state.**

One can see that since any male or female is higher than the other in the Light of God, this would bring cries of opposition throughout the world. The male aspect has predominated for 2,000 years, and women were refused to be held within the same light, as it was believed the male alone contained the light. Every man and every woman in the world have been in opposition to one another for centuries as either one was denied in God. But God is neither male, nor female. **God is everlasting Light that flows through all of mankind.**

As prophets became more sensitive and

were magnetized, each prophet in some way, felt the Holy Spirit in his spirit, and declared his own spirit to be the one and only God.

Mankind in every country, has fought many wars over whose God is the Supreme God. And confusion has been rampant within this New Age because so many disciples hear the voice of God and receive the truth along with knowledge and revelations. To hear the voice of God increases one's faith within one's self in a greater and stronger faith in the belief of one's own God.

When the angelic beings are speaking from the Heaven World, they do not reject any man's God. Should we not also accept God within one who believes God is with him or her in the world and do as we see the angels do? Should we not also accept the Pure Light in each one as being that portion of God that the divine being represents?

The angelic beings, each one, once lived upon the earth within a human body, but they have become purified just as Jesus had done. Each angelic being has built the Temple not made by the hands of man but by the Light of His Father Mother God within his being where God dwells within his soul. All the knowledge and truths about God are recorded within each one's soul, as each one follows and obeys his Celestial Light, his Father, a higher evolved shining One. The disciple will hear his Father speaking to him from the Heaven World.

Prophets who hear the voice of God are still being taught by these highly evolved beings.

The human mortal disciples are being guided and taught how to consecrate their all to the **One God**. Followers everywhere who hear the voice of God are in a state of learning, as though they are within a divine school whose teachers are the Angelic Beings.

Knowing that God is Love, each divine being has become One with God's Love and represents this Love for All, in what each one would say and do. Are not the angels within the Will of God, the Wisdom of God and the Truth of God? Are they not the brothers and sisters of Jesus within the One Christ Light? Do not all the angels have God's Prosperity in His Heaven world? Has it not been written that all were first to seek the Way to the Kingdom of Heaven and all things shall be added to you--*all* **things!**"

Did not the "**Ancient of Days, Sanat Kumara**" say that **He** gives all twelve Rays to the **Universal Mother** who is **Lady Master Venus Kumara**, who is **One** with the **One** of the **Great Central Sun**. It is **She** w h o represents the **Pure Love** from the **One** within the Divine Mothers. The **Pure Love of God** which **She** carries flows through all of the Rays in the world from the Heaven World to the Earth and then this Love is stepped down in frequency and given to the children of the Earth.

As you are a son or a daughter in the world, so too can you ask the questions in prayer from the **One God**. "**Ask** and you shall receive an answer." It is the Angelic Beings who hear the voice of the One, and then they represent Him and answer the questions to bring understanding to those who pray and ask. For the children of the Earth are not to: "Lean on their own understanding."

Each son or daughter in his time will one day make the ascension and be with his divine brothers and sisters. These are the divine beings who obey the Will of God just as Jesus said. And then, each one becomes enlightened gradually, and will be illumined by the One Light. The teachings are continuous within the Heaven World and are available to the sincere seeking ones who themselves now learn to love God. Eventually, each one will represent various aspects of the One God of the Great Central Sun.

For eons of time, there have been thousands of gods, but each one has some attribute which stands out as a virtue of the One God.

All are to accept that God enlightens His sons and daughters with His Light which is formless in its purity. But this Light forever flows from the highest frequencies and is stepped down from the Heaven World by the saints and the light flows to the level of each one's own frequency.

Be not confused about the names of angelic beings or the names of leaders and teachers within the world. Henceforth all the names circulating and even name changes are constantly taking place in the world. Likewise there are name changes in the **Heaven World.** It has already been illustrated that as the consciousness is transformed, a new name is given. Simon illustrated this, as well as other followers of the Lord who were given new names. But the Celestial Soul gradually purifies the light of the son or daughter in the world and the light brightens and increases to a higher frequency after purification, as more knowledge is gained.

Before one becomes aware of God within his own spirit, each one is to understand and know his own light within the world, which one receives according to each one's own state of consciousness and being on his own level. **"Man, know thyself."**

Know that the Celestial Soul is created and formed from the Universal Light of one's Celestial Parents. After one has made the complete dedication of himself to God in the Law of Balanced Interchange, and one is transformed and learns how to follow the Higher Light within the Angelic Beings, they become the Master Teachers of the mortal teachers in the world.

Although countless women are receiving understanding and knowledge as they hear the still small voice, since the women are being purified, they are accepting the duality of the Universal soul as being Father and Mother in God. Many purified women are accepting God as being within the men. But because the men have rejected the **Universal Angel Mothers,** the knowledge of the **duality** of the **Celestial Soul** has not yet been revealed to the men. Among these Angel Mothers is the **Universal Mother, Quan Yin** of the Far East, well-known and revered by millions. the complement of **Lao Tse** who

Generally and phenomenally in individual roles as Celestial Father, and Mother—over the Pan, the Supreme God.

Neither male nor female expresses the All of God. Since has the All of the All in any mortal role does all the power of the world? No, that is impossible.

"The Earth is the Lord's, and the fullness thereof," which is all of mankind, all the resources in the world, and all that is in the universe—the entire moral being. All belongs to the Lord, the Creator of all.

I AM THAT ONE IN ALL.